BLACK

An African American Guide to the Zodiac

SUN SIGNS

Thelma Balfour

D0068352

A Fireside Book
Published by Simon & Schuster

New York   London   Toronto   Sydney   Tokyo   Singapore

FIRESIDE
Rockefeller Center
1230 Avenue of the Americas
New York, New York 10020

FIRESIDE and colophon are registered
trademarks of Simon & Schuster Inc.

Designed by Elina D. Nudelman

Manufactured in the United States of America

1   3   5   7   9   10   8   6   4   2

Library of Congress Cataloging-in-Publication Data
Balfour, Thelma.
Black sun signs : an African American guide to the zodiac /
Thelma Balfour.
p.   cm.
"A Fireside book."
1. Afro-American astrology.   I. Title.
BF1714.A37B27   1996
133.5′089′96073—dc20   95-54013
CIP
ISBN 0-684-81209-6

To my husband, Gabriel, and my sons,
Erin and David, for your love, support and patience

Table of Contents

Contents

Acknowledgments

And to those who died before the dream became a reality:

My mother, Gwendolyn Lattimer Hudson
My grandmother, Hortense Lewis Lattimer
My aunt, Thomasine Lattimer Jones
My cousin, Michael
My fellow choir member, Derek Taylor

In alphabetical order:

Jesse Balfour
Rico Balfour
Sam Balfour
Joyce Blackmon
Jan Clemons
Melanie Few

Kimmie McNeil
Deanie Parker
Otis Sanford
Vern Smith
Carolyn Watkins

Thanks for your help and encouragement:

Peggy McKenzie, my friend, whose constant support and encouragement propelled me through some of my lowest periods

To all of you who responded to my questionnaires, consented to interviews or phone calls and provided valuable contacts, I thank you

Acknowledgments

My friends, my confidantes and my sisters: Dorretha Balfour, Ruby Balfour, Delois Beckley, Claudette Campbell, Rita Gatlin Hall, Edna Ingram, Evelyn Matthews, Norma McBride, Renee Dozier McCarley, Minister Shirley Prince, Denise Suggs Rixter, Gwen Robinson, Bernestine Sanders, Ida Scott, Sandra Vaughn, Eva Watson, Ruth Nelson Wright

Venita Steppe-Smith, who taught me how to use the computer and saved me from a mild coronary when I thought I had deleted seventeen pages from the manuscript

Cheryl Hudson, my feisty niece, who helped with clerical matters and my son David

Special thanks to:

My mentor, Miriam DeCosta Willis, for encouraging me to participate in the Black Writers Workshop

My family: my father, Limuel Lockard; my sisters, Levennette and Adrienne; my aunts, Agnes Lattimer, M.D., and Camille Lattimer; my cousins, Michael, Sandra, Terry, Bernard, Keith and Holly; my stepson, Gabriel, Jr.; my nephew, Cedric Hudson; my goddaughter, Candace Shelton

The Roxie Gunter Singers of Friendship Baptist Church and the Friendship Baptist Church family for all their support

My agent, Marlene Connor, whose vision of a black astrology book made this project a reality

And finally, my editor, Dawn Daniels, whose enthusiasm, moral support and editing have propelled this project to its completion

Introduction

This book is about astrology and how it relates to the African American experience. It's a book about us, about our culture, about our parents, our grandparents, our friends, our relatives and our lives. And, it's an idea whose time is long overdue.

With the recent renewed interest in and resurgence of astrology, 1-900 telephone numbers, soothsayers and novice predictors of the future abound. However, none of them address the black experience. Consequently, this book provides an Afrocentric approach to astrological substance, compatible mates and personalities in general.

Granted there are some commonalities among astrological signs that serve the majority. But when writers of astrology identify people born under the sign of Aries as having red hair or a red skin tone, for example, they exclude the African American community. How personalities are molded by culture, folkways and mores is also pertinent to this book.

This book will differ from other astrology books in a number of ways. I will not use vague daily predictions that read as though they could be recycled under a different sign the following day, because the information is so general. I will use Afrocentric cultural references and examples. For example, if I note that a particular sign will not wear Jheri curls, black people will understand what that means. If there are references to "the brother" or "the sister," we won't be talking about siblings.

Under some Sun signs, both black men and black women have an overriding need to succeed, over and above the pressure we put on ourselves as blacks to work like slaves to be looked upon in a favorable light. The pressure is there already when we are one of two or three blacks on jobs that some whites think we don't deserve.

In general, we have the same hopes and dreams as nonblacks, but in reality, our dreams, hopes and aspirations are sometimes derailed or put on hold permanently because of our circumstances. Those circumstances come in the form of layoffs, racism, drugs, violence, deadly diseases and situations beyond our control.

In addition, the general African American experience has a profound effect on how our individual personality traits manifest themselves in certain instances. For example, the Capricorn personality in general and the Sun sign in particular represent a serious-minded, nose-to-the-grindstone born leader with an unwavering drive to make it to the top. But when variables such as being black in a racist society come into play (translation: loss of a job and having to move back home with his single-parent mom, who has a part-time job to support three children), the Capricorn's drive to succeed comes to a screeching halt. In its place, we find the need to eat and survive. He remains the born leader and he's conscientious, but he has to lead in other ways—like orchestrating the budget or the workload and household responsibilities. It's not that the Capricorn's personality has changed, but the general characteristics are not readily visible because there's no time to be personable, friendly and engaging, at least not on an ongoing basis. This man has to eat and find a way to help support others in the household. His personality won't be like the white Capricorn's because of his circumstances. Granted, the white Capricorn has adversity in his life. But that ever-looming monster called racism adds insult to injury. Therefore the black Cap is more frustrated, angrier and more distant.

Astrology is certainly not a cure-all for life's struggles, twists and turns. It's merely an innovative and fun way to determine compatible mates, career paths and overall personality traits. In general, it's human nature for people to be interested in finding out about themselves. Black folks are no different.

And whether we like it or not, astrology is all around us. How many times have you heard the question, "What's your sign?" Most folks hear it in some sort of social setting. The question can serve as an icebreaker and a way to talk to people when you're kickin' it at a party, hoping to meet that all-important potential soul mate. Trying to impress that sister with what you want her to think you know about astrology. Nodding your head when the sister responds and says, "Pisces." It's all part of the games people play—like you actually know what astrology means. Yeah, right.

Usually what we know about astrology is what we hear others saying, like "Girl, Scorpios are mean" or "You don't need to deal with Geminis 'cause they're moody and two-faced." But aside from all that we hear and think we know, what *does* it all mean? When asked, "What's your sign?" some of you who are trying to be cute will say, "Dollar sign." But what does being a Gemini really mean?

It means that Gemini is an air sign and one of the twelve signs of the zodiac. Astrology involves the study of the planets and heavenly bodies, including the moon and the sun, to determine how and what effects their changing positions have on human behavior. Folks, what goes on in the heavens has a direct bearing on what's going on down here!

I conducted hundreds of interviews and sent out hundreds of questionnaires to determine, astrologically, what men and women of African American origin were about. And the masses responded to everything—from being turned off by colored contact lenses (specifically blue), to men asking women for money, to men acting macho and needing constant stroking, to Jheri curls, polyesters, blind dates, insensitive people and control freaks. There were plenty of upbeat notes, too. Men wanted women who were more sensitive to their needs. Many of the brothers commented that they were simply tired of playing cat-and-mouse games with women. The brothers felt that the rules to those games had changed and no one had bothered to tell the other principle players, namely, the men! Ladies, are you listening?

I never expected to get the kind of response I got—from young and old alike. I was flabbergasted! From Washington State to Florida, it was as though someone had pushed a button and there was a chain reaction. The response of those who wanted to be heard was phenomenal. My approach in writing this book was to accommodate us, an underserved group of people who are interested in this popular phenomenon called astrology. This book, *Black Sun Signs: An African American Guide to the Zodiac,* will be the first to do so. Enjoy!

PRIMER

Astrology Can Help You Find Love

"You've got the right one, baby" is the punch line in a very popular commercial and the words that singer Ray Charles echos over and over in the successful ad. Maybe there's an underlying reason for the ad's popularity. Really, the theme of the ad is what successful court-ships are made of—finding the right baby (if you'll pardon the pun).

Astrology can help you find that all-important person, that soul mate or that love of your life. I know some will say, "I don't care what the sign is, there are jerks in all twelve signs." So true. But before you write off this whole concept, read further. I was also once the skeptic. However, when I started to pay attention to the various signs, talked to people directly and discovered personality traits all on my own, I thought, hey, there may be something to this. And there was, for me, anyway.

For the purpose of this book, the Sun sign aspect of astrology, the most noted and popular portion of the zodiac, will be examined. The sun is the central most important celestial body; therefore, your Sun sign is the most important aspect of your birth chart. [The birth chart is determined by the position of all the planets, including the sun and moon (the two luminaries), at the time of your birth.]

The sun moves around the earth each year and travels through all twelve signs of the zodiac. The Sun sign is the astrological sign that the sun is moving through at the time of your birth. For in-stance, the sun will move into the sign of Libra on September 23 and exit on October 22, so anyone born between September 23 and October 22 is known as a Libra, the sign of the scales.

From an astrological standpoint, the Sun sign controls your

personality, style, general demeanor and outward appearance. For example, if you're a Leo, you are usually likely to be impeccably dressed, outfitted in the most expensive clothing or the most provocative that the ol' checkbook can stand. Therefore, you may be attracted to members of the opposite sex who are well-dressed too, such as Virgos—and they to you. Generally, however, Virgos and Leos are not compatible. The initial impression of being dressed to kill is what catches Virgo, but little else will hold these two together. Virgo is an earth sign and Leo is a fire sign, and earth and fire don't mix.

Here's how the mix works. There are twelve signs of the zodiac, and these signs are divided into the four elements of the universe: earth, fire, water and air. The earth signs are Taurus, Virgo and Capricorn. The fire signs are Aries, Leo and Sagittarius. The water signs are Cancer, Scorpio and Pisces. And the air signs are Aquarius, Gemini and Libra. Each element, earth, fire, water, and air, reveals tidbits about the twelve Sun signs. We don't need a Ph.D. from the School of Astrology to pick up the juicy and illuminating clues that these elements provide.

Earth signs: Taurus, Virgo and Capricorn. You're down-to-earth, practical and cautious. Basically, you're always the same—predictable, reliable, grounded. (Ground-ed, ground, earth—get it?)

Fire signs: Aries, Leo, and Sagittarius. Like the element of fire, you're unpredictable, feisty, aggressive, impulsive and hard to control. (To put it more bluntly, it's going to be your way or no way at all!)

Water signs: Cancer, Scorpio and Pisces. In reality, people generally love to be close to lakes, rivers, oceans and ponds. If you're a water sign, people love to be close to you because you're reassuring, emotional, intuitive, soothing and nonthreatening.

Air signs: Gemini, Libra and Aquarius. If you're an air sign, you're independent, aloof, analytical, intriguing and very hard to keep up with. You must have freedom. Like air itself, air signs cannot be contained, harnessed or backed into a corner. If either happens, you'll simply disappear.

From a practical standpoint, earth and water signs make beautiful mud together. And fire and air make a bonfire that's hard to put out.

Here's the breakdown of the Sun signs:

- *Aries* (March 21–April 19)
- *Taurus* (April 20–May 20)
- *Gemini* (May 21–June 20)
- *Cancer* (June 21–July 22)
- *Leo* (July 23–August 22)
- *Virgo* (August 23–September 22)
- *Libra* (September 23–October 22)
- *Scorpio* (October 23–November 21)
- *Sagittarius* (November 22–December 21)
- *Capricorn* (December 22–January 19)
- *Aquarius* (January 20–February 18)
- *Pisces* (February 19–March 20).

Compatible mates:

- Aries works best with Sagittarius, Leo, Gemini and Aquarius.
- Taurus is compatible with Virgo, Capricorn, Cancer and Pisces.
- Gemini is more suited to Leo, Aries, Aquarius and Libra.
- Cancer is better with Pisces, Scorpio, Virgo and Taurus.

The four signs listed within each group are also compatible and interchangeable. For example, in addition to Cancers, Scorpios are also compatible with Virgo, Taurus and Pisces.

And please, please, please don't send those cards and letters declaring that you and your husband, your boyfriend, your man or your woman of twenty years are not listed here as being compatible. I didn't say all of this astrology business is foolproof. I'm simply saying this method will enable you to leap over some of the many frogs before you meet Prince or Princess Charming, as the case may be.

Your opposite sign is generally about six months from your

birth date or directly across from your sign on the circular horoscope. The following signs are opposites:

- Aries–Libra
- Taurus–Scorpio
- Gemini–Sagittarius
- Cancer–Capricorn
- Leo–Aquarius
- Virgo–Pisces.

If you pay attention to astrology or know the birth date of your companion, you will probably realize that you're constantly meeting your opposite and the encounters are usually quite interesting. The conversations are stimulating; there's definitely chemistry. As you're trying to emphatically leave this courtship, exchange, date or whatever, you'll constantly get this "Wait a minute, baby" plea. The magnetic attraction is so deep that the two of you won't be able to accept that the relationship ain't working! And you'll spend most of your time making up. But on the real tip, you know that after the morning after, reality sets in. You need to give it up and you know it!

But understanding astrology may crystallize a few issues and help you bring closure to a relationship or help your relationship blossom. So chill out, and enjoy the book for what it is, an exercise in fun! Then when you're asked, "What's your sign?" you'll know what the question means. And after you find that lovely creature or that handsome devil through the stars, you may want to become a member of the "Uh, huh" chorus!

ARIES
March 21 to April 19
Symbol: The Ram

Positive traits: Optimistic, energetic, courageous, innovative, assertive, enthusiastic, adventuresome, free-spirited

Negative traits: Selfish, quick-tempered, impatient, tactless, impulsive, self-centered, accident-prone, given to procrastination

Ruling planet: Mars is associated with initiative and courage.

Get set for the whirlwind experience of your life—the Aries' movements and demeanor are mesmerizing. When you first encounter an Aries, swooping into the room and stopping on a dime, meeting and greeting people with a self-assured smile, you'll wonder if a tornado has just touched down.

Like a spinning top that bounces off each object it touches and never loses its spin, Arians keep on bouncing back, undaunted by life's twists and turns. And if you attempt to get to know this ball of energy, your head will be spinning too. Aries people have amazing resilience, for they simply won't let most things put a damper on their zest for life.

Those ruled by Mars are cheerful, enthusiastic and gung ho about everything in which they're involved. They love life and life loves them. The phrase "You can do anything you really want to do" is a favorite of theirs. And that's pretty much how they live their lives. They face life head on and they're definitely not leery of taking chances, striking out on their own and testing new waters. They must have excitement in their lives, and there's no fear of the unknown for them. They make a fine science of living life to the fullest, mainly because they're really making sure that their lives are comfortable in every way and they are enjoying themselves.

Arians are energetic, upbeat people who usually have an overabundance of projects, duties and social functions that they couldn't possibly get to in a twenty-four-hour period. They are the cheerleaders of the zodiac. They're usually charged up about most projects they initiate and never finish. They will sit down and tell you what the plans will be for the weekend, including fixing the storage room door, pruning the hedges, and cooking their famous catfish recipe. But don't turn your head for too long because you'll be in the yard or the kitchen all alone after your Aries disappears. The cheerleading efforts must be spread around, you know. He will be off helping a friend with his stalled car; she'll be showing a group of senior citizens the latest dance steps.

Aries are very intelligent and quick thinkers. Some will say that they are know-it-alls and that may be true. One Virgo sister commented that an older Aries brother with whom she worked drove her absolutely batty with his condescending air during most conversations. Said the Virgo, "I don't care what the subject is, the Aries brother knows more than anyone in the room. Even if the discussion is about the Ku Klux Klan or the skinheads, he has a friend or a worker who was involved with these groups, so he would know!" Are you listening, Aries?

Although they're involved in so much, getting to know them may be difficult unless the friendship begins when they're young because they're very comfortable being alone. The key word with Aries is "self."

The element for Aries is fire, and like the element, Aries are bold, hot-tempered and hard to control. They're also brave, innovative souls, and they have their own way of approaching issues in their lives. For example, an Aries woman who became a mother in her teens decided after the baby was born that even though she grew up in Chicago's housing projects, she would not become a statistic. She didn't hold out false hopes for her relationship with the child's father, which ended after two years. She saw that all too often women were in unfulfilling relationships, taking care of their men and children with only their meager welfare checks. She obtained her general equivalency diploma and went on to become a lab technician and support her child without help.

You'll find these rams where the action is—provided they're not at home resting up for their next conquest. They love sports, the arts, theater, poetry readings. They also love to dance or be in the middle of an exciting game, like a scavenger hunt or even strip poker.

Don't ever dare them to do something, because you'll be left holding the bag. They'll meet the challenge, but the problem is, they'll run off half-cocked without thinking things through. Consequently, Arians can suffer several disappointments in their lives before practicality sets in and they understand that planning comes before execution, not vice versa. One Aries who tried to start a trade school for African American boys couldn't understand why he couldn't get the financing he needed, though he tried at several black lending institutions. Each unsuccessful attempt found him more and more sullen. But he failed to understand that he needed a business proposal, a business plan and collateral. He was so pumped on this great idea, that he automatically assumed the bankers would be too.

Getting to know Aries people may be difficult sometimes. For the most part these people are loners. Aries people can be totally self-absorbed and preoccupied with whatever they are about. They will readily acknowledge their selfishness if you point it out to them. But just because they acknowledge it doesn't mean that anything changes. Nothing changes with Aries but the weather. For example, an Aries insurance salesperson asked her sister to charge a television set on the sister's account, promising payment in full when the bill arrived. But when the bill came, the ram proceeded to make excuses for not paying, saying her rent was due. And all the while the two argued, the Aries never addressed the real issue of the bill, but went off on a tangent about her sister's yelling.

Physically, Aries are quite striking. They're usually medium tall to tall. They have larger than average heads with lots of hair. If you look a bit closer there's usually a scar or mark from some accidental injury. Both men and women are broad-shouldered. They have an unmistakable charm and a winning smile.

Aries parents are also very aggressive in child rearing, placing a burden on the child to achieve. This can be detrimental to children who are introverted and quiet. However, Aries parents are fun-loving with their children. They will instill a sense of adventure and risk taking in their children at a very early age. They are also the first to challenge any perceived injustice with their children. For example, an Aries mother demanded a parent-teacher conference after her ten-year-old son informed her that his teacher never called on the three black children in the class. In a firm manner, the Aries mom outlined the situation and requested an explanation. The teacher assured her that it was an oversight, and after the meeting, the child was frequently the line leader and was called on quite often.

The Aries Man

Aries brothers are hard to get to know sometimes. This brave, confident man is a loner. Sure, he can be the life of the party, keeping you doubled over with laughter with his great story-telling skills. But when the party's over, the Aries goes back into seclusion, unless he discovers an outlet of some sort that piques his interest. That outlet may be you. But if that is the case and a relationship develops, he must be first in your life. The Aries motto is, "Thou shalt have no other before me." The sign of Aries is the first sign of the zodiac, and these rams plan and expect to be first in everything they do.

When you meet this brother, the thing you'll notice is his confidence. He does have a sense of style. But many rams wear outdated clothing. This brother may even show up in a leisure suit or bell-bottom pants. They simply don't take the time to shop for clothes. They're too impatient and they have better things to do. It's only when they're standing in front of the closet, trying to determine what to wear to a club or some other function, that they realize they haven't been shopping in months—even years.

Although they can be very supportive when it comes to problems that friends and relatives face, they are rational thinkers who do not act on emotion. So if you're bawling, you may get a curious look rather than his loving arms, soothing voice, and assurances that everything is going to be all right. Aries men are attracted to women who are independent thinkers and those sisters who want a sense of adventure in their lives, no matter what their age. They can't deal with the clingy types of sisters and those whose lives are totally dependent on theirs for too long. Aries brothers want and encourage you to do your own thing. This brother will not stand for your livelihood hinging on his. He doesn't plan to see or be with you every day, either. He simply doesn't want that. The routine and the predictable bore him. And spending every Saturday night at your house watching movies and eating popcorn come rain or shine is not a part of his agenda. Don't fret—just find something else to do so you won't feel left out.

They will forever be looking for the unique date. The mundane or the routine will bore them out of their minds. An Aries related one such exceptional date that he experienced. His date had a pilot's license and the couple decided to fly one hundred miles away to a neighboring town for dinner. They were picked up at the airport by limousine, then they met some interesting people, went to dinner and flew back the same day. That is an ideal dinner date for an Aries.

Save your breath, ladies, these rams will only lock horns with you regarding what to do, because they're only going to do exactly what *they* want to. The best approach with any Aries is to plan social outings that don't necessarily need his involvement. You'll definitely spend some time together, but your recreation needs to be independent of his so that when he shows up late or not at all because he simply forgot, you won't get into a "How could you do this to me?" routine. The Arian's actions have nothing to do with you. This same scenario could be played out with him at a family wedding or baptism, an employee picnic or his best friend's bachelor party.

As husbands or lovers, they will never give you a dull moment. The roller-coaster ride you experience is for real. And they expect you to be as enthusiastic as they are about everything they do. He will sweep you off your feet with cards and poems sent to you daily. At first, you'll admire his honesty and candor until that directness is turned toward you. His tongue can be biting. His intent is not to hurt feelings, but to improve you or the relationship in some way.

As for improving him, well, as far as he's concerned, you've got the best. What's not to like?

And he'll approach the relationship as though you're his first and only love. But if it doesn't work, he'll be off again writing more poems for his new lady love with the same passion and commitment he once had for you. When the relationship is over, he's the first to say good-bye.

He's a stickler for promptness because he doesn't have any patience unless you're waiting for him. A date with an Aries man will probably include a long drive to an out-of-the-way spot. This may sound a little sneaky—but don't worry, he won't harm you. Aries males feel that this is one of the best ways to get your undivided attention because they don't like competition of any type—children, dogs, relatives or noisy surroundings. The other consideration is, once you're out of familiar surroundings, you'll have a tendency to relax and become a little less inhibited.

If you don't plan to deliver, don't accept the invitation to the house of this Aries brother. That would be a grave mistake. They may charm the pants right off you. Conversation will be lively and on a variety of subjects. But beware, don't go in with the attitude of "I know I've got it going on," because you'll be in for a rude awakening. The Aries also has a lot of confidence, and the relationship can end as abruptly as it began.

If he's a bachelor, everything will have a place and everything will be in its place. If you're married to this ram, don't waste your time requesting that he accompany you to the grocery store. The grocery shopping will be reduced from the planned one hour to about fifteen minutes. He'll bellyache all along the way as he impatiently grabs items while saying, "Let's go!" After you're hurried out of the store with only a third of the items you planned to buy, he'll return home and sit smiling in his lounge chair, declaring he couldn't miss the basketball game.

Both the men and women of this sign are very courageous and determined people. One Aries brother I knew quit a very lucrative job. He saved enough money and paid off the bills so that he could live comfortably during his two-year sabbatical that ended up being six years. Aries males are very comfortable being single. They're very much into themselves and spend many hours reading, mapping strategy for a new project or enjoying some new adventure.

The Aries Woman

When you meet this dynamic ram, you'll be totally in awe of her confidence, cheerfulness and overall good looks. You will be intrigued and definitely interested. But if you look a little closer you'll determine that she's like that with most people, so don't get the mistaken notion that you're the one. You might be, but the relationship will move along when the ram is ready. Whatever the moves, they'd better be well thought-out and slow-going because if this Mars-ruled sister isn't interested, you'll be told in an instant. You can't make any assumptions with this lady ram.

This sister may be more interested in your dog than she is in you. Just because you see her on a regular basis doesn't mean that a relationship is blossoming. She may be hopelessly attached to Harambee, your golden retriever, and may be mentally calculating how she can convince you to let the dog become her companion and not you. Aries females are the mystery women of the zodiac. You'll never be able to predict her moves because this fire sign is too restless and impatient. She will forever keep you guessing about whether her intentions for romance are legit. That's part of the lady ram's intrigue. She hates the routine and the predictable. Being bored is one of her greatest fears. So if you're interested in keeping up with this fire sign, you'd better not be squeamish in your approach. By the time you muster your courage, she'll be long gone.

One of the best ways to get the Arian's attention is to be spontaneous. On the first date, take her hiking in the local state park, include some fishing and eat the fish right on the creek's bank. She'll love it. Try introducing some little mini-adventure she hasn't tried, like roller blading or hang gliding. This lady ram is not a wimp. She'll definitely not lay down like a lamb; she'll stand up like a ram and face any challenge head on.

This woman is the Sojourner Truth of her time, but she usually sees beyond race; therefore, dating outside of her race with Latino, Jewish or even Polish companions can be an option. She's usually looking for someone to meet her needs. The key word here is "her." And when she has selected you (usually, it's easier when she makes the first move), she'll expect all of your attention. She won't expect the chivalry routine. But she will expect—and demand—that you only have eyes for her when you're dating.

Also, these courageous women of the zodiac want strong men, not physically, but in spirit and outlook. The Aries woman wants to feel secure in knowing that her guy is a take-charge person, because if the man doesn't, she definitely can and will. She will definitely dominate if you let her, but she's more content to be your equal partner.

For example, a single lady ram and a Gemini man decided to start a catering business. Aries was an excellent cook and Gemini ran the money side of the business. The relationship began as a courtship, but eventually changed into a purely business arrangement. After years of success, Gemini met and began a courtship with another woman. Aries eventually left him and started her own business. Gemini swears the lady ram left because he lost interest in her romantically. "Not so," said Aries. "You needed financial help, and I gave it. Now it's someone else's turn."

As wives or live-in companions, Aries can be very supportive. If you've decided to start your own business or leave an old job for a new one, Aries will be there as your own personal cheerleader. These sisters love to take chances, so you'll be supported and admired for taking chances too. On the other hand, if she perceives you as a wimp, forget it. Such was the case with a lady ram who was an account executive for a major advertising firm and fell in love with a steelworker. No problem there. But as time wore on and he refused to take chances, buy a house or try to get a part-time job to offset the travel expenses for these two, Ms. Ram saw the writing on the wall. Although she loved him, his insecurity about her job and his constant digs at her, saying things like "You're a legend in your mind," made her realize that homeboy would soon be history.

They can definitely hold down the same jobs as men. Aries women are usually working side-by-side with their male counterparts in factories, as executives or as surgeons. If you happen to become Mr. Mom for a while, an Aries spouse won't quibble.

Aries

If this sister is single, the card and Tupperware parties, along with baby and bridal showers, will be at her house. She loves to be where the action is and she's an excellent hostess and cook. So brothers, you'll have to get use to playing second banana sometimes. Also Aries women appear to be more comfortable being single. Many men can be intimidated by this sister because she exudes self-confidence. By the time you meet her, she will probably own her home, be in business for herself or hold a high-profile job. But deep down, she longs for that take-charge kind of guy that she can look up to.

When she falls in love, the relationship will go full throttle. She's very loyal and faithful in a relationship. Having two companions at once is not to her liking because all her attention must be on you. And you can bet that all of your attention will be on her. She'll shower you with attention, plan adventuresome trips and keep you guessing as to what the lady ram is up to next. And she'll expect the same from you.

Her strong, direct and sometimes insensitive approach to your agenda will have you in a quandary. And yes, she'll definitely rant and rave when she's upset. Hopefully, for your sake, it won't be directed at you. But as strong and confident as she may seem, there's a soft, vulnerable side to the lady ram that belies the rough, tough exterior of this fire sign. If she's working around the clock, she'll expect you to put what you're doing on hold to come to her aid. She may need you to pick up dry cleaning and toiletries and go by and cut her mother's grass. She's usually the designated person for yard work at her mother's house. Although there may be brothers, she simply doesn't have the patience to wait until they decide to do the work.

One of the biggest turnoffs for any Aries is boredom. If you only want to fall asleep in front of the TV, you're reading the wrong section of this book. The relationship will be over without any regrets and the Aries sister won't look back.

An Aries sister has definite ideas about what she wants in a man, and if you don't fit the mold, well, brother, you need to get you some business. As one lady ram put it, "I want a man who's tall, dark and handsome, owns his own business, drives a BMW and speaks English."

Love Connection

Are you sure you're up for the challenge of a relationship with an Aries? If you're doubtful about having a relationship with the ram, I suggest you rethink this whole thing. I'm not trying to scare you off, but these fire signs are very aggressive. To give you a good indication of their aggressiveness, observe how they eat. When they're hungry, they attack food. Similarly, when they're interested in a certain person, they want the relationship when they want it, and that's that. You want to be attacked (I hope). But if you're the potential mate, you'll have no time to think. They'll definitely put a rush on you. Both the men and the women go in for the "kill" early and don't waste precious time. While you're giving them the "I'll think about it" routine, they've already planned their next move. This approach is true of both men and women Aries, but more so with the men.

But if you decide to make the first move before knowing if he or she is interested, you might get your feelings hurt. They have to have the challenge, so playing hard to get is the best strategy. In love relationships with the rams, the initial courtship will be of an overwhelming nature. You won't have time to catch your breath. You'll be inundated with cards and calls and showered with attention. Ladies, you must look alluring at all times (no rollers or fuzzy pink house shoes), with only eyes for him. And men, you've got to be neatly dressed. But the lady ram also likes that Marlboro country look of jeans and cowboy boots. All the dates will be creative and spontaneous, with plenty to do and no thought to being bored. The Aries' stamina is phenomenal. You'll start the day with a delectable breakfast prepared by your Aries and set out on the patio. Then off for a drive to the country, followed by lunch with homemade wine and a game of checkers at a quaint roadside inn. Then back to the city for ordered-in Chinese food. Time to shower (maybe together) and change to go out for some late-night jazz at a nice cozy club. And then. . . .

As for the bedroom antics with Aries, both male and female, I issue the same warning: If you're squeamish or fearful, run for your life! By the time you reach the boudoir, you should have an inkling of what's to come. Any or all of your sexual fantasies could be fulfilled with an Aries in one night! They don't have any hangups about any kind of sex play known to man or woman—they can do it all, and their aggressive nature will have you begging for mercy. And they expect their companions to bring something to the party as well. Like the Scorpios, Aries people have an insatiable appetite for sex.

If you want the ram to stand up on his hind legs with passion, massage his face, scalp and head, or in the case of the woman, scratch her dandruff, comb her hair or massage her scalp. Also ear nibbling and kissing around the hairline and near the temple ignites the flames of this fire sign. In short, any leanings to the head area are of the blue ribbon variety.

Aries people are extremely jealous, so don't even try giving someone else some play. When they feel the need to end the relationship, they'll be gone long before the fat lady sings. Tenacity is not one of the virtues you can count on with the Aries. And they're loyal only to themselves. The relationship could be short and sweet, but it will be remembered. Once they figure out the relationship is not working to their advantage, they're not good at pretending. And you can bet, it won't be long before the curtain call.

If you're a Libra, an air sign and Aries' opposite, he won't want to let you go because of the strong magnetic attraction between the two of you and the downright good sex. You'll hear him say, "Wait a minute, baby, can't we talk about this" a lot, not willing to accept the inevitable fate of the relationship. If presented with the challenge, they could probably talk their way into heaven. So if you plan to stick to your guns, don't listen.

After her on-again, off-again relationship was no longer bearable, an insurance executive in Atlanta decided to end it. When she called her Leo companion at home at seven in the morning, only to hear his second girlfriend's voice on the phone, the lady ram demanded to speak to her friend. The Leo brother, upon hearing the Arian's voice, retreated into the Academy Award-winning performance of the year, pretending there was a bad connection while the two talked on the telephone. The conversation went like this: "Hello, hello, I can't hear you . . . hello, hello, we must have a bad connection, I'll call you back." After the conversation that never really happened, the Aries decided to end the relationship. They had agreed to see other people in addition to their relationship. But her annoyance and impatience came after his deception of pretending the telephone connection was bad. The relationship between the two ended as quickly as the last telephone conversation!

Aries, a fire sign, is generally more compatible with the two other fire signs, Sagittarius and Leo, because persons born under these signs have many characteristics of Aries. They are bold, aggressive, spontaneous and not easily intimidated, and they can give Aries a run for the money, which is the main factor needed to offset the whirlwind behavior of the ram. The two other air signs that mate best with the ram are Aquarius and Gemini. These air signs are independent and successful and have good self-images.

How to Get Next to an Aries

• Seek advice from the Aries. They're usually well versed on a variety of subjects.
• Don't play the damsel in distress or the dumb-jock role. Arians are intelligent people who must be stimulated mentally as well as physically.
• Be complimentary—Arians love flattery because they are their own biggest fans. But don't pour it on too thick.
• Timid and shy people, stay away and don't bother. If you can't "hang," or if you have any doubts or inhibitions, don't waste your time or the Arian's.
• Don't nag or dictate. All of your efforts will fall on deaf ears.
• Be spontaneous. Arians are usually impulsive and they love surprises. For goodness' sake, don't be a wet blanket.
• Wigs, toupees and hair weaves or reasonable facsimiles are okay with the rams because these props can be a part of the sexual fantasy in which you and the Aries may be participating.
• Aries people are not usually interested in those who are impeccably dressed. They could care less because they're more interested in what's in your head, instead of what's on your body. Some Aries people are known for wearing outdated clothing.
• Aries sisters don't care for men with permed hair or colored contact lenses. They want what they consider a "real" man, who doesn't need enhancements.
• As for the brothers, attractiveness counts, but not as much as intellect.

The Aries Child

From infancy to adulthood, the Aries requires most of your attention even if there are other children in the household. The key word here is "self." For the ram, that's the one word that sums up this Mars-ruled sign. It will be I, me, my and myself all through life. And your Aries youngster will want and expect your undivided attention. They're considered the babies of the zodiac.

As toddlers, they will walk, talk and potty-train earlier than most children—the little Aries is always interested in conquering the next challenge. Parents, you must provide in abundance stimulating toys, erector sets, strategy games, lots of dolls and clothing, paints and coloring books that will challenge your child's inquisitive, restless nature. For if he is left idle for too long, he will most certainly get into trouble. "An idle mind is the devil's workshop" must have been coined for an Aries. Therefore, an early introduction to sports, scouting and other competitive outlets will help to channel some of that energy. But they are accident-prone and will give you a mild coronary as they dive for the baseball, flip over in an effort to kick the soccer ball or eventually trip and fall as they are mounting the stage to receive an award for outstanding drama student.

Even as early as the toddler stage, the beginning years of an Aries' life must be carefully monitored with strict discipline. If the ground rules are not laid in no uncertain terms, this child will control you, their siblings and their teachers. She's a born leader and has the ability to lead other children into mischief such as playing hooky from school (she'll offer her house), rock throwing, picking fights and even shoplifting.

They have somewhat of a rebellious nature and a hot temper, but their temper usually cools down just as quickly as it flares up. The key is not to emphatically tell them that they can't do something but to make the situation a challenge that they will be compelled to meet.

For example, a single parent who had a four-year-old Aries couldn't monitor her little ram as needed because she worked at the telephone company during odd hours and had to rely on baby-sitters. The little Aries was one of two black children in the day care center—and the worst and the most defiant of all of the children.

The white middle-aged teacher was beside herself when the mother came in for a parent-teacher conference. The teacher tried to explain she hadn't had much experience with black children, implying the child acted this way because of his race. The teacher outlined all of the child's indiscretions and the parent readily agreed. After the teacher threw up her hands, called the child a brat and gave up on the situation, the mother decided to use a little child psychology or "Aries psychology." She explained to the child that he needed to be the leader of the class so that he could help the teacher with the other students. It worked for her. The child became a model student, which meant fewer gray strands of hair for the weary teacher.

Aries children are independent with pioneering spirits, which means that they will initiate new projects others won't try. They will probably be the ones who initiate safe-sex campaigns or volunteer to speak at the school board meeting on the need for condom distribution to the students in the high school.

Parents, you'll come to admit that they are enterprising little people with lots of creativity and nerve. For example, one parent explained that when her Aries child graduated from sixth grade, the principal came over to praise the little ram, saying the child was one of the best students to ever graduate from the school. The child had written her a letter explaining how much he enjoyed being in her school. He also commented on how wonderful the principal was and gave examples of all that he had learned. The trouble was, however, he had given the same letter to three of his teachers, who were also gushing with pride.

As teenagers, their grades may falter when it comes to tedious schoolwork such as math or subjects like German that involve repetition and detail, because the Aries child has very little patience. But here's the trick: If they become interested in something like basketball or science, their other grades should improve as a stipulation of being involved in what they truly enjoy. And they will.

The black Aries child learns very early about the ramifications of being African American in a predominantly white world. However, she doesn't let the philosophy hamper her efforts. Her ego, determination and pioneering spirit can usually triumph over most adversity if she's interested enough in the matter. This child is stimulated by the novelty of being the first black senior class president or the only eleventh-grade finalist in the science fair competition.

Participation in sex at an early age may be a problem. Both girls and boys are always willing to test new waters. When you begin your explanation of the birds and bees, don't be surprised if your Aries child already knows many of the things you're going to tell him. And he may even tell you a thing or two. Don't panic and start hyperventilating! It doesn't mean he's sexually active. Like everything he's curious about, he will want to know more. But it's up to you, the parents, to demystify sex. Consequently, the Aries child won't think anything of it. (Let's hope so!)

The Aries Employee

If you're considering the Aries for a desk job where he will be corralled and confined to quarters with very little creative input, you better think again. Aries are not interested in the mundane, the safe or the tried and true. Work as a dispatcher, a doorman, a security guard or an insurance clerk would bore them to tears. It would be the same as caging a wild animal. It would never work: The Aries would be miserable.

If the job is unfulfilling to the Aries, a huge salary with great benefits, though attractive, is not the carrot you dangle in front of this ram. A chance to run things is more to her liking. For example, an Aries carpenter worked closely with his older brother, who owned a small construction business. The brother was so bossy that he even wanted the ram to emulate his method of holding the hammer. Fed up, the Aries quit and found another job. Since that time he and his brother have reunited and are again working together, but now the Aries is the property manager and his own boss.

Aries people are at their best on jobs where there is tension, noise, hustle and bustle and possible conflict in the workplace. They make great supervisors because they can give orders more effectively than taking them. They love a good challenge and can usually hold their own in cliff-hanger decision making. This fire sign performs well as a salesperson, pro athlete, mechanic, butcher, dentist, re-

porter, stockbroker, surgeon, scientist or long-distance driver—
namely, in jobs where there is a risk involved.

Because of their pioneering spirit, they are very adept at figuring
out how they will fit in to the workplace where automation and
technology are taking hold. One Aries man, who was an X-ray technician, read materials on nuclear medicine and then talked his supervisor and hospital administrators into buying equipment for nuclear
medicine, a new, advanced procedure for finding abnormalities in
the body's organs. The ram took an introductory course and eventually headed the new department.

Rams are extremely comfortable testing new ground and looking for the unconquerable area in their lives to conquer. One retired
police officer, who volunteered to become an undercover detective
when drug use was at its height during the 1960s, found a way to
stay clean during exchanges with drug dealers. The Aries officer
would bite the tip of the marijuana joint with each inhale, thereby
giving the appearance that he was indeed smoking. Because he
wasn't high, he was able to make mental notes of all of the goings-on
during the meeting with buyers and sellers. Although onlookers
watched with suspicion, he was able to convince the dealers that he
was one of them. This resulted in several arrests and the breakup of
a major drug ring in the South.

The throw-caution-to-the-wind attitude of this high-spirited
sign makes careful bosses reluctant at first to allow the ram free rein.
But she grasps responsibility quickly, so any reluctance to hire this
fire sign should be put aside. Now that's not to say that they won't
leave a job. Aries people have been known to leave a job one day
and get another the next. If Aries knows that he is valued in the
workplace, he will give 110 percent.

Yes, she will be somewhat disorganized. Her desk will be clut-
tered with sticky notes, like confetti, as reminders to herself. *Ebony
Man, Popular Mechanics, Home Gardening* and trade magazines will
be piled in a mound in the corner of his office. (There's simply no
more space on top of his desk with all of the memos, budget outlines
and day-old ham sandwiches in the way.)

They won't always be on time or adhere to office procedure and
the chain of command. And they might not always be a team player

either. But they will go beyond the call of duty to accomplish the goals you set or any task you require, for the Aries genuinely believes that no one can do a job better than he or she.

As an employee, he wouldn't ever be the little mealymouthed underling in the workplace. Aries people are usually respected on their jobs, not for being overly friendly but because any job they attempt, they do well. They are very direct and will tell you in a heartbeat what they think, whether you want to hear it or not. They are not intimidated in the least by being the only black on the job. Race is never an issue with the ram. He simply knows it exists, but doesn't allow it to ruffle his feathers. And any confrontations of a racial nature will be met head-on.

If you're the boss, their unorthodox manner in completing assignments will have you pulling your hair out. For example, your Aries employee may ask you to let her work at home on weekends and have two days off during the week to help save day care expenses. If you agree to the arrangement, you won't be sorry. Your reward from the Aries will be a job well done.

Health Matters

Eating well-balanced meals, drinking lots of water and avoiding alcohol are all essential to the Aries' overall good health and well-being.

Arians are overly confident that their bodies can withstand the demands of their hectic, and most of the time unorganized, schedule. Their bodies will hold up, but only if they get rest and eat balanced meals—at least sometimes, anyway.

They are justified in believing that they can run on sheer will, and many times they can do just that. But when the doctor says slow down, get more rest and take blood pressure medicine daily, take it daily, not weekly! For example, an Aries runner repeatedly ignored advice from his physician about giving up the sport and ultimately began to run ultra long (52 miles) marathons. After two hip replacement surgeries, though, he finally got the message.

Their impatient nature won't allow them to eat healthily on an ongoing basis unless they're athletes. Aries jump from one thing to the next without giving much thought to completing most projects, including a daily regimen of "three squares." Either they forget to eat entirely or they wolf down their burger and fries so quickly they may not remember eating it.

Since their calendars are brimming over and very little time is slated for relaxation, grocery shopping, food preparation and cooking are very low priorities, so low that when they do shop for groceries the frozen foods stay that way—frozen. They impatiently move about the store picking items at random and giving little thought to what they're buying. The approach of the Aries is to just get enough groceries for three days or to buy impulsively, picking up impractical items just because. One Aries woman bought a large 32-ounce can of coffee just because she had a dollar-off coupon. She didn't drink coffee and neither did any member of her family.

They have better things to do than grocery shop, you know. For them learning to eat, not to mention learning to eat healthily, will be a major hurdle. They rarely have time to cook or even feel the need to do so. It's not that they can't cook. Of course they can, and like most things they attempt, they do it well.

Aries, the first sign of the zodiac, rules the head and face. The Aries usually has a larger-than-average head, healthy, thick hair and a broad, chiseled face. Aries are usually prone to migraine headaches, sinus congestion, colds, eye and ear infections and some dental problems. They are also prone to accidents or minor injuries because of their fast-moving and impatient nature.

The Aries should drink milk and eat seafood, lots of dried beans for protein and energy, salads with bean sprouts, and broccoli and cauliflower. An abundance of vitamin C should reduce the onset of colds and congestion that are so common among Aries people.

Avoid excessive use of alcohol. I know, your "boys" want you to have a drink with them. Or you're the life of the party and your girlfriends want you to meet them for happy hour. And yes, you feel you have to accommodate. Feel free, only don't close down all of the local bars with your loud revelry, because the next day you'll pay with a hangover that may have you bedridden for a day.

Aries

Famous African American Arians

Marcus Allen
Maya Angelou
Pearl Bailey
George Benson
Tony Brown
Randall Cunningham
Henry O. Flipper
Aretha Franklin
Al Freeman Jr.
Marvin Gaye
Al Green
Lani Guinier
Lionel Hampton
Herbie Hancock
Dorothy Height
Billie Holiday
Robert Hooks
Alberta Hunter
Maynard Jackson
Jack Johnson
David Justice

Chaka Kahn
Bernice King
Martin Lawrence
Wilbur Marshall
Stephanie Mills
Eddie Murphy
Teddy Pendergrass
Colin Powell
Keshia Knight Pulliam
Paul Robeson
Diana Ross
Bessie Smith
Meshach Taylor
Ernie Terrell
Debi Thomas
Rufus Thomas
Luther Vandross
Sarah Vaughan
Harold Washington
Billy Dee Williams

TAURUS
April 20 to May 20
Symbol: The Bull

Positive traits: Strong-willed, reliable, persistent, solid, affectionate, practical, warmhearted, trustworthy

Negative traits: Stubborn, greedy, possessive, lazy, resistant to change, inflexible, resentful, violent

Ruling planet: Venus is associated with feelings and the power to love.

If you're looking for stability, security, loyalty and a solid foundation on which to build a relationship, Taurus is the ticket.

Taurus is an earth sign, which means you'll find this bull grazing at home just chillin', on a farm or any place where there is a close tie with nature. They love the great outdoors and seem to be tranquilized and revived during long walks in the park on bright, crisp autumn days or on a picnic, with all of their favorite foods and the bright blue sky as a backdrop.

Although the term "homebody" aptly applies to Taurus, they enjoy church activities and sporting events. You might even find them at happy hour or meeting coworkers after work at a bar to support another coworker-musician who's playing his first gig. The Taurean man won't be the loudmouth roustabout, swilling beer and trading war stories; he'll be the laid-back brother somewhere in the background taking it all in. He'll be checking out the scene, flirting subtly, making eye contact and sending over drinks anonymously.

The Taurus woman will more than likely be surrounded by the brothers as they ooh and aah over her voluptuous body, confidence and genuine earthiness.

People born under the sign of Taurus are down to earth and practical; rarely do they act on impulse. The ruling planet is Venus, which is associated with acquisitiveness and the power to love. Most Taureans are collectors. One Taurean female, a mortgage loan officer living in Alabama, collects fish, vases, elephants and all sorts of items. She also collects old clothes because she has yet to discard any of her wardrobe from the 1970s, including those hip-hugger bell-bottom pants.

Taurus people revere a good and stable home life and are prone to long, long relationships. Even if the relationship has long ago gone sour, Taurus people have a tendency to stick and stay, though this may not always be the best move. A Taurean woman who migrated to Oakland, California, over thirty years ago with her alcoholic and abusive spouse stayed on even though she and the children were miserably unhappy, saying her husband needed her. He died of cirrhosis of the liver without ever once acknowledging her contribution to his care.

Taurus people are fiercely loyal to family and friends. That loyalty also extends to the workplace, and what you tell them won't become the office gossip, even if the boss is having an affair with two women. A city editor of a major newspaper, who was hired by the editor and taken under the editor's wing, decided not to support a union drive. He also came out publicly against it, much to the chagrin of his colleagues, who had counted on his support. After deciding that the salaries were good and the editor was fair-minded, he was ultimately loyal to the editor who had hired him.

You'll usually find Taurus people at home in their peaceful, yet semiluxurious surroundings. They are sometimes collectors of fine things and can readily assess quality. They love jewelry (preferably diamonds) and fine furnishings that give them a sense of the security that they are forever seeking. The song "Money, Money, Money," by the O'Jays, had to have been written with a Taurus in mind. Money means a great deal to the Taurean, who will save and manage on even the smallest of paychecks with an expertise unmatched by most. Taurus will hold on to a dollar until it hollers. They have an affinity for saving money, and, therefore, they won't jeopardize their jobs for any reason.

The sensible and practical nature of Taureans won't allow them to make rash decisions or take on radical causes. They will not be among the nature group that decides to walk across the continent of Africa. Their initial reaction would be, "Are you crazy?" Although they don't mind getting down and dirty, planting a garden, hiking or camping, their practical nature would question all the details of such a trek across the motherland: Will there be snakes, wild animals and bottled water? And what if you smoke? There ain't no cigarette machines and convenience stores nearby.

Taureans, however, can usually adapt to most situations without much effort, even living in a foreign country. One Taurus brother who played basketball in Europe for five years believed his marriage failed because of that reason. He was able to assimilate more readily than his Cancerian wife, who suffered from a chronic case of homesickness. By the middle of the second season, he was speaking French and interacting very effectively with colleagues, local countrymen and the like and became a star in his own right. His wife became jealous and resentful and felt overlooked. She returned to the United States after the second season and gave birth to the couple's only child. The situation eventually created a wedge between the two that was never bridged.

As parents, Taurus people can be overprotective. Their children are their prized possessions; therefore, they want to shield their children from what they perceive as hurt, harm and danger. Their children often see such behavior as smothering and most of the time rebel. Save your breath, kids, your Taurus mother or father rules the roost. And most of your cries for freedom will be met with fierce resistance and slow action.

The Taurean has a scorching temper, but only when provoked. He usually minds his own business until someone waves a red flag in front of him, and then he charges without any warning. For example, don't buy a new car if you haven't paid the Taurean the money (there's that word again) you owe him. You'll be introduced to a person you never thought existed. He may even show up at your job on payday demanding his money and refusing to leave until you comply. And if all else fails, he'll kick your butt right there.

But beneath the surface of the raging bull is a gentle, sentimental and caring lamb. Although they hoard money, Taureans are generous to family and friends in need. They are a sucker for a sob story and will rescue friends and family at a moment's notice.

Taurus people are the mainstays of the zodiac. Whatever their disposition was when you met them, it won't change over the subsequent months or the long haul.

The Taurus Man

This brother is one of the most laid-back signs of the zodiac. You won't find him out front, bragging about his job, his women or his fine car or clothes. He doesn't have to because he's a very secure person. He's a quiet, unassuming bull with a power that speaks louder than words. This brother can also be rather shy and somewhat reserved. He's more of a behind-the-scenes kind of brother, working or playing slowly, methodically and carefully as he plods through life.

Remember, ladies, Taurus is the bull, and it takes only one bull to service an entire cow pasture. Not that he's a lover boy or ladies' man, but he could compete against the best when it comes to physical prowess.

Taurean males are the epitome of manliness. There's something about being around this brother that automatically makes a woman feel secure. Other women feel it too. So if you're married to one or considering a relationship with a Taurean, you're going to have to share him with the world. It's almost as if this broad-shouldered person has imaginary arms that provide a cocoon of security. And that cocoon is what most women want, that take-charge kind of guy, that brother who lets you lay all your troubles on his broad, broad shoulders.

This bull usually has more female friends than male. He's the one the sisters call on for advice about their love relationships. A sister might ask her Taurean friend about the feasibility of dating a man who makes less than she—would it make a difference? The

Taurus brother will give it to you straight and more than likely tell you it will.

It was probably a Taurean you witnessed last summer jumping into the pool to save a child from drowning. Or it may have been a Taurean who loaned you the $500 when your car needed repairs. It could even have been a Taurean who carried your elderly grandmother's groceries.

His calm and even nature, coupled with his masculine appearance, makes any woman turn for a second look. She may be thinking, "Why did I look at him again?" She may not be able to figure out why the magnetism between her and the bull is so strong. Don't sweat it, babycakes, just go with it!

His appearance won't include the Armani suit, a Countess Mara tie, Perry Ellis shirt or Italian shoes. It may be clothes by Wal-Mart. At first glance, you may be turned off because of his clothing; the outfit may not be polyester, but it may be its first cousin. But don't be fooled by first impressions, and don't despair. He will be well-groomed, but he won't be dressed to the nines. So what do you want, a man who spends all his money on clothes or a man who has money to spend on you?

Any woman with the Taurus man is going first-class. He may hedge when it comes to outfitting himself, but his companion will be treated like royalty. The money he's saving by not buying the most expensive clothes will go toward the nest egg that he will share with his mate someday. He's a builder, not only figuratively, but literally. But like his personality, which is even-tempered and calculating (with dollar signs dancing in his head), he will build the relationship and the future in a slow, systematic manner.

One Taurus man I know spent fifteen years building a 2,000-square-foot home from the ground up while his Capricorn wife looked on, keeping him company during the entire process. He would work at the defense depot until four in the afternoon, leave work and pick up his wife, who was a teacher. Then he'd head for the vacant lot that he'd bought years earlier, building the dream home for his wife, who was his first and only love.

Remember, he's an earthy, meat-and-potatoes kind of man— no vichyssoise and caviar for this earth sign. He doesn't like frills, fluff and fanfare, and he feels the same way about his women. He doesn't go in for the "fortress hair" look or the hair that has so much gel in it that it won't move, even in a tornado. For the Taurus brother, extremes throw him off. When a sister is transformed from a black Rapunzel to the Tracy Chapman look after one week of courtship, the brother is put off. As one Taurean put it, "You meet this lady with hair all down her back and by the time you end up going to bed with her, you wake up and her hair is an inch long and the rest is on the pillow. You're now dealing with another person!" Taureans are not hung up on hair. In fact, it makes no difference to them if the hair is long or short. It's the *deception* they take issue with. Braids are okay—but they need not extend past the waistline. Besides, he doesn't want a stranglehold during sex.

He doesn't like a lot of controversy or strife. One Taurus, who was dating a woman who was separated, found himself in a very uncomfortable situation. He and his mate were enjoying life and having fun. The drinks were flowing and a good time was being had by all. He went to the bathroom, and just then the doorbell rang and her husband came in. Consequently, the Taurean was stuck in the bathroom for about twenty minutes while his mate and her estranged husband argued. Meanwhile, Taurus' bladder suffered because he didn't dare use the toilet for fear of discovery.

As a husband, the Taurus brother is devoted and generous to his spouse. He will buy her lavish gifts and furnish the house as his wife sees fit. One note here: Wives, you won't be able to decorate the bedroom in pink and green, red and white, blue and white or any other sorority colors. That's where the Taurus draws the line. The only other requirement for the Taurus is that he must be in charge of the checkbook so he can curtail sporadic and needless spending. How else will you be the recipient of those lovely gifts?

The Taurus Woman

When this sister dresses up, she's unstoppable. From her newly permed hair to her fresh pedicure, she projects an air of confidence when she struts her stuff, and heads turn. The look, when it all comes together, includes manicured nails, jewelry, shoes, matching purse, and a killer outfit. When she goes out, she's usually dressed to the nines. But the secret is her entire outfit is half the cost of what others would pay. She shops until she finds "that dress" that's within her carefully planned budget. Money is something she plans to have in abundance one day.

Unlike the Taurus man, the sister enjoys dressing up and going to fancy restaurants. This sister also expects her companion to be well groomed and, hopefully, dressed in the latest styles. One of the mottos of the Taurean woman is—Clothes make the man.

The Taurus woman downplays her ability to attract men, waiting, for the most part, for them to come to her. But make no mistake, this lady bull gets her attention and plenty of it. And when you make a move, your line better be a good one. None of this "Haven't I seen you somewhere before?" or "You really look familiar to me." That won't work. The line needs to have punch and originality because this may be your only chance. Something like "You're the first woman I've met in a while that I sincerely want to get to know" may work. She'll stop, smile and turn her attention to you, even if it's temporary.

One Virgo man who met this young Taurus sister at a party wanted her phone number. But when he confessed that he was married, she emphatically said no and headed for the bar on the other side of the room. Frantic, the brother decided that in this case honesty wasn't the best policy. Instead, he approached the lady bull again, this time saying that he and his wife were separated. He then added that he and his wife had been apart for only six months and it was hard to accept. The Virgo was, of course, lying, but decided to use drastic measures. But before the Taurean consented to the relationship, she discovered the lie and the exchange ended quickly.

Taureans aren't impressed with the social standing and possessions of other people. They can be mildly impressed with your new BMW or Benz, but don't praise the car more than you do this woman. If you make that mistake too often, she'll be long gone. She wants a man with all the layers of pretentiousness, phoniness and deception peeled back to uncover the real man. She wants a man who's in control and who won't be intimidated by her straightforward and independent nature. Her down-to-earth and easygoing manner, however, make most who know her comfortable and at ease.

During your first meeting with this lady bull, she may ask if you can grow a beard. That may be a sign that she's interested. Taureans usually have out-of-the-way requirements for their potential guy friends. If they are complied with, the Taurean will undoubtedly fall in "like" with the brother. Those quirks may include no gold teeth, shined shoes, or dressing in a decent or up-to-date manner (within the last ten years).

A pleasant evening for the Taurean woman is basically a cheap date. Her idea of relaxation or recreation is chillin' at home with a good book or watching a good love story on television.

The biggest turnoff for the Taurean woman is to be asked for money. She's not stingy and a dutch-treat lunch or dinner once in a while is acceptable. But don't get carried away, dude. They don't play that! Money is the key word with this earth sign, and you'd better spend it wisely. She doesn't like wastefulness.

They don't like to be smothered with attention either. They expect to be complimented when they're immaculately dressed. But because they are comfortable with themselves and who they are, there's really no need to shower them with kisses—not daily anyway.

This sister is a very independent person with an uncanny determination to succeed. She is not the kind of woman to merely sit back on her heels and wait for you to support her. One Taurean doctor, who was the oldest of six children, was her father's favorite child. Even though there was a boy in the family, from as early as age twelve, this little bull was taken to her father's office and shown the ropes of the family insurance business. Although she grew up in the 1940s when independent women were few and far between, she never wavered from her quest to become a doctor. First getting a full scholarship to college, then working her way through medical school, she was driven by her ultimate goal. Her two marriages ended in divorce, in part because of her independence, but her integrity was never compromised, and she became one of the most successful physicians in the country.

The independence of Taurus could be a real problem for some

men. The Taurus sister doesn't want to run the show, but her mate may feel that if he doesn't run it effectively, she can and will.

They have an affinity for organization, especially when it comes to money. When married, they will sometimes have a separate checking account from their spouse. One Taurean I know organizes all of her canceled checks by year and month. Her reasoning was that she had to know where every check was located for easy access; in case she needed a check from 1976, she wouldn't have to look all over for it. Her receipts for bills are organized by amounts and months. If she is missing a single one, everything is put on hold until it's found. (Whew!)

The Taurus sisters are capable of making great sacrifices and are fiercely loyal to family and friends. They take a strong, practical approach to problem solving and adversity. They are usually the glue that holds together the family, marriage, friendship or any situation with the potential of falling apart.

Love Connection

Taurus people move at a snail's pace when it comes to love relationships. Cupid's arrow doesn't score many direct hits with the bull. But Taureans are worth the wait. Like most everything they attempt, they have to think about it first. The Taurus female may think that her potential mate is a fun-loving, down-to-earth "cutie pie." But when the pertinent questions surface, this sister will consider: Is he financially stable? Is he a mama's boy? Is he possessive? If he lives at home with his mom, will that mean he'll want to spend a lot of time at my house? After such considerations, all of the good looks, earthiness and fun in the world is not going to convince the lady bull the relationship is workable. It's thumbs down on this one.

Most Taureans find it hard to show their feelings openly. They will shower you with gifts, but the words "I love you" or "You mean the world to me" may never roll off their tongues. It's not that they are trying to be cool. It's as though they're anticipating rejection and they don't want to get their faces cracked.

When a Taurean finally falls in love, he takes off in hot pursuit of his potential companion most of the time with an insatiable desire to absorb all there is to know about the person. The love-struck bull is giddy and will have you in stitches as he cracks one joke after another. He is also like an octopus with touchy-feely tentacles to a fault.

A Taurus man or woman would be a fine catch for anyone. However, Taureans are stubborn! And I do mean stubborn! You will need a crowbar to get this person to move. They see no reason why they must change or alter their thinking about a particular subject. Their motto is, If it ain't broke, don't fix it!

Like breathing and eating, sex is an essential part of everyday life for the Taurus and a recreation they enjoy. But they want the tried-and-true approach to sex, with very few surprises.

If you want the fireworks to start immediately, the throat and neck areas are the erogenous zones for Taureans. Any touches, strokes or kisses to those areas will make these bulls stand up on their hind legs. And speaking of sex, well, since the bull doesn't talk much, let's just say that he's more of a doer than a talker. Most Taureans won't rest until they feel that the woman is completely satisfied. For the Taurean, if the sex act isn't "complete," they take it personally. Most of the time, it isn't anything that has to do with the Taurean's lack of knowledge, but more fatigue, mental stress and distractions on the part of his companion. Don't worry, Mr. Taurus, the general consensus is that you're doing the job! And "very, very well," says one woman who was dating a Taurean, adding, "Ladies, make sure you get plenty of rest and you're feeling up to it."

As for the Taurus brother, affairs of the heart won't blossom too quickly because he's stubborn and he's not moving until he gets ready—be it toward you or otherwise. Which brings us to the relationship. By the time this man makes a commitment to a marriage or a courtship, you may be out grazing in what you perceive as a greener pasture. But the real field is with the Taurean. He won't make impulsive decisions or offer false hopes and promises that he won't be able to keep. This bull is a man of his word.

The lady bulls have a similar outlook on relationships, but they're not as slow to act as the males. Although the Taurus females are careful, they'll usually know before their male counterpart if a certain brother has potential. When she decides she wants a man, she goes after him. Lady bulls are full of self-confidence. That quality can be somewhat intimidating to men, and it can carry over into the boudoir. The female Taurean will expect her mate to know his way around the bedroom. Sex is important to the females of this sign—and so is a sense of humor. (You might need it if things don't work in the bedroom.) The Taurean sister loves to laugh and be carefree.

Taurus, an earth sign, is most compatible with the two other earth signs, Virgo and Capricorn, because their like personalities generally complement each other. Earth signs are practical, careful and down to earth. Taurus people are also compatible with Cancer and Pisces, the two water signs. Water signs who are emotional and intuitive can provide a nice balance for the serious-minded, practical personality of Taurus. The third water sign, Scorpio, is the opposite sign of Taurus. There is always a strong magnetic attraction between opposites, and the Taurus-Scorpio combination is explosive at best. These two are so passionate together, it's scary. Generally, people born under opposite signs can't seem to get it together other than in the bedroom. These two will argue continuously over major and minor matters—and there won't be much room for compromise.

How to Get Next to a Taurus

• Take these earth signs to a fancy restaurant or cook a good meal at home. The way to a Taurean's heart is through his stomach.

• Don't play games. Taureans appreciate the straightforward approach.

• Be complimentary, but not to excess. Taureans love to feel wanted but not smothered.

• A sense of humor is key. Taureans find that laughter breaks the ice pretty easily.

• Don't be impulsive or spring surprises on this mainstay of the zodiac. They must have prior notice for most things. If you want to go bungee-cord jumping on the first date—or any date—they must know ahead of time.

• Don't ask for money. Money is a sore spot. They are constantly concerned about how to keep it and get more of it, so they certainly don't plan to give you any of their carefully saved nest egg.

- Don't be too consumed with your successes, career and social standing. Taurus people are down to earth and pretty grounded, and they expect their mates to keep the hoity-toity attitude at a minimum.
- To the men: Lay off the Jheri curl or, as one woman called it, the "scary" curl. No polyesters, no tattered or outdated clothing. The Taurean sister likes a man to be well groomed. (The polyesters are now an endangered species!)
- To the women: Keep the hair weave, the electric orange–painted false nails and matching lipstick, and the blue-tinted contact lenses out of sight until after the first date. If you don't, this man will be history.
- If you're overweight, that won't be a problem because Taureans have a tendency to be heavy, too. Moderation is the key, however.

The Taurus Child

Remember the crowbar I mentioned you will need for the stubborn Taureans of the world? Well, while you're at the store, you might as well get two—a baby crowbar for the youngsters and regular one for the big bulls.

Taurean children are strong-willed children, with minds of their own from as early as the toddler years. Using brute force with this little bull will never work—it will only serve to frustrate the parents, and they will have very little energy to discipline the other children. Taurus children thrive on plenty of love, attention and affection; this is the best way to handle any potentially troublesome situation with the Taurus.

The Taurean boy will run home to mommy or daddy to show off the bird he caught that's now mashed from being in the pocket of his jeans all day. Don't faint, mom. Just get used to it. The males are "all boy," showing an early interest in scouting, baseball and any sport where getting dirty is involved. The girls are perfect little ladies, emulating mom with jewelry and makeup or playing with their collection of dolls. If there are boys in the family, however, the girls can be tomboys and will want to "take it to the hoop," playing basketball or any other male-dominated sport.

Taurus children want to belong and be liked, and they are usually readily accepted because of their steady, down-to-earth nature. But in rare situations they can be the victim. For example, a Taurean female teenager was cornered by another female teenager holding a rusty knife during lunch at school. The incident was a culmination of months of arguments, threats, and taunts. The Taurean teenager was cute, along the with the LL factor (light complexion, long hair). The teenager with the knife had a severe case of acne and was overweight. In addition to being envious of Taurus' good looks, she was also jealous of the Taurean's popularity and would constantly pick on the Taurus at every opportunity. When the exchanges finally came to a head, and the Taurean teenager, who was somewhat timid, was cornered by the acne-riddled teenager, the Taurean's best friend fought for and interceded on behalf of the Taurean. Through the entire school year and to this day, the Taurean never understood why her classmate despised her so.

There won't be a lot of punishments for these children. They are pretty even-tempered. They are generally obedient kids who give their parents very few problems. In some cases the Taurean child may emulate an older sibling, who will lead him in the wrong direction. In that case, punishment could occur daily.

The boys are usually the apple of their mother's eye, helping mother with chores, carrying the groceries and hanging out in the kitchen to lick the bowl after the cake batter has been poured into the pans. The girls are usually daddy's little girl and remain so until the grandchildren come along.

Although these children don't grasp schoolwork as readily as other signs, once they grasp Algebra, their powers of recall are phenomenal. And they will be able to pass their knowledge of math along to the grandchildren. They're usually good students who give their teachers or coaches very few problems.

As teenagers, many Taureans are hypercritical of themselves and see themselves as awkward, lackluster geeks with very little to offer. Discussing the birds and the bees with the Taurus child won't be as traumatic as with other children. When the talks start around age ten or eleven, more than likely your Taurean won't even have started "playing doctor" by then. Taureans are sometimes late bloomers and don't usually experiment with sex too early. In other areas, like learning to dance, they may be awkward, stiff and self-conscious. If you ever felt as though you were dancing with a surf board when you were a teenager, it was probably a Taurean.

For example, one female Taurean teenager was so shy that her father ended up finding her a date for her junior prom. Although she protested, she relented when her father (also Taurean) threatened to take her himself. In the 1950s, it was unheard of for girls to attend the prom unescorted. Her date, a first-year military man, guided her on the dance floor even though she couldn't dance and kept her there most of the night. Although he knew all of the latest dance steps and supported her as she tried, dancing was a recreation she never mastered.

With the Taurean, the poor self-image changes once the members of the opposite sex start to notice (and they will!). The second glances, smiles and requests for dates will pick up steam and as a parent, so will your nerves. The telephone will ring off the wall for the little Taurean, and you'll wonder why no one ever calls you anymore.

Taureans will go along with just about anything as long as they feel that there is a logical explanation. A Taurus child in the third grade gave the ball and bat designated for the third grade section to some junior high kids after they explained that someone had stolen theirs and they had to prepare for a game later in the day. The little Taurean's two best friends were against it, but he took it upon himself to make the decision. His friends were furious and gave him a hard time. He eventually got the teacher to retrieve the bat and ball but remembers vividly how his friends dissed him. The recovery process was slow.

Parents, give your little bull love, support, quiet and pleasant surroundings in which to nurture his potential and growth, and you and the family will reap the benefits over time. The adult Taurean will impart the knowledge that he learned from his parents to his own children—and, if need be, will support his or her parents.

The Taurus Employee

Job security is more important to a Taurus than a job with creative control. Working at the post office instead of managing a nightclub would be a more acceptable job for a Taurean. The nightclub business, though high profile, is too risky to attract a Taurean long-term. The income would be too sporadic, and if his paycheck hinged on patronage, he would be miserable. Taureans work at their best when they know they will get paid, come hell or high water.

The best way to get the bulls' goat is to mess with their money or treat them unfairly in the workplace. Generally, Taureans are hard workers and pride themselves on doing their jobs and doing them well.

Taurus employees work best in jobs where they feel that there is a significant need and that they are making a difference. Jobs such as teaching, the medical field, banking, reporting, real estate development and music are positions that highlight the many talents of Taurus and are more suitable for her steady and consistent personality.

Taureans can function effectively as leaders or followers. However, as a follower, his steadfast, conscientious drive to overcome adversity in the workplace makes even the poorest of bosses appear effective. Bosses can usually sit back and relax and know that "ol' reliable" has everything under control.

As supervisors, they will support their employees right down to the wire. They're usually well respected. You won't find any Oreos among this sign. Taurus people don't talk out of both sides of their mouths or straddle both sides of the fence. Once their position about a particular subject is known, it's written in stone.

However, don't misinterpret this trait as wimpishness or lack of courage, because this is simply not the case. They definitely will stand up for what they believe is right or unbecoming on the part of other employees and supervisors. For example, a Taurean in a work situation during a strike crossed the picket line. Some of her coworkers were angry, and one in particular wouldn't give the bull her union newspaper, saying she wasn't a member of the union anymore. This Taurean promptly informed the coworker that union dues continued to be deducted from her check, and as long as there was a deduction she was getting the paper! Even after the supervisor was called to mediate, the Taurean stood firm. This bull received the newspaper.

If any racial slurs or confrontations occur, don't expect the humble Taurean to "cow down." She will quickly challenge any stereotypical comment such as, "Blacks don't score well on tests or college entrance exams." The bull will immediately point out that many of the tests are culturally biased and not representative of African American culture, and she'll more than likely offer statistical documentation. Taurus people also have a tendency to come to the defense of persons who are being dominated by stronger individuals. The Taurean may chime in, "If you want to pick on someone, pick on me." When it comes to confrontation, you better have your facts straight, because they can definitely hold their own during most altercations.

If treated fairly and with respect, they will hang in there through thick and thin with you and your company. Even though they will not walk off a job on impulse, they are not to be taken lightly either. If you accuse a Taurean of negligence in the workplace, you better have detailed documentation, because they will have their own personnel file too.

They are usually well organized, with a system that they painstakingly put in place. All files will be labeled in a system that everyone in the workplace will be able to access. Don't go "festicating" around with it either. The system, I mean. Your innovative suggestions in terms of making changes will fall on deaf ears. You may as well find another person to be innovative with because the Taurean is not interested. And for the most part Taurus people are resistant to change: It's not that they can't do most jobs effectively, it's just that they function best in a predictable situation without abrupt changes.

The Taurean employee never forgets how he is treated initially in the workplace. Those who were unfair to this bull in the beginning will probably have to pay later, no matter how minor the payback. For example, when one Taurean teacher began her teaching career in the late 1960s, it took the all-white office staff twenty minutes to help her when she first arrived at her assigned school. A secretary called the school board to verify that she had indeed been assigned to that school. Once the school year began, many of her white colleagues wouldn't say anything to the five black teachers. One white teacher never said word one for five years until she turned to the Taurean during a staff meeting and asked if she could put her cigarette out in the bull's portable ashtray. With a cold glare, the Taurean said, "No, you may not!"

Health Matters

Taureans are generally stubborn and adverse to change, so this section of the book may be met with some resistance. Although Taureans have strong bodies generally, their weakness for fattening foods such as cake, peach cobbler, liver cheese, yams, corn bread (Southern style, of course, with sugar added) and beer will take its toll over time and force Taureans to diet.

Obesity could be a real problem for Taurus people. One reason for this is that their palates are finely tuned and they are connoisseurs of good food. Because they are stubborn, more than likely they will not be willing to sacrifice the full taste of regular beer just for the sake of "lite" beer and a few calories.

Not only do they enjoy good food; they pride themselves on being excellent cooks. Entertaining at home with loads and loads of culinary delights is a favorite pastime for Taureans. Being a homebody doesn't help the situation either, because after all of the hoopla is over, the Taurus man will retreat to that easy chair or the sister will nestle herself in the corner of the sectional couch amidst the throw pillows for the evening.

Taureans have natural vitality, and although their movement and activities are not deliberate and nonstop like, for example, a Gemini, their activities are nevertheless steady and even, like their personality. They make only moderate attempts at regular exercise. Since the Taurus is not prone to rigorous exercise, walking or activities such as tennis, racquetball or aerobics should be considered.

Physically, they're usually well proportioned, with strikingly beautiful and even skin tone from the darkest cocoa to the paleness of café au lait. The women are usually what is known as "sturdy" or "healthy" in the black culture. They usually have a rather substantial bustline and either long legs or big calves. The Taurean men are hefty as well, with large chests and wide shoulders. Even if they're short in stature, the chest is usually larger than the rest of the body, adding to a virile appearance.

Taurus people should eat foods high in iodine, such as seafood, to keep the thyroid in working order. Also eating plenty of green vegetables and fresh fruit can be a great substitute for pound cake after church. Drinking at least six to eight glasses of water will keep the system flushed out and water retention at a minimum. Here's a tip when grocery shopping, which can become an agonizing experience because of all of the sweets, baked goods and snacks. Have someone accompany the Taurean to the store, blindfold this earth sign and lead her past all her favorite foods. Once she makes it home, she will not likely venture back out for these treats.

Taurus rules the neck and throat, the base of the brain and the lower jaw. Therefore, Taureans are susceptible to bronchitis, thyroid problems and throat infections. When at a football game or in cold, damp weather, this earth sign should always cover the throat area with a scarf or a turtleneck sweater to avoid sore throats and other related problems.

Many Taurus people have thyroid problems and may even have to have them removed. If this happens, the lack of a thyroid can also slow down metabolism of the body, which can also result in weight gain.

As a weight loss measure, one Taurus sister I know went on a sex diet. She informed her Scorpio boyfriend that she enjoyed sex and being at home. She saw no reason why she couldn't lose some weight and at the same time enjoy what she loved. Of course, the Scorpion was more than happy to accommodate her.

Famous African American Taureans

Byron Allen	Ella Fitzgerald
James Brown	Greg Gumbel
Roscoe Lee Browne	Lorraine Hansberry
Joe Clark	Janet Jackson
John Conyers, Jr.	Reggie Jackson
Duke Ellington	Charles R. Johnson
Louis Farrakhan	Coretta Scott King

Black Sun Signs

Sugar Ray Leonard
Sonny Liston
Ronnie Loft
Joe Louis
Ollie Matson
Willie Mays
Dr. Alvin Poussaint
Adam Clayton Powell Sr.
Ma Rainey
Max Robinson

Sugar Ray Robinson
Dennis Rodman
Bernard Shaw
Emmitt Smith
Isiah L. Thomas III
Thurman Thomas
Stevie Wonder
Granville T. Woods
Malcolm X

GEMINI
May 21 to June 20
Symbol: The Twins

Positive traits: Versatile, energetic, a communicator, adaptable, logical, witty, intellectual, spontaneous

Negative traits: Superficial, cunning, inconsistent, restless, secretive, flighty, nosey, devious

Ruling planet: Mercury is associated with intellect and the brain.

The saying, a rolling stone gathers no moss, was probably written with a Gemini in mind. Geminis are constantly on the go and you'll be hard-pressed to keep pace. The symbol of the Gemini is the twins, which means two distinct personalities, so you're actually dealing with or involved with two different people. And, of course, the movements or activities of two people would definitely outnumber those of one. The duality of their personalities finds Geminis with two jobs, sometimes two companions, two hobbies, two lifestyles. The diligent, conservatively dressed office worker by day can become a leather-clad, wild-dancing swinger by night.

Geminis will make the most of any situation. They can easily adapt to most situations without much bother. You won't find them moping around when there's nothing to do; they definitely know how to amuse themselves. If alone, the Gemini may tape-record his philosophies of life to be used later to improve his diction. Or if he's bored, he may simply yell out loud while driving his car. Don't be alarmed. Although this behavior may be bizarre to some, this is simply Gemini's way of breaking the silence, the ice or both.

The men and the women of this sign love change and new situations, so moving on to a new companion, new job or new city is something that the Gemini looks forward to. For example, one Gemini sister, who had a successful career in computer operations, decided to open a braiding salon in Hawaii after she visited the state during a vacation. The tropical, humid climate of Hawaii was not conducive to maintaining black hair in straight styles. Besides, she realized there was a need for this kind of service because there were very few black beauty salons. After conducting her research, she learned of the military bases on the islands. Black women in the military, as well as the wives of men in the service, needed good hair care. I don't have to tell you what a success story this situation turned out to be.

One of the problems with the Gemini is the stick-and-stay attitude: Like the rolling stone, they won't slow down long enough to be caught or carry any excess baggage (if you get my drift). A Gemini might stick around for a while if there's excitement around the clock (you might even have to resort to a few magic tricks, the promise of fame and fortune to begin the next day), but their staying power is sorely lacking. We're talking maybe three months to a year if the Gemini feels the relationship is going nowhere.

Both the men and women of this sign are restless and won't tolerate the routine or boring. They must have excitement and a variety of activities, associates and places to visit. They love being in the spotlight. Get prepared for impromptu comedy routines. He'll be the one to volunteer to go on stage to try and make the audience laugh. She'll be the one to allow the magician to saw her in half or the psychic to hypnotize her. Don't be surprised if you hear something about her that you haven't heard before, for example, that she was a founding member of the Black Panther Party or he was a former member of a nudist colony. The "former member" designation came about because he had a brainstorm: He introduced "swinging," a new form of recreation, to the colony. Oh, well.

The ruling planet for Gemini is Mercury which is associated with intellect and the brain. Like Virgos, whose ruling planet is also

Mercury, Geminis must analyze and examine everything from all angles. So when you meet the Gemini, she probably saw you first and assessed whether you would respond if conversation came up. On the other hand, she also weighed whether to respond to you if you decided to make the first move. In short, Geminis have considered what the overall potential would be of accepting you as a friend, associate, contact or whatever. Even as the conversation progresses with a Gemini, the analysis in his mind is ever present. They'll be enthusiastic or cordial, depending on which personality you are introduced to first. Hopefully, the upbeat personality is the one you'll meet initially. Like it or not, you'll have to get used to two distinct personalities.

Geminis are usually thin, but rather tall people, with long willowy arms and distinctive-looking hands. Their eye-hand coordination and keen intelligence create the gift of manual dexterity. They usually excel in carpentry, sculpting, playing a musical instrument, typing or any undertaking that requires using the hands.

Like the Aquarian, the Gemini will dress in the latest fashions, with all of the details down to a fine science such as nails, cologne or perfume, hairstyle and color-coordinated accessories. If you have the notion of dating a Gemini, I would suggest that you go shopping first. Subscribing to *Ebony Man* or *Essence* magazine to bone up on a few fashion tips first is advisable. When Geminis meet people, appearance will be what strikes them initially. And you may have only one chance to make a good first impression.

Most Geminis are extremely successful because they are extremely intelligent and their brains are constantly working overtime to determine how to keep, make or break a dollar. They will work hard to attain the Lexus or the yacht. And they're not too proud to ask their companion for what they want. For example, the Gemini brother who's trying to save for a Lexus will hint around to moving in with you until he saves enough money for the car. Of course, he may already be living with his mother, cousin or brother, but the goal right now is the Lexus. This approach may be putting the carriage before the horse, but he's got it all figured out (in his mind, anyway).

The sister of the sign won't spend her money readily on you

although she doesn't mind occasionally taking her mate out to dinner, a movie or both. But I would suggest if you plan to start a relationship with a Gemini, you may want to consider a second job, some new duds and some definite ideas on keeping this restless person amused.

The men and women of the sign are the charmers of the zodiac. These air signs have very pleasant-looking faces. Usually, their lips are relatively thin and they have broad grins. Their faces are generally oval in shape. For the most part, the women wear their hair cut short in various styles—a short 'fro, braids, a fade, or they may even go bald. As for the Gemini brothers, they're certainly not above putting texturizers or relaxers in their hair for that added silky look. You just never know with a Gemini.

However, with both the men and women of this sign, getting too emotional with them is a no-no. Emotional behavior makes the Gemini too uncomfortable, and expressing emotions is a sign of weakness. Although inwardly they have their own insecurities and misgivings about personal achievements, they find it very difficult to express how they really feel, even to loved ones. Whenever a questionable situation surfaces, Geminis view the situation logically and won't ever allow emotions to blur their vision.

The Geminí Man

If by chance you have captured this brother's attention, congratulations! Most of the time they're so preoccupied with the thought of their next move, they hardly notice people in general, and women in particular. The Gemini man, however, has the capacity for love, and when he is in love, he puts all his energy in that direction—for as long as he's interested. The relationship will be full of fun, with loads of interesting outings and stimulating conversation. However, because of the dual personality traits, Geminis can also be cheap. It's called self-preservation. They do have expensive tastes, and during Christmas and birthdays, the gifts will be on it. But the "just because" trinkets may be on the cheap side because this air sign must save his money for early retirement.

As the companion of a Gemini, you won't be able to believe

what a class act this brother is, including champagne, roses and maybe a serenade. He may even write you a song or two. But, you know, sister girl, there's got to be a "but" there somewhere. The Gemini brother, with his dual personality, will definitely be a challenge to keep up with. His temperament, moods, and general outlook run hot and cold, but thankfully, not all at the same time. When the cold side of this brother surfaces, and it will, just back off. Don't continue to ask him what's wrong or if it was something you said. This tactic will not bring him out of his funk, but will only add fuel to the flame and make matters worse. In an effort to get you to back off, he may say some unkind words. Leave him alone. Give him some space. Don't expect to see your Gemini mate until you see him. And above all else, don't take it personally, because you'll be constantly licking your wounds. Later, when this air sign resurfaces and acts like nothing has ever gone wrong, take it with a grain of salt. That way, you won't be disappointed.

One Aquarius sister became so fed up with the disappearing acts of her Gemini companion that she ended the relationship without telling him. This brother would call and say that he was on his way to pick her up for a drive to the country or shopping, but then he wouldn't show up. What the Aquarian didn't realize was that several projects came up between the time he left home and when he made it to her house. Check the Gemini's story out: "As I was pulling out of the driveway, my homeboy from Chicago came by to say hello and he was only in town for a day. After I talked to my homeboy, my mom wanted me to go and pick up her medicine. The prescription couldn't be refilled, and I had to wait around until the doctor called it in. The reason I didn't call was because I knew you'd be mad and I knew that I'd be over there the next day. Then next day, I couldn't find my keys, and my sister wasn't home, so I couldn't get my second set." The point is, this scenario, in which this air sign is the central figure with all of his many activities and intentions, will be played out over and over. He does have good intentions (most of the time). Just kidding! The brother simply has a million and one activities in the works.

As friends, Geminis will definitely be there through thick and thin, if you can locate them. They're usually always upbeat and can keep you laughing and your attention diverted from any depression. But like everything else in his life, the Gemini seeks new challenges, including friends. Don't get upset if he doesn't call. He's probably out of town, on a new job, simply out of his mind for the moment or distracted by a new adventure.

To get his attention during the intimate hours of the relationship, you might have to resort to a tabletop dance or even a striptease routine. Again, the preoccupation with all the many aspects of his life finds this Gemini brother distracted.

If you happen to be married to a Gemini man or if you're considering matrimony, you should know that the marriage is going to be unpredictable and anything but boring. The key to dealing with a Gemini husband is to be flexible and roll with the punches. Here's a typical scenario with a Gemini: The phone is ringing off the wall as you're walking in the door with groceries in one hand and the dry cleaning in the other, all the while stepping over building blocks and newspapers. It's your husband on the telephone. "Honey, the district manager is in town for one day, and I invited him over for dinner." As he's talking, you're looking around the house at what looks like the aftermath of a tornado. Before you can go completely off on your husband, he puts the district manager on the phone. "Ms. Jones, thanks so much for inviting me to dinner. My wife and I will have to return the favor when you come to D.C." Well, you're stuck now, so you might as well start flying around the room to get things rolling. Your Gemini husband played that scene just right—and there will be plenty more where that one came from. But what you perceive as irresponsible behavior on the part of your mate is in actuality a means to an end. Your Gemini husband definitely has plans to get closer to the manager because one never knows when the dinner invitation will be useful as a payback of sorts. In short, everything he does is analyzed, thought out and examined. So be prepared and be flexible.

Even in college, the Gemini brother will expect his girlfriend to come over to help with the cleanup of the apartment in preparation for the fraternity party that he volunteered to have at his place the entire semester. During the party, if you happen to glance over and see him flirting shamelessly with your roommate, and she's loving every minute of it, well . . . that's the Gemini charm. When the party's over, this brother will still want you to remain to help clean up.

But aside from what may be perceived as frivolity, a Gemini can hold his own and take the brightest and boldest to task on most issues. For example, when a Gemini brother graduated from a traditional black university in the South in the late 1960s, he was hired by one of the top automakers as an engineer because at the height of the civil rights movement, company executives were doing the right thing and giving blacks a chance in positions traditionally only held by white men. Although this brother had to compete with graduates of Massachusetts Institute of Technology, he was undaunted and stayed up most nights reading background materials and playing catch-up. And the Gemini brother caught up.

The Gemini Woman

The Gemini sister will be a real challenge to understand. If you know anything about chess, you know that one game can go on and on and on before a conclusion can be drawn as to who's going to win. Thus is a relationship with a Gemini woman. With Gemini women, you just never know until, maybe, when it's over.

There are some pointers you need to proceed and some to succeed. First and foremost, just because she was warm and friendly initially, don't make assumptions that she'll be ready to sit in your lap and feed you grapes on the second meeting. I hate to keep harping on this subject, but Geminis *are* the sign of the twins. So in the course of the relationship, platonic or otherwise, you'll be meeting two personalities. (Hopefully, that's all. Sometimes there may be more if other planets in her birth chart are Gemini. But, that's another talk show altogether.) And, heaven forbid, if she's literally born a twin, you'll need all the energy, gusto and nerve you can muster to keep up with this air sign.

Also, these sisters must feel that they can do their own thing. And you as a friend or companion won't impede progress. Gemini sisters are fiercely independent, so they won't generally feel compelled to constantly cater to a mate. Geminis are full of fun and love to embark on new adventures. They'll most definitely support you in all of the new projects, cheerleading on the sidelines and offering a few well thought-out suggestions. But remember, she's got her own fish to fry. And if I were you, I wouldn't sit in the kitchen waiting for her because you might go hungry.

One Gemini sister, a songwriter and businesswoman, ended up leaving her Scorpio husband after a few months of marriage. Her husband, ten years her senior, was demanding and controlling and wanted his wife to more or less put her career on hold for the sake of the marriage. When this Gemini woman married her husband during the 1960s, at age twenty-five, she was already established in her career, owned a house and drove a luxury car. Back then this was virtually unheard of for a woman her age, black or white. This brother couldn't take her independence, and she ended the relationship as abruptly as it began: When her husband came home from work one day, she and her belongings were gone.

These sisters work hard to achieve their goals and they expect the same from friends, family or companions. They won't readily buy into the "I'm a black man trying to survive in this racist society" routine. It's not that they feel a person can't fall on hard times. Rather, Gemini women believe that if they can be successful, so can all of those who bellyache. It's a matter of doing something about the situation. For she believes that men, both black and white, should have a commitment to their philosophy and ideals of life and be able to deal with problems without a lot of complaints or excuses.

Some people feel Gemini women are unapproachable. When a guy looks at a Gemini woman who's dressed to the nines with not a strand of hair out of place, he may feel a bit intimidated. Don't. That may be her goal—but again one never knows. The Gemini woman is what brothers consider "high maintenance." She's the sister who works hard, has a good job, and usually treats herself well, and she expects her companion to do the same.

If and when you approach the Gemini sister, the line you give her better be original. Please don't come up with a lame line like "Don't I know you?" It won't work. A better line would be something that is open and honest. Try, "I was having a not so pleasant day, but all of that changed after I noticed you."

Gemini

Even if the line is good, Gemini sisters won't lose sight of what they want. If you hesitate, you might be left in the lurch. One Gemini sister, although very intrigued by a Virgo brother, never lost her momentum as she moved from Memphis to Atlanta to Houston and then back to Memphis, all in a three-year period. Oh, by the way, she's back in Atlanta. And where is the smitten Virgo? He got married after a four-month courtship to forget the Gemini. Good luck, sweetie!

If you happen to be the one who is pining away for the Gemini woman and you finally win her heart, trying to force her into domesticity will be the same as breaking a wild stallion. It's going to be tough! The domestic scene for the Gemini sister won't be at all what you expect. There won't be any aprons, baked cookies, homemade pies or rolls. Many Gemini women can cook, but because they don't have time or won't take time, the cooking scene is something they do only if it's an emergency. For example, if her mother is sick, she'll make the chicken soup. But if you look a little closer, it may just be doctored-up Campbell's.

Gemini women are very comfortable being single. They're so busy enjoying themselves, they may not even stop to consider matrimony. Why should they if life is simply grand as it is? Why screw up a good thing?

If they get married, Gemini women make good parents because they're a lot like their children. They are fun-loving mothers, they love life and they won't be stern disciplinarians. They will want their children to follow important rules, like keeping up grades and doing homework, but these air signs will sometimes vacillate and give in to their children. Gemini parents give their children a zest for life, but one word of warning to the free spirits that Gemini women can be: In exposing your young children to adult-related issues, you must never treat them as equals.

Love Connection

By this point, your head is probably spinning from all the requirements or stipulations that the Geminis have undoubtedly placed along the paths to their hearts. But if you can hang in there, the

Gemini experience, or should I say the Gemini *phenomenon,* will last a while even if you're no longer involved. Gemini people are the charmers of the zodiac. An experience with any Gemini will leave you thoroughly entertained. They are almost always the life of the party, telling great stories or great lies. They're usually well versed on a variety of topics and are generally lively and flirtatious by nature. They will lead the group in song, either playing the piano, singing, directing or all three.

Once you get this air sign's attention, the chase or the wooing will be a wonderful experience. They enjoy the chase more than the actual capture. The key here is to play hard to get—Geminis love a good challenge. A challenge is mentally stimulating to this Mercury-ruled sign. All you have to do is tell them that they can't have something, and they will use all their feminine wiles or manly tactics to let you know (if that is what they seek) that it's just a matter of time.

A Gemini sister endured an on-again, off-again relationship with her Aries mate for ten years. The brother eventually married someone else and then later determined that he had married the wrong woman. When he approached the Gemini about marriage, admitting that he had made the wrong choice, the sister was no longer interested. You see, the chase was over.

For the Gemini sister, the idea of a fun date does not include being taken to her mate's mother's house to enjoy small talk or going to an eatery with a big handwritten sign that reads No Checks Accepted. Instead, she would rather go horseback riding, take a weekend trip or just be surprised with a spontaneous outing where you've planned the entire evening and all she has to do is show up. A date that included getting on a commuter airplane and enjoying champagne as the two of you flew over the Atlantic Ocean would definitely be to her liking.

If you're considering dating a Gemini man, you'll get a clear sense that he's interested in your mind and not necessarily your body (not right away, anyway). For understanding women and how they think is the key to understanding subsequent female relationships that he's sure to find himself in.

With the Gemini, the relationship will be kind of like playing tennis. (The difference here is you'll be playing a singles match and he will be playing doubles.) The Gemini will jockey for position, and the potential companion will counter with some moves of her own. But let me caution you against making your move too soon with a Gemini: If you're wrong about this air sign's interest in you, you'll be totally embarrassed. For example, a Gemini woman who attended a party with a first date pretended that she didn't know the dude after he got a little too drunk and started talking too loudly. When the party was over, the Gemini had disappeared back to her secure abode.

Remember, Gemini is the sign of the twins. Even if you're given the go-ahead on the relationship and everything is proceeding as planned, you may still encounter a person you don't know when the other personality rears its ugly head. It's called the Jekyll and Hyde syndrome—they simply can't help it. So when this occurs, make yourself scarce.

Once you find yourself in a bedroom situation with the Gemini, if you're an emotional person who's full of passion, you may feel like you're going to bed with a robot. The sexual encounter will be complete with all of the right moves, but the emotional drama of the entire connection may be lacking. Again, don't take it personally— Geminis can't help their lack of emotion. They do have a little, but they're usually preoccupied with all of life's twists and turns. Even in the bedroom, you probably won't ever have a Gemini's undivided attention.

However, stroking the hands and arms of the Gemini may get their attention. Hand kissing and massages, along with feathery touches on the arms and shoulders will make the Gemini come alive, for a while anyway. And again, remember the dual nature of the Gemini. On any given day, their sexual appetite may become adventuresome. They love to experiment sexually and sometimes find themselves participating in perverted behavior that may even include multiple sex partners. It's really hard to predict what Geminis will do, because most of the time they don't know themselves.

Geminis are compatible with Aquarians and Libras, the two other air signs, particularly those who allow them to have their freedom while at the same time supporting them in their many endeavors. The element air knows no boundaries: No matter how a person tries, he or she cannot contain air. And Geminis will not be controlled and manipulated—they simply won't stand still long enough.

Aries and Leo are also compatible mates with Gemini. Both these fire signs have plenty of self-confidence and won't be intimidated by Gemini's flirtatious nature, charm, good looks and outgoing personality. Of the elements of the universe, air and fire mix well together.

The opposite of Gemini is Sagittarius. Opposites are the most intriguing of the horoscope because opposites attract. And boy, with these two, I do mean attract. But the physical activity and the stimulating conversation will not salvage this liaison alone. After the initial sparks, the relationship will die down because Sagittarius will forever seek the next new fun relationship, and Gemini simply can't stand to be bored even for a minute. The problem here is that these two are much too different to stick and stay.

How to Get Next to a Gemini

• Be sincere; they can tell intuitively when someone is shamming.
• Dressing neatly in the latest styles will always score points with a Gemini. If you want to accompany the Gemini, you must look the part. Image is everything.
• They love intelligence. Don't conjugate the verb *to be,* by saying "I be, you be, he, she or it bees." They don't acknowledge black English. You'll get corrected every time.
• They detest the routine and the boring. They are intrigued by original ideas and spontaneous adventuresome dates.
• A good sense of humor will be a plus in dealing with the Gemini's dual personality.
• A variety of looks excite Geminis and pique their interest. Wigs, hair weaves, braids and dreadlocks are generally acceptable. For Gemini, it all adds to the deception and mystery of the potential mate.
• You will need to get plenty of rest to keep up with a Gemini. They are constantly on the move, involved in a variety of projects that *they* can barely keep up with. Just be prepared!

• When buying presents remember to purchase gadgets or items that are mentally stimulating, such as computer games, puzzles or books.
• Don't wear sunglasses at night. Image is everything to a Gemini. And instead of projecting the cool look, you'll be accused of the country look.
• You need your own life. Don't play twenty questions with a Gemini. They value their privacy. You'll only know what they allow you to know.

The Gemini Child

There's never a dull moment when this feisty little youngster is around. The ol' saying, Having children around keeps a person young, was probably created with a Gemini child in mind. These children are constantly on the move, even as babies. And if you're the lucky parent, you'll be constantly on the move as well, chasing after him in the house or on an outing or in later years chauffeuring her to cheerleading practice, the debate club meeting, choir rehearsal, shopping or basketball practice. You may also find yourself playing the role of the answering service when the telephone is ringing off the wall and all the calls are for your Gemini youngster. In any case, the weekend will be lost.

As infants, they will walk, talk and get into trouble very early. You absolutely cannot leave these children alone because their motor skills develop very early. And sometimes with these children, the hand is quicker than the eye, so monitor them closely. They understand very early that they can get away with a lot more when mom or dad is not present. Potty training is a horse of a different color. The little Gemini shows his two sides very early; their little personalities evolve just as quickly as they do. On one day, the potty training will go really well, but on other days, this child will be cranky and annoyed and simply will not sit on the pot, not even for a minute. So throw away the potty-training books, because each attempt will be a different story.

Even as a toddler, the little Gemini needs lots of mental stimulation in the form of books, building blocks, and colorful toys with a challenge. Also providing these youngsters with musical instruments or exposing them to music of all types will calm their restless little spirits, and enrolling this little air sign in music lessons of some type is always a good idea. For example, the father of a Gemini boy introduced him to music as a toddler by placing the earphones of the stereo against his tiny ears; the child listened intently. When the boy started piano lessons at age five, the teacher was amazed at his sense of rhythm and the ease with which he was able to play.

During adolescence, their ability to communicate and to persuade will have you as parents marveling over their ability to entertain and their creativity of presenting details of an out-of-town trip or a trek to the movies. But sometimes Gemini youngsters can become so adept at presentation that they have a hard time separating fact from fiction. If these youngsters find themselves in a tight squeeze, they are not above telling a lie—and not just a yes or no lie, but a tall tale with full details.

At school, this child will be the center of attention. If everything doesn't go her way, she's prone to temper tantrums. She figures out very early that this is one way to get what she wants. But her attention span is short, and enrollment in a strictly regimented school with few creative outlets may be more of a detriment than an advantage for the Gemini child.

Learning to complete projects and pay attention in school will be hard for Gemini children. They will be most interested in new projects or subjects; maintaining and sustaining the interest of this air sign will be the real challenge. The problem here is that, like the adults, Gemini children invariably have too many interests, and schoolwork, if not monitored, will be the sacrificial lamb. The key is to allow these children social activities on condition that they maintain good study habits. And stick to your guns!

All the young Gemini needs is five minutes of your time to convince you of how important being a member of the Social Gents is, and how he simply, absolutely and definitely couldn't miss the initiation meeting, and how he would be thrown out of the most exclusive club in the city if he wasn't allowed to attend.

When they start driving as teenagers, I suggest that you keep an extra set of car keys as a backup because they will forever lose such items as keys, jackets, sweaters, books, even tennis shoes if these items aren't nailed down or surgically attached to this air sign. Sometimes you'll be lucky if she can find her way home when she is totally preoccupied with so many endeavors at once.

Just to let you know, Gemini children won't be all that organized either. So when you awaken them every morning for school, be sure to allot some extra time for last-minute "I can't find my books, project, house keys . . ." scrambles. This move will save you from pulling your hair out—and it will also keep you from being late for work.

Also, an early introduction to the birds and the bees is almost always warranted. These young air signs are extremely popular with the opposite sex, and as a parent, you won't be able to monitor your Gemini, who is elusive, secretive and curious. Without a detailed talk about the dangers, ramifications and detrimental effects of early involvement with sex, teenage pregnancy could be a problem.

When these children are very young, they may have an identity crisis about their African American heritage. These children will interact with children of all races. As observers, Gemini youngsters will readily grasp the race factor and what it all means. And as a parent, you need to have a full discussion of racism, the importance of being black and proud, and how this little Gemini fits into the total scheme of things. Later, as the child develops and understands, he will become more conscious of his own ethnicity and will definitely develop his own style in dress, demeanor and personality.

The Gemini Employee

Geminis are the communicators of the zodiac. These people are so agile verbally and mentally that they could most assuredly sell you some swampland in Florida. And you'd probably be pleased about it and totally convinced that the venture was a good investment. They definitely have the gift of gab. And when they make the ol' sales pitch, it's been analyzed, examined and well planned before the execution. So by the time the Gemini has your attention, the deal is basically history. For example, a very successful Gemini car salesman constantly moved from dealership to dealership, forever seeking the new challenge. The only time this brother slowed his quicksilver approach was when a lovely female entered the showroom. Then during the transaction, his comment to her would invariably be that just in case a courtship was imminent, he needed to give this lovely creature a good deal so it wouldn't cost him so much money. Even though the comments were made in jest, there's always method to the Gemini's madness.

Geminis also excel as journalists, receptionists, salespeople and writers and in fields where their written and verbal skills can be used to their fullest potential. They hate being bored with mundane, tedious work. Jobs as a security guard, a clerk filing and purging old records, a telephone operator or a no-brainer position where there is very little movement, creative input or responsibility won't ever hold a Gemini's interest. If, by chance, Geminis are in such a position, they will be compelled to create an additional outlet to channel the mental overload that this Mercury-ruled sign dictates. For example, if he's a social worker or counselor, he may be a promoter, bringing jazz groups such as Grover Washington or Ramsey Lewis to a city that has very little exposure to jazz. There must be at least the prospect of a job that will awaken many of the Gemini's creative juices; otherwise, they will create it.

A warning to bosses: Don't stifle the Gemini's creativity or pigeonhole her in a situation in which she feels unappreciated. Geminis can do it all. They're so versatile and fast on their feet that you won't be able to keep pace. Remember, you're dealing with two personalities, so they can actually do the work of two people, or maybe more. For example, the Gemini sister will organize the fundraiser for the congressional incumbent, write the speech, convince the sponsors to support the event, step in for the musician who's running late and even cajole the spectators, contributors and passersby. In short, any jobs that provide unique and changeable situations are best suited to the Gemini.

And handling racism and strife on the job is no problem either. Although Geminis have a pretty easygoing, nonthreatening nature, they usually get what they want in the workplace by outsmarting their adversary. This air sign will finesse the situation without ever raising his voice. For example, when a doctor ignored a black registered nurse, who just happened to be a Gemini, to address issues of patient care with a white nurse's assistant, the assistant turned to the

Gemini nurse to get the answers. After several questions, the assistant told the doctor that he needed to ask the nurse. Turning to the nurse, the doctor assured her that he hadn't been aware of her position. The sister kindly pointed out that he knew that nurses wear white and assistants wear pink, and that therefore the oversight must have been intentional because he wasn't interested in talking to a nurse in white who was black.

If you're the boss, you'll simply marvel at the creative ability and intelligence of a Gemini. But while you're in the marveling state, the Gemini will convince you that she needs to either be put in charge, promoted or given a substantial raise—or all of the above! And she will eventually achieve that goal.

She simply must have an avenue through which to express herself. And expression means allowing her to have flexible hours and not watching the clock or her every move. Granted she may be a few minutes late getting back from lunch—for a Gemini, having her nails done or going to the sale at the exclusive men's store takes precedence over being back from lunch on time—but the image and style that she projects will make you stand up and take notice.

Although Geminis can lead effectively for a designated period, they're far too restless to remain in a supervisory role. They simply don't have the staying power to even aspire to such goals. They are the creators and implementors of the ideas. That doesn't mean that after the ideas have progressed to realities, the Gemini will be interested in overseeing the life of the project. The challenge for Geminis is in coming up with the idea. Their attention span isn't long enough to supervise the end results.

Health Matters

Wait a minute! Hold it! These commands are for the Gemini who is in perpetual motion. Even as they rest in a reclining position, their minds are continuously at work. They are constantly analyzing, debating and strategizing their next move. The analysis is probably reminiscent of how the decision was made about whether apartheid would continue in South Africa—in the terms of how many years it took to abolish it altogether.

Mercury, their ruling planet, is associated with the intellect. If

Geminis don't take heed, the mental stress will translate into physical stress. They probably won't take the time to read this entire section, so I better get to the point pretty quickly.

1. Geminis have lots of nervous energy that they must channel. They are restless and live on the edge. Geminis must slow the pace and find ways of relaxing, such as meditating, sitting in a sauna or listening to classical music or soft jazz to soothe their nerves.

2. Geminis have a tendency to run, run, run until they drop. There are only twenty-four hours in a day; therefore, properly planning activities and giving priority to those ventures that are most important should be addressed.

3. This air sign has a tendency to eat sporadically and are the kings and queens of the junk food world. Geminis must eat well-balanced meals as often as possible. Substitute a few carrot and celery sticks for that microwaved burrito sometimes. I know that the burrito can be held in one hand while the Gemini is driving and talking on the car phone, but so can the carrot sticks.

4. Geminis' mental dexterity has them biting off much more than they can physically chew. With their dual personality, they are completely comfortable doing more than one thing simultaneously. Therefore, rest, regular working hours and a good balanced diet are essential for the well-being of this air sign. And take a multivitamin supplement, too.

5. The sign of Gemini rules the lungs, arms, shoulders, hands, and nerves; therefore, these areas of the body are susceptible to injury or ailments. You can sometimes keep a nagging cough indefinitely because of your frayed nerves, lack of good nutrition and inability to rest. To help keep lung and throat ailments to a minimum, eat such vegetables as green beans, asparagus, carrots and cauliflower. Also, dairy products such as milk, yogurt and cottage cheese help to promote stronger bones.

Taking the time to shop for groceries is not even an idea that enters Geminis' heads, especially if they are single. If they're married, the shopping usually falls to the spouse. Grocery shopping for the Gemini is an exercise in futility. They simply don't see the point in wasting all of that time shopping for food when they can eat out, run by mom's or grab a bite on the run.

Gemini

Geminis are generally slim, and they see being slim or looking good as justification for their erratic eating habits. But there's certainly no substitute for being healthy as well as slim. Avoid excessive amounts of caffeine, cigarettes and alcohol. They shouldn't ever be substituted for nutritional foods. I know that it's hard to convince Geminis of the validity of any information that's of a long-term nature, such as eating better for better overall health, but since Geminis only really stand up and take notice of a point if it affects them immediately, go to the library and check out the statistics on good health and see for yourself. If you won't take the time now, I hope you won't be perusing medical journals later while you're in the hospital suffering from anemia and exhaustion.

Famous African American Geminis

Raymond Andrews
Dusty Baker
Josephine Baker
Lou Brock
John Carlos
Bernie Casey
Benjamin Chavis, Jr.
Miles Davis
Charles Drew
Marian Wright Edelman
Morgan Freeman
Nikki Giovanni
Louis Gossett, Jr.
Marvelous Marvin Hagler
Roy Innes
LaToya Jackson
James Weldon Johnson
Gladys Knight

Patti LaBelle
Curtis Mayfield
Hattie McDaniels
Davey Moore
Eleanor Holmes Norton
The artist formerly known as Prince
Phylicia Rashad
Lionel Richie
Gale Sayers
Betty Shabazz
Bruce Smith
Tommie Smith
Henry Ossawa Tanner
Leslie Uggams
Keenen Ivory Wayans
Paul Winfield
Coleman Young

CANCER

June 21 to July 22

Symbol: The Crab

Positive traits: Receptive, sensitive, sympathetic, kind, shrewd, intuitive, thrifty, emotional

Negative traits: Moody, changeable, hypersensitive, messy, unforgiving, unstable, overly emotional, overindulgent in self-pity

Ruling planet: The Moon is associated with emotions, feelings and intuitive powers.

If you've ever talked to a person to whom you felt compelled to pour out your soul, it was probably a Cancer. And if you wondered why you did such a thing, it was probably because the nurturing and sympathetic vibe of the Cancer made you feel so at ease. Cancers are down-to-earth, practical and sensible. They're usually the voice of reason.

These people (males included) are the mothers of the zodiac. They will give advice whether you want it or not. It's usually good advice too. For example, one young man decided to tell his girlfriend's mother off. His coworker, a Cancer brother, cautioned him against making such an impulsive move. The girlfriend was only sixteen and the mother was skeptical about having a nineteen-year-old date her daughter. The Cancer pointed out to his coworker that the girl's mother was the only link to his girlfriend, and then told him to chill out and be patient. Eventually, after several short visits and reassurances from the nineteen-year-old, the mother relented. Now, of course, the Cancer brother is bombarded with questions about what the coworker's next move should be. But Cancers love that! Cancers love feeling needed.

Cancer is the sign of the crab, which means they'll hold on for dear life and never let go, either in love relationships or friendships. Cancer people will be lifetime friends—reliable and there for you no matter what their present station in life is. Their ruling planet, the Moon, is associated with emotions and feelings. In short, these people are one big lump in the throat. If you've ever noticed the man in the moon, he has somewhat of a jolly look about him and so do Cancerians. Consider the various stages of the moon—new moon, full moon, crescent moon, and so on. Such are the various changes you'll find in this water sign. There will never be a dull moment with this chameleon of moods. One minute she'll laugh in reckless abandon as she tells you the story of her husband's great-aunt's funeral in rural Mississippi. Of course, the subject matter is serious enough, but when the Cancer's creative sense of humor recounts the whole or (hole) details, there won't be a dry eye in the room. "The grave was too small, it had rained torrents the night before, and when the coffin was lowered into the ground, it became apparent that the grave was more square than rectangular. While all the folks are standing in mud up to their ankles, dressed in their Sunday best, trying to determine what to do next, a nonfamily member suggests placing the coffin in an upright position, and next, an argument starts." Enough said.

Then the next minute, this Cancer sister will be complaining about the wideness of her butt, a cross for black women to bear since the beginning of time. The point is, that trait is not changing. It won't matter to this sister that she has a brick-house figure. She'll always hang on to some minor detail of her physical appearance that will cancel out all of her positive attributes.

The physical appearance of Cancerians runs the gamut. They can be either tall or short and sometimes pleasingly plump from all of the family gatherings. The Cancer is the designated cook who'll prepare all of the long, drawn-out meals like peas, fried corn, chicken and dressing that usually take all day. The meals are so good they make you want to slap your mama and then go to sleep. Even the men of the sign love to eat and cook. Their chubbiness comes from being totally immersed in the process. These crabs have nice, full moon-shaped faces. The arms of Cancer people are usually long and slim in proportion to the rest of the body. The hands and feet of a Cancer are usually large, even if the Cancer is small in stature. The mouth is wide, with a broad grin.

Cancer men are just as moody as the women, even without premenstrual syndrome to add insult to injury. They will sulk in silence, and you'll never know what the problem is. Moody Cancerians either overcome their moodiness or allow it to plunge them into the depths of despair. In the latter case, don't bother trying to coax this moon child out of it—it will be futile on your part. The phrase "Leave me alone, I'm having a crisis," was probably coined by a Cancer.

As a rule, Cancers spend their money wisely. They love to dress when they do go out, but the outfit won't cost as much as their last paycheck, and it won't be the gold metallic jumpsuit or the skintight leather pants either. They know how to dress, but these frugal people are going to spend only so much on clothing or on you. A Cancer man who's a driver for a courier service has a pet peeve: "Women kill me. When you try to buy them a drink, they want to order the most expensive brandy or cognac. Before I made the offer, she was drinking cheap white wine." Hmm.

Cancer people are doting parents. As one Cancerian flight attendant put it, "My daughter is the air I breathe." I think that about sums it up for most Cancers. Sometimes these parents find it hard to allow their children to grow up. Cancers love living in the past; so many times, they're unwilling to see their children as mature and responsible teenagers or adolescents. Stop smothering and hovering, Cancers. It's going to be okay. Living in the past also carries over to love relationships. "The Way We Were" is the theme song for most Cancers. If you're an old flame from high school or the first person the Cancer fell in love with, chances are, he or she hasn't gotten over the relationship. And you probably haven't either. There may be weddings bells in the future after all.

On the other hand, if you're the new companion, and the old

flame won't let go of the Cancer, there could be trouble. Long after a relationship with a Cancer has ended, the ex may often have trouble moving on. The reason: Many times Cancerians overindulge their companions by spoiling them with gifts and pampering, and during this process, the ex doesn't appreciate the relationship until it's over. Stand your ground. Remember, you (meaning the new mate) have it going on now.

You'll find Cancers hanging with the posse at the club, at a party, on a picnic, watching a game with friends or simply shooting the breeze and chillin' at home. One of the favorite outings for Cancers is watching a full moon while snuggling close to a loved one. There doesn't have to be any sex involved. Stimulating conversation, a bottle of wine, good oldies and you—that's all that's necessary.

The Cancer Man

This brother put the W in Wonderful, so sit back and enjoy! He will wine and dine you and send flowers even before the two of you determine that you're in a courtship. He's a very caring, romantic and considerate person. The water signs, of which Cancer is one, are emotionally charged people who are sympathetic to whatever a person is going through. The men respond in a way that they know will touch the emotions and support the person. A card with a thoughtful message—"Enjoyed meeting you. Let's get together soon."—is his way of ensuring that he won't get his face cracked by coming on too strong or by making certain assumptions, namely, that a sister is interested before she gives him the go-ahead.

Besides, this brother's overtures will be subtle. He doesn't like a woman being too forward with him either. Actually, he's the old-fashioned type from the old school. A wink from a female across the room is okay, but bumpin' and grindin' on the dance floor in front of strangers with the bright lights on is out of the question. He has preconceived notions of how women ought to act. You see, as a youngster, his mother was the first female he knew and adored, and he'll be looking for those same characteristics in you as a potential companion.

If you're dating a Cancer man, or thinking about it, you need to plan to get to know his family in general and his mother in particular. Cancer people have strong emotional ties to family, especially mom. You'll be seeing a lot of his mother. Try to look as interested as you can when his mama relates story after story on how quickly he was potty-trained, when he took his first steps or even when he hurled the chocolate cake in the air during his birthday party at age two. If his mother calls him "Junior" or "June Bug," you're in trouble—Cancer men are mama's favorite most of the time. The biggest mistake any woman could ever make is to say something derogatory about his mother, even in jest.

Yes, Cancer men can be mama's boys and may even be considered kind of nerdy or even geeky. But please don't buy into the false philosophy of appreciating another man who'll dog you out more than the Cancer who's the nice guy. If you don't appreciate what he brings to the relationship, you'll be the loser.

Although black people love to jump sharp and be dressed, Cancer men are the casual dressers. This brother would rather wear a jogging suit than a Brooks Brothers suit any day. They just don't understand what all of the commotion and fuss is about. If they're white-collar workers, working hours will probably be the only time you'll see them dressed—except maybe for church. So if you're preparing for a date and the Cancer brother needs to be dressed, I would advise you to tell him so beforehand.

However, Cancers are resourceful. One Cancer lawyer who was in his fifties, decided he no longer wanted to wear Jockey shorts because the underwear was too tight and cut off his blood circulation. Although he wanted to impress his companion, he felt that wearing Jockeys was a waste of time except on days when he was pretty sure he would score. In that case, he made sure he had a pair of french-cut bikini pants in a leopard or tiger print in his briefcase handy. When it was time to disrobe, he would simply go into the bathroom for a quick change.

The Cancer brother likes a woman to be somewhat intelligent, although it's not a requirement. Physical contact is important, but one Cancer brother commented that his last relationship didn't get off the ground because his companion was as dense as the tropics. There was never any discussion of world issues, which he liked to talk about on occasion, because for that woman, world issues didn't extend past her neighborhood. Early on in the relationship he was "too through."

Cancer brothers, like the females of the sign, can also be very nurturing. They do love family life and are more comfortable married than single. However, if he's single, he'll be the child who'll be more than responsible for caring for his elderly mother. Such was the case with one Cancer brother, the baby of six children. Although there are two daughters and three other sons in the family, this brother, who is the sole provider for his mother, bathes, feeds and provides what she needs.

The Cancer brother has an excellent memory and will remember every detail of a chance meeting. When you happen to see this brother years later, he'll be able to tell you how the two of you met and even what you talked about. He's a loyal and devoted friend and will not only stay up all night at a coffee shop with you while you hash out the details of a relationship gone sour, but serve as a witness in the divorce fight, too.

If you happen to have a Cancer parent, well, you'll have two parents in one. The first will be a stern disciplinarian who won't want you to go to the dance with that new boy that he's suspicious of. On the other hand, he's a cream puff of a guy, who simply loves his family. He's glad that you're his son or daughter, and during this mood, life will be grand and he'll laugh, joke and be your best friend.

Cancer men are good husbands and revere the home and family and even sometimes cutting the lawn; it's the total family package that they want. The Cancer man will be looking over his wife's shoulder, trying to determine what she put in the vegetable broth to make it taste so good.

Since he's so money-conscious, instead of hiring someone, he'll volunteer to repair the trim around the house. Even if he doesn't know how to do the repair work, there are always books. If all else fails, he'll find a friend who'll charge half the cost.

The Cancer Woman

One of the first things that has to happen with a Cancer woman is, she must feel you're being yourself. If you're acting, you'll definitely get off on the wrong foot. Her antennae are always up, and she can spot a phony a mile away, so don't even go there. Cancerian women are interested in how the person treats other people first and in material things last. Case in point: Her companion will need to have a car, but it certainly doesn't have to be a Benz. Constantly bragging about what you have or may have in the future won't get you to bat, not to mention home plate.

If you're married to a Cancer woman, you might as well go shopping for a backyard storage barn because your moon child will keep every birthday, Mother's Day, going-to-a-new-job, you-just-got-a-promotion, or just-because card. These cards and trinkets will be in a shoe box in the bottom of the closet and any other available space in the house. And if you're trying to clean up, I would suggest that you ask her first before you start going on a rampage of throwing away anything. Like a wounded child, she'll simply retrieve them, thinking how could her husband have thrown away her mother's one earring that the Cancerian found stuck between the couch and the pillow in the den or the old doilies that are as limp as dishcloths that her Aunt Pearl crocheted just for her. And don't ask her why she keeps all of the single earrings from years past—it's almost as though she expects the mates to show up in the her jewelry box one day.

The other footnote here is that she'll be the counselor for every-one. Her strong intuitive powers also enhance her level-headed ad-vising skills. So while you're waiting for her to come to bed, she may be counseling a brother whose wife has a drug problem, or encouraging a friend who was recently fired or talking with a friend and catching up on the latest gossip. Don't even bother trying to wait up. She's like the emotional doctor for all of her friends, and even some strangers.

Usually, when the Cancerian listens to others, the bottom falls out of everything. But when this sister follows her own intuition, she's better off. For example, a Cancer woman in her fifties began living with a guy who was twenty-eight years old. Problems surfaced with the man when he wanted part ownership in her company and she refused. He became abusive. When she returned home one day, the door of her apartment was kicked in. Shortly after, the police arrived and searched the apartment. The Cancer sister begged the police to wait until the repairman arrived to fix the door, but they refused. By the time the police officers had reached the parking lot, a gunshot rang out from the apartment. Intuitively, the Cancerian had checked her gun to make sure it was loaded. As soon as she cocked the chamber back in place, her lover lunged from the closet. She shot and killed him. Of course, she was traumatized by the whole ordeal and it took several months to recover, but she did recover. She later learned that her lover had been released from jail a year earlier for killing his wife in Minnesota.

Cancer women love strong men. They want the man in a take-charge mode. This sister must feel a sense of protection similar to what a child feels when a parent hugs and cradles her. But if the man doesn't live up to her expectations, she won't last long. For example, a Cancer woman who married and had a child found out later that her husband didn't want children, but only said he did to pique her interest. When the child was age two, she traded her marriage license in for a real estate license and set out on her own.

The Cancer sister also wants a classy man, and not one whose idea of recreation involves cruising the bus station. And don't think for one minute that you're going to waltz out of her life as easily as you walked in. It ain't gonna happen. Cancers are like flypaper: If they fall in love with you, you're stuck. You'll be called, poked, prodded and coaxed about coming back "home." If the relationship doesn't get back to its original way, she may call you after a few glasses of wine and scold you because you married someone else.

And men, it's not unmasculine to use lotion. The Cancer woman likes to snuggle, but she doesn't want abrasions or scratches left from rusty knees or ashy feet. If those limbs are not treated regularly with some type of lubricant, "they feel like steel wool when you're close to them," one Cancer woman said.

During the home-life state of the relationship or in marriage, you'll think you've died and gone to heaven. For a Cancer, home is a haven, warm and inviting, and she'll worry you about eating properly, pick the hair out of the bumps on your face and even scratch your dandruff.

Love Connection

If you plan to connect with a Cancer, you need to run out and take a crash course in the art of kissing. They will demand lots of kisses and hugs. And I don't mean any pecks either—I'm talking the real deal! The art of kissing is very important to this water sign whose emotions run high. And while you're at it, a visit to the dentist is not a bad idea. Your mouth will get a full workout!

One Cancer woman who dated a Scorpio man for several months said that although the sexual encounters were good, she remained unfulfilled because there was very little kissing involved. The Scorpio had little interest in kissing, generally, but she took it personally.

When you think of romance with Cancer people, think of waves washing up on the shore. The full moon is suspended in the darkness as the two of you, barefoot, gaze dreamily into each other's eyes and then turn to look wistfully into the distance. If this sounds corny, don't bother planning a strategy to spur this moon child's interest because Cancers are the romantics of the zodiac.

For both the male and female of this sign, lovemaking begins long before these moon children reach the bedroom. For them lovemaking is caring for the other person, hand-holding, intimate conversations and simply being content to be in each other's company without feeling any pressure to "perform." When the pressure is off, that's when the Cancerian comes alive. If you get lucky and he or she consents to a liaison between the sheets, you can bet the rent that it won't be a one-night stand. Cancers want romance and sex in that order, not the reverse. If you're married, she may even consider an affair with you, provided she knows that she's the only "other" woman. But in any case, proceed with caution.

For the sister of this sign, romance and courtship means more to them than the actual roll in the hay. They enjoy sex, but they enjoy the hand-holding, flowers, intimate talks and family-oriented matters best. I know this may sound strange, but the total package is what they must have: no bim bam, thank you ma'am for the moon child.

Although the women are sometimes shy and too cautious in

their approach to sex, when they are secure in a relationship, they are capable of great passion. They don't want to run the show; they prefer to be perceived as damsel-in-distress types, but they can definitely hold their own in the bedroom. They will immediately grasp what you prefer and add their own creative spin to it.

The erogenous zones for both men and women are the breast or chest areas. They love to have this area caressed gently at any time or any place. To these water signs, foreplay is all important. Consequently, kissing, caressing and nibbling are always good starting points for these moon people and can ignite a fire in this water sign that's hard to put out.

But sister girl, the men of the sign are a different story. They may insist on running the show. This brother doesn't have the confidence of, say, an Arian; nevertheless, he can hold his own when it comes to bedroom matters. He may need some encouragement at first, but if his companion is receptive, this man will undoubtedly be the man of the hour. Warning: I advise you women out there to try to "play dead." During intimate moments, you need to kind of pretend that you don't know your way around the bedroom, if you get my drift. But the key here is to allow him to run the show, or at least *think* he's running it. The Cancer brother remembers minor details. He has total recall when it comes to sexual encounters and remembers what works and what doesn't. The sex will be mostly traditional with a few kinky fringes.

As far as the compatibility situation, here's how it goes: Cancer is a water sign, and they get along with the two other water signs, Scorpio and Pisces. Water signs govern the emotions, so these two signs will provide insecure Cancers with all the emotional support they need. All three complement each other. The two earth signs that are most compatible with Cancers are Taurus and Virgo. Earth and water make beautiful mud together. Virgos, who are practical as well as analytical, won't allow Cancers to drift too far into left field with their moodiness and emotions. And Taureans, the mainstays of the zodiac, won't give in to the many moods of Cancers and will provide stability in their lives.

If you're a Cancer, you'll be running into lots of Capricorns, your opposite sign. When you meet them, the conversation will be stimulating and you'll laugh a lot. You and your Cap won't want to leave each other's side, not even for a minute. If you're asking yourself, How will I know when I meet this person? You'll know. There's an automatic, intense magnetic attraction between the two of you.

However, very few relationships of opposites work. The truth is, you'll be spending much of your time kissing and making up because of the almost insurmountable differences in your two personalities. For example, Cancer's moodiness and emotional eruptions will drive a controlled, quiet Capricorn batty. Caps are usually unemotional and aloof. Cancerians absolutely must have emotional reassurance and support.

How to Get Next to a Cancer

• Cancers love compliments and praise. But don't pour it on too thick; their intuitive powers will alert them to any insincerity on your part.

• Cancer people sometimes wear their feelings on their sleeves, so be cautious. Don't be overbearing, tactless and impatient. Although you might not get that immediate yes, this water sign is worth the wait.

• They love music, especially oldies. Jazz, blues or R & B concerts are always a good idea. They also love being taken to dinner. Even a carefully planned meal at your place would pique a Cancerian's interest. Knowing how to cook is a plus with them.

• Seek advice on any subject, including career goals, relationships or in-law problems. Cancers are very insightful and have the ability to dissect problems down to their basic elements to present clear-cut solutions.

• Romantic outings such as long walks near the ocean, river, lake or any place there's water will relax the crab and make her more receptive to your ultimate advances.

• Don't brag and constantly talk about yourself. Cancers are good listeners, but even they can get tired of all the "I" strain.

• Don't discuss previous relationships with your Cancer. They have no interest in hearing about your former lovers. Subconsciously they will feel that they don't measure up.

• Cancers are pretty diplomatic when it comes to wild clothing. But
don't make a habit out of rubber or vinyl hot pants with matching
combat boots or spandex clothing that constricts the circulation.
• Leave the nose ring at home on this date. It'll only be a distraction
because the Cancer won't be able to take his eyes off it.

The Cancer Child

The Cancer is a joy to rear. As a parent, you'll have very few problems with these devoted, moody, social and friendly little moon
children. But you may find yourself constantly jumping up after the
baby is born because he or she may cry constantly, seeking to be
held and comforted. A Taurus mother had to hold and comfort her
newborn Cancerian boy constantly. She couldn't leave the room
even after he fell asleep because after about fifteen minutes, the baby
would awaken instinctively, realizing that his mother had left the
room. After weeks without any relief, the mother started to resent
the child, but was later assured by her mother that her resentment
was normal given the circumstances.

Cancer children have memories like steel traps. They remember
all of the pleasant areas of their life—visits to grandmama's house,
baking cookies, learning to sew or going on summer fishing trips
with granddaddy. But they also record negative occurrences that
have far-reaching effects on their lives. For instance, a Cancer child
who grew up on a small farm in Tennessee was traumatized when
he moved to the city at age twelve and witnessed neighborhood
bullies, drugs, and what he perceived as the intimidating bigness of
the city. This moon child now believes his reclusive behavior and
conscious decision to stay out of the mix and clear of the influences
of city life are the reasons he's succeeded in life and remains alive
today.

Another Cancerian adult has total recall of one of the most
traumatic situations of her childhood. At age fifty, this sister hasn't
gotten over being made to take cornflakes from a variety pack to
school for lunch in first grade. And how mortified she was when the
teacher offered to buy milk for the cornflakes and allowed her to
remain in the classroom so that the children in the cafeteria wouldn't

make fun of her. The teacher was a lifesaver to the vulnerable Cancerian, who to this day remembers every detail of the event.

As adolescents, both girls and boys will have lots of friends. They'll be well liked by students and teachers alike. These children will constantly beg to go to movies, parties and other functions with their hordes of friends. And sorry, but the house where the Cancer lives will be a neighborhood house where most of the kids congregate. Moon children have a great sense of humor. Yes, they can be the class clowns.

The moods of the Cancerian child vary greatly, so watch out. They will declare their love for you after you make their favorite meal of fried pork chops, but then in the very next minute won't be able to tell you what their homework assignment is or when the project is due. Cancer adults are notorious for procrastination, and so are the children. During the grade school and junior high years, homework assignments may have to be monitored closely, because they simply are not interested in keeping up. These children have more important things to think about, like the opposite sex, what they're going to wear to school the next day, and whether they can muster the courage to ask a schoolmate to accompany them to the dance. Generally, Cancerian children are good students, but their moodiness can sometimes interfere with real progress. And, they internalize every emotional hurt. For example, one Cancer adolescent whose playmates made fun of her early development became sullen and quiet and no longer wanted to associate with her friends. She declared to her mother, who'd told her about the birds and the bees, that she never wanted to grow up and wanted everything to stay the way it was.

Although Cancer teenagers are well liked and have no problems being noticed, a serious situation may develop if they are noticed by an adult. One Cancerian teenager found herself in a compromising position with her mother's boyfriend when the boyfriend made attempts to fondle her. If this happens, please listen and don't blame the child.

They're sort of late bloomers, which means there won't be any mad rush to experiment too early. But the birds-and-bees discussion should proceed as scheduled. There's always an exception to the rule. Besides that, they're pretty intuitive and instinctively know when a member of the opposite sex is handing them a line. These children are much too insecure about themselves to believe a bunch of bologna.

Which brings us to racism and the theory of black male prowess. Although at times Cancer teenagers can be influenced by friends, they are generally independent thinkers. They generally make their own decisions about such nonsense and won't buy into a bunch of stereotypical innuendo. Cancer children are very observant, and they keep their eyes and ears open. If parents are discussing such issues at home, the Cancer child will listen intently, picking up bits and pieces wherever possible. These children understand the ramifications of racism in America. They usually have understanding beyond their years.

How they handle being in a white environment or school will depend on their parents. First of all, Cancer children need love, and lots of it. These moon children must feel a strong sense of security at home before they will be able to tackle the many problems of everyday life. They must feel that they're loved unconditionally. If a strong family base is in place, then this crab will blossom, knowing that the foundation of support will be there forever.

The Cancer Employee

Job security to Cancer employees is second only to their families. Therefore, Cancers are reliable and hard-working employees. Cancers, like Taureans, are usually preoccupied with money, saving it, hoarding it and having lots of it.

Most Cancerians are insecure regarding some aspect of their lives, and having money saved can provide them with the sense of security they so desperately seek. A Cancer brother will work much harder if he knows that he's appreciated on the job. Money is important to this crab, but having a satisfying job and a pleasant work environment rate a close second to monetary gains. But if you're a friend or a companion, you'll never know if he's got money or how much, because he won't ever brag to you about it. He'll simply build his empire with as little fanfare as possible. The Cancer brother will open a barbecue restaurant and hire the entire family, including all of the unemployed cousins. He readily knows the value of good help. And reliable employees will be rewarded with raises and work incentives, including an attractive investment option in the business.

Both the men and women of the sign are born leaders, but they have a tendency to lead indirectly rather than being the pushy, out-front types or the look-what-I've-accomplished kind of person. A Cancer woman who owns her own construction business rehabs old buildings for resale in the Chicago area. In an effort to allow her mostly black employees some say in the goings-on, she constantly encourages their input. The black men resent her success and the white male employees complain that she's not a man and doesn't know about certain aspects of the construction business, but despite this, she knows that, ultimately, it's her business and it's successful.

These crabs function best on jobs as public servants, including social workers, salespersons, curators or teachers. They also come alive in jobs where creative ability is needed—as writers, chefs, caterers, interior decorators and musicians. They must be appreciated in the workplace. The crab employee is the sensible, practical one of the group. She won't throw caution to the wind. She won't be the one who suddenly announces that she has met a record company mogul who promises fame and fortune and so she is leaving without notice. Instead, the Cancer will save enough money to live on and then give you enough notice to find a replacement.

In many cases, they will help other employees who aren't up to par in their responsibilities. The nurturing and protective attitude of a Cancer spills over into the job performance: They will be the mothers and fathers of the office as well. For example, a Cancerian nurse frequently finds herself in the middle of disputes involving management and employees. Although this moon child is not the floor supervisor, she's frequently in charge. The employees feel more comfortable coming to her, and she knows it. She loves the attention, but the disputes become so frequent that she finds it hard to get all of her work finished.

Cancer people are usually very effective in the workplace unless they determine that they're unappreciated. This water sign is highly emotional, volatile and insecure, which is potentially dangerous if the crab doesn't get the proper support. Generally, Cancers expect their employers to display the same attitude to everyone on an equal basis, and they admire a sense of fairness. Sometimes this lack of appreciation may have subtle racial overtones. Racism is very hard for the Cancer brother or sister to take. They may become disgusted and aggressive or abruptly leave the job. Such was the case of a Cancer man, who left a Fortune 500 company after he was repeatedly passed over for promotions. He had managed to save $100,000 and started his own warehouse storage business. However, the business eventually folded, and so did his marriage, because he simply couldn't focus on anything else but his company. He became a different person, not communicating with his wife or other family members, as he watched his fortune slowly dwindle. Undaunted, this Cancer brother will eventually try again, but certainly not to the exclusion of family and friends.

As supervisors, the Cancers can hold their own. In fact, Cancers would rather lead than follow, but they're very adept at playing both roles. Their nurturing spirit and easygoing nature will promote harmony in the workplace—but don't look for this same harmony in their office or work area. The desk will be a mess, the files won't be in order, and there may even be coffee stains on the report, which the Cancer will notice minutes before it's to be submitted. But the work will be complete, accurate and on time.

Health Matters

One of the biggest problems for Cancers is that they harbor grudges, lick old wounds, internalize emotional concerns and may drink alcohol to forget their pain.

Cancer people have a tendency to be heavy because they use food as a source of comfort. When a Cancerian is upset or feeling put upon, sweet potato pie, homemade ice cream or lasagna will make everything all right, at least temporarily. Excess weight for the Cancer is difficult to lose because as they get older, they become more sedentary. They'd rather be home curled up with a good book than out on the town. These water signs love to be near water so swimming or walking along the river or beach is a sure bet for them.

Moon children provide the shoulders that everyone cries on. Both men and women are good listeners, but they can internalize the problems of others as well as their own. Their sensitive stomachs and digestive systems simply cannot hold up against the weight of the world and health problems surface.

Cancer rules the breasts and the stomach. Tension, emotional and job stress, financial woes or concern for friends and relatives can take their toll. Cancers are prone to tumors, arthritis, ulcers and digestive problems.

Lean meats, green vegetables, fruits high in vitamin C, and milk products are foods that moon children should eat in abundance. Also, drinking eight glasses of water a day will help control water retention. Cancers should avoid sweets, salt and excessive use of alcohol. Also staying away from hot, spicy foods that you simply adore will give your sensitive stomach a needed break.

The lives of Cancers are busy with hectic schedules that include scout meetings, church socials and family-oriented functions. But once the dust clears, they're usually at home reading to their children, taking in a football game or asleep in front of the TV. Cancers are great cooks and really get into cooking the big spread for all the family members. If there's going to be a Thanksgiving feast, it's usually at the Cancer's house. Both the men and women who cook really get into it by tasting and sampling everything so by the time the meal is ready, the Cancer has no interest in it.

Although Cancerians don't really care for it, grocery shopping is easy for them, especially if there are lots of sale items. But stay away from the cookie aisle. They love a good sale and will sometimes go from store to store in search of a bargain.

The lessons that Cancers must learn are varied when it comes to their health and well-being. First, Cancers cannot be the mothers and fathers to everyone they meet. This is unhealthy because people must be responsible for solving their own problems. And the Cancers who give excellent advice cannot be there for everyone all the time and still be there for themselves. Second, Cancers need to substitute an exercise program for alcohol consumption, especially when alcohol is used as a means of relieving stress or forgetting problems. This approach will give them more energy to handle family-oriented projects and relieve some of the job stress and general anxiety. And third, getting more rest and learning to truly relax will go a long way to promote overall good health and well-being.

Famous African American Cancerians

Louis Armstrong
Arthur Ashe Jr.
Regina Belle
Mary McLeod Bethune
Ed Bradley
Octavia Butler
Stokely Carmichael
Diahann Carroll
George Clinton
Bill Cosby
Charles N. Dinkins
Clyde Drexler
Paul Lawrence Dunbar
Katherine Dunham
Lee Elder
Danny Glover
Roosevelt "Rosie" Greer
Lena Horne
Phyllis Hyman
Ann Marie Johnson
Eddie Levert
Carl Lewis
John Lewis
Thurgood Marshall

Daphne Maxwell-Reid
Harold Melvin
Denise Nicholas
Satchel Paige
Calvin Peete
Brock Peters
Bonnie Pointer
A. Philip Randolph
Willis Reed Jr.
Della Reese
Martha Reeves
Beah Richards
Wilma Rudolph
Barry Sanders
O.J. Simpson
Leon Spinks
Michael Spinks
Clarence Thomas
Mike Tyson
James Van Der Zee
Faye Wattleton
Spud Webb
Ida B. Wells
Forest Whitaker

LEO

July 23 to August 22

Symbol: The Lion

Positive traits: Generous, dramatic, enthusiastic, broad-minded, creative, organized, powerful, optimistic

Negative traits: Intolerant, patronizing, conceited, egotistical, snobbish, extravagant, attention-seeking, dogmatic

Ruling planet: The Sun is associated with vitality and authority.

Leos strive to reign supreme. Of all of the signs of the zodiac, Leo is as close to royalty as you'll get. Leos are a proud and dignified bunch who will want and expect your undivided attention. Once the guidelines have been set regarding what's acceptable in terms of behavior and demeanor, the encounter will be a rewarding one. They also strive to be center stage, where they are most comfortable: With center stage comes all of the melodrama they can muster.

And they detest being ignored. If you want to get their goat, ignore them or overlook their opinion about a subject that they feel is crucial and for which they have a certain passion.

Leos have a definite presence. Most Leos are tall and statuesque. But even if they're short, the lions command attention. They walk straight and proud with a smooth gait like a feline, head up, shoulders back with the "Yes, I'm all that" look. And yes, they know you're watching. That's why they're dressed in the unmistakable Leo style. Sometimes they may be taken to extremes—like the "git it" girl look, horizontal-striped two-piece spandex outfit that lifts and separates, or the hip-hop, yo, boy-from-hell outfit that's so baggy it swallows the guy's body. But, generally, their style of dress is quiet and elegant.

They usually have lots of thick hair, even if it's very short. The lion's eyes are very direct and intense. The mouth is wide with big full lips. Their bodies are well proportioned; they're neither top-heavy nor bottom-heavy, and they are generally slim.

You'll find the Leo conversing with hordes of people, and you'll no doubt conclude that they're not only the life of the party but *the* party. You'll find this social butterfly wherever the action is. Expect the unexpected with them. A Leo may be the guest who pops up out of the cake during a birthday bash or the one to join a band member on stage for a dance and a duet. They will give you their opinion whether you want it or not, spewing out their comments on Haitian refugees, sexual harassment in the workplace, getting closer to God, the best homemade brownies or the issue of skin color. For example, if you're in the middle of an argument with a Leo about why black people are still color-struck, he will maintain that it's merely coincidence that his dates are all LLs (light, long hair). The Leo woman won't offer any apologies for her preference for the curly-headed beige-complexioned brothers. If she's a dark cocoa color, she might offer in her defense that opposites attract, or she may merely say, "That's what I like." As a rule, though, color is not a big issue with this fire sign because they are also pretty open to relationships with other ethnic groups such as Latinos, Iranians, Indians or any other race for that matter.

But in most of their love relationships, there will be some burning issue, whether it's interracial dating, his decision to become a minister, her plans to leave town for a new job or the other person in the picture that they just can't seem to give up. For example, although a Leo law student has been dating his Aries for five years, he can't fully resolve a relationship with a Libra sister he met at an NAACP convention. She was going up the escalator as he was going down. Their eyes met and the rest was history. But what the Leo probably doesn't realize is Aries and Libra are opposite signs, which means the personality traits that Libra has, Aries doesn't, and vice versa. He's seeking that consummate woman. Good luck!

Leos will be fun-loving friends and confidantes to their children. But they do have a tendency to be overbearing, with unrealistic expectations. For example, one Leo mother, who was determined to make her Arian tomboy a little lady, had her child's bedroom decorated in Pepto-Bismol pink with pink and white foil wallpaper. The wallpaper's design of white cloud-shaped puffs with sparkles of silver that resembled stars gave the room an open, outdoor quality. Wicker lamps with pink shades and a white canopied bed completed the dainty, soft look. While Leo was decorating the room, the little ram was out playing football with the neighborhood boys. The lion even tried to send the little ram to charm school. Although Leos can be bossy by nature, their children shouldn't be dictated to, but as they develop, the youngsters should be allowed to make responsible decisions without the interference of the Leo parent.

Leos enjoy outdoor events, movies, picnics, plays or going to clubs. The lion is also at home coaching Little League baseball, being the scoutmaster, teaching Sunday school or any activity that has a family orientation to it. The sisters love to entertain. They know how to lay out the table settings with the fine china and crystal. They know how to create the image of class with very little money. But they can also spend money so fast it will make your head spin.

They are usually generous people and will give you the silk shirt off their backs—even if they have to borrow the shirt from a another friend.

Oh, by the way, there's no middle ground when it comes to their general approach to keeping areas tidy: The Leo is either a slob or meticulously neat. If they're slobs, it's usually because they're so busy looking in the mirror, outfitting themselves or determining what they're going to do next to get attention, the underlying theme of their whole existence. Or it may be because they're working two jobs or pulling so much overtime that they simply don't have time to color-coordinate clothes in both closets or keep their countless pairs of shoes stacked neatly in the boxes.

They're also equal opportunity–minded: They'll spend your money with the same enthusiasm that they spend their own.

Let's consider the Leo's ruling body, the Sun, for a minute. The Sun is essential for Earth's survival. Very few life-forms can survive without its illumination. Thus is the Leo's attitude about himself. Just think of how boring life would be without your Leo friend, sibling, wife, or mother to guide you through life. Whether you ask for their guidance or not, you're going to get it anyway—they're very adept at giving advice to those who hang around long enough to listen.

The Leo Man

If you're thinking about becoming involved with a Leo brother, it's going to be first class all the way—well, in theory anyway. He's not the type to be stingy on a date or cut corners. Even if there's little money, and even if he's a college student, he'll want to take you to a restaurant where a sign reads, Please wait to be seated. And any wine will have a cork in it. He loves creating the glitz and glamour in his life. He loves to show off. One Leo described his early twenties in a midwestern city as being the life of pimps, players and part-time movie stars. This brother believed people who worked for a living were squares. Back then he was proud of his career as a hustler who sold drugs and was even involved in a shootout. This brother, who is now a Christian, felt innately that his life would evolve into one with more meaning; he was drawn to the glamour and the attention that the street life afforded him.

Ladies, Leo is a proud man who can wrestle very effectively with being a black man in America and maintain his dignity at the same time. In other words, Leo plans to be all that. He is forever striving to keep it together and to have it going on. And just to impress you with his clout, he'll offer to pay the check when he knows full well that his credit card can't possibly hold another charge. For many females, this "I know I'm tough" attitude is a big turnoff. It's only show and done for the attention the Leo feels he'll reap. Although a Leo man is very conscious of his image and of not appearing weak, he's vulnerable and needs your support and reasurrance. Of course, he'll never admit this in a million years.

Even if you're not interested in a relationhip with Leo, he's friendly and outgoing and a valuable friend. He's got a great sense of humor and can coax you right out of your blue funk in a matter of minutes. Leo is a fire sign, which means he is upbeat and usually in a good mood. These lions are very stubborn, and they simply must have their way 99.9 percent of the time. Yes, they will share why their opinion must be valued and also why you should listen.

One Leo describes meeting a Sagittarian woman on campus when he was a junior and she was a freshman. To his amazement, she stood him up on the first date. He thought he was cute enough and had, of course, bought the corked wine. He had his own apartment. What's up! Actually she totally forgot about the date, but getting stood up got his attention. Leos hate to be ignored and love a good challenge. Now, of course, they're married.

Once you're designated as "his" woman, you'll be expected to conduct yourself accordingly. This Leo brother will be turned off by loud and what he feels is unbecoming behavior. Chauvinism at its best. Your role, as his companion, will be to wait on him, cajole him, flatter him and give him the attention he craves. I know this directive may sound a little one-sided, but he's a very generous, caring, loving person, and you will be rewarded handsomely for your efforts. For example, although you might have cooked this Leo a soul food feast of mustard greens, baked chicken and dressing, yams, potato salad and rolls, he may still request that you fix his plate. Don't balk, just do it because he would have done it for you had you asked.

Leos can also have the carefree attitude that everything will be all right, and I can do this just because I can. One Leo man I know said he jumped in the deep water at the YMCA without knowing how to swim. He said he had grown up watching the old Tarzan movies and when he jumped in the water he felt that he would be able to swim like the ape man himself.

Leo brothers are very jealous. When you're with them, it's best not to look around, period. They want your undivided attention. So if you're caught talking to a male, it had better be your uncle or cousin. If not, to be on the safe side, you'd better introduce this brother as somebody who is related to you.

Leo men want to be seen with beautiful women on their arm. But that is not a requirement. Leos are drawn to sisters who are smart and enterprising and who make them feel good about themselves. He also assesses what the woman is able to accomplish on a physical level with what she has to work with. Consequently, enhancements like hair weaves or extensions don't turn them off. Many times Leo men will have their hair texturized to give it a more curly appearance. (Not the Ike Turner hairdo in *What's Love Got to Do with It?*, but a more subtle appearance.)

As husbands or companions, Leo men are kind, generous and hardworking. They will be the Mr. Fixit in your life. They thrive on being needed. They are very mechanically inclined, and they will program your new VCR, hang the blinds, fix the lawn mower or even cook. If their mates have children from previous relationships, not to worry: Leos are very adept at making children feel comfortable by including them in activities of the day. A Leo man may ask his companion's daughter to show him the latest dance steps.

The Leo brother will have his own gallery of adoring females, laughing at his jokes and enterprising spirit and noting this cutie pie's overall good looks. There won't be any visits to the polyester farms for this brother: He knows how to dress appropriately for all occasions. He's the type of man you could call if you're in a pinch for a black tie date. He would pick you up on time, be elegantly dressed and make an impressive armpiece for any occasion. He's a social animal anyway, so you wouldn't have to concern yourself with improper language or substitute phrases like "duh ruh." He prides himself on looking good at all times. Even when he dashes out to the store, he makes sure that he's well groomed. His motto is, You never know who you might run into.

The Leo Woman

This sister will expect you to all but bow down as she sits on her imaginary throne. She's overly dignified or sedate, what some of us might call "sedidy." But in all honesty, this sister is a genuinely warm and generous person to all who can hang around long enough to get past the facade.

When you first meet this woman, you'll notice that all eyes are on her because of her dazzling outfit, with accessories right down to her ankle bracelet. She will expect you to notice, and she'll expect loads of compliments, for, you see, this sister is testing you. If you're not going to notice the end results of all the painstakingly detailed preparations she's made for her public, she won't have any time for you.

But if by chance she looks your way, you must realize that you must live up to her expectations of being taken to fancy restaurants, symphony concerts or banquets, where she can flex her regal muscles and show off her latest sequinned strapless dress.

One Leo woman, a full-figured person, is not ashamed of her weight. She maintains that black men like "substantial" women. She's even a model for the plus sizes and knows how to accentuate the positive with carefully applied makeup. She has that certain air and feels good about herself. Whenever she's told that, with such a pretty face, she would have a long line of admirers if she would only lose weight, she proudly proclaims that she's happy just the way she is. Most Leo sisters have that general attitude. They know how to coordinate clothing with accessories that always create an elegant appearance even when they're just wearing jeans. These women work hard at looking good and they expect their men to follow suit.

And know this—they don't like cheapskates! For example, a brother who was taking this Leo sister to the movies waited until they got to the theater to ask if they could go dutch. Well, I guess you know that they didn't go at all. She politely told the brother to take her home and on the drive back to her house, she demanded that she stop by a fast-food place with his money and buy fries and burgers.

Leos, like Arians, are sometimes hard to get to know. Her personality is a lesson in contradictions. She can be warm, yet distant. She's prone to tantrums if she doesn't get what she wants and even sulks in silence because she feels she's unappreciated. If the courtship or marriage doesn't work, she will sometimes give a long list of reasons for the breakup but never implicate herself.

When they finally get married, they won't be content to be just housewives. Being a housewife will never suit the Leo, who must be directing and motivating people. She is usually multitalented and can do most things without much effort. But being a homemaker doesn't have as much luster as, say, being director of the community theater, chairperson of the local cancer society fund drive or a part-time CPA. There must be some passionate cause involved in order for Leo to jump in headfirst and throw caution to the wind. A teacher once told me she took it upon herself to take home a student whom she suspected of being sexually abused. Never mind that the police weren't called initially. This sister felt there was too much bureaucratic red tape with calling the cops and the child needed protection immediately from the abusers. She felt it was her duty to take charge of the situation and not pass the buck.

Before you attempt to talk to this lioness, I advise you to put a shine on those dusty shoes. If you don't, you may get a nice pair of shoes from the Leo as your Christmas present. Also, being in shape is always a winner with the lady Leo. They detest those tummies that have progressed from playgrounds to state parks. Leos pride themselves on keeping their weight down and all of the excess bulges to a minimum.

If you're invited to her house, you'll enter a mini art gallery. She loves artwork, antique furniture, and luxurious surroundings. There will be candles galore and other atmosphere enhancers.

They make devoted friends, good wives but better live-in companions because they can get bored very easily. And then their attentions wander elsewhere to something more tantalizing.

If you have a Leo wife, everything will have to be just so. I would also suggest separate bank accounts. That way, you'll be able to separate the household budget account from her expense account. And she will have one whether you like it or not, so get over it.

Love Connection

So now that you know a little bit about the Leo man and woman, it's off to the races! The race for the bedroom, in the case of both males and females, will be a matter of control and sheer will. Leos expect to have total control in the bedroom. They are the kings of the jungle, born leaders, and the boudoir is no exception. And by taking the lead, they know that they can't pussyfoot around. Most of the time this lion will do what's necessary to make his partner feel special. If you like lots of foreplay, you may be somewhat disappointed because Leos like the *actual* play, as they perceive it, saving all of their energy to be used where it counts.

These fire signs are generally very creative in bed and may

engage in some kinky behavior because they can't stand to be bored even for a minute. However, lions are more experimental than lionesses. The Leo brother doesn't really mind complying with what his partner wants sexually. He's not intimidated, but he can't read minds either. Just tell him what you want and he'll do it. You won't hurt his feelings, and you'll be glad you did. *Warning:* Don't have too many mirrors around in the bedroom because you may find yourself becoming the second banana as the Leo brother stares adoringly at himself during sex.

Leo sisters, on the other hand, take the lead in a more subtle way. But even as they take the lead, they're mentally noting details of what the brother will and won't do. If it's not up to snuff, you'll be told. When it comes to taking care of business, they generally don't mince words. The sign of Leo rules the spine and back. Any massages, back rubs or touches or kisses to the spinal column delight Leos and make an exciting beginning to any intimate exchange.

Both the males and females of the sign have a tendency to fall head over heels in love at the drop of a hat—and sometimes with more than one person. When the Leo falls in love, the whole world knows it. They love romance, courtship and the whole idealized view of love itself. They desperately want the Romeo and Juliet or the Antony and Cleopatra liaisons—those to die for. They can also fall *out* of love just as quickly and dramatically. Their idealistic concept of a relationship sometimes overshadows the realities. When their companion exhibits human behavior such as burping or lack of enthusiasm for all Leo's many interests, the relationship can die down just as quickly as it ignited.

Leos are generally more compatible with Aries and Sagittarius, the two other fire signs of the zodiac. Air signs such as Gemini and Libra are also a good bet for Leos because air signs are usually more apt to allow Leos space to explore their varied interests, and they generally have as much confidence as Leo and a full agenda as well.

The opposite sign of Leo is Aquarius, the third air sign. You may believe upon meeting the Aquarian that you have met your soul mate, and the same goes for the Aquarian. The conversation will be stimulating and sexual encounters may be mind-boggling as passion overtakes the practicality and feasiblity of the relationship, but with opposite signs, over the long haul, the relationship will turn into more of a liability than an asset.

Getting to know a Leo will be a snap. They love attention and eat up compliments the way the Cookie Monster devours cookies. You'll find them wherever they can be the center of attention, on the dance floor, surrounded by suitors discussing current events, at the helm of a company, giving orders or simply at home planning the Sunday school lesson for next week. The Leo sister will be surrounded by male suitors. She'll be dressed to kill, in orange, lavender or a seductively tapered black dress for which she searched for weeks. For, you see, Leos spare neither expense nor time when it comes to what they want and their all-important image.

How to Get Next to a Leo

• Don't plan on being a cheap date. Leos go first class all the way.
• Even though many times they will have champagne ideas with only beer money, they will forever reach for the stars. Don't be a miser or spoilsport when it comes to spending money.
• With Leos, pour the compliments on thick. The more outlandish the compliment, the better. For they simply believe that they indeed warrant such praise.
• If you're lucky enough to have a date with a Leo, you need to dress for the part. Leave the casual dress for your bowling night. This sign will expect you to wear your Sunday best because you must measure up if you're to accompany her.
• Leos are upbeat, optimistic people and they will expect you to laugh at their jokes. Having a good sense of humor will score high with this fire sign. They're entertainers and they expect the same from you.
• Besides lavish dinners, Leo loves the arts. An opening to a play or an exhibit of one of his favorite artists is always a winner.
• Take them to an outdoor concert with Nancy Wilson or to the symphony. Pack a picnic basket and include wine or champagne. You won't need to enjoy the fireworks after the concert—you'll start your own.

- Wigs, toupees, braids and hair weaves are okay with Leos as long as you don't take it to the extreme. They appreciate the extra effort to look attractive.
- When you're with a Leo, pay attention. A roving eye may earn you a fat lip (just kidding) because Leo wants your undivided attention.
- Leos love to give advice. They love to be needed. They are generous people who treasure family and friendships.

The Leo Child

Leo children require more attention than the average child. You will need a few pairs of kid gloves for this little fire sign. Even as youngsters, the ego of a Leo must be stroked. There are serious lessons the little cubs must learn, like sharing and being considerate of the feelings of their playmates, which you must enforce early. And they cannot have everything their way.

That's not to say that they shouldn't be encouraged to be the born leaders that they are and be supported and pushed to excellence. Encouragement and support are essential for their well-being. They must be constantly made to feel that you have confidence in them. Lots of hugs and praise are recommended when they perform well in school, especially if they feel they're not getting enough encouragement from the teacher. You must explain that the teacher can't possibly provide all of the attention they crave because she has thirty other children in the class who need attention, too. Leos must also learn that as wonderful as they think they may be, they must accept their failures as well as their successes.

The typical Leo child is happy, upbeat and playful, but your little cub may become sullen or depressed if he feels he can't cope with some facet of life or he's not getting his way. Usually that means not being fully appreciated or acknowledged by friends and family members.

Oh yes, and parents, let your Leo child decide what she wants to wear to school. As early as first grade Leos have some definite ideas about clothing, so rather than put yourself through the daily morning argument over what to wear, let them make the decision some of the time. By all means, take them with you when you shop for them. This will eliminate some of the clothing hassles.

Leo

A Leo youngster who was a happy, well-adjusted child and a good student suddenly became listless and unmotivated after his cousin, who was mixed (white mother, black father), moved to town. The mixed child, who had a lighter complexion and curly hair, was a bright kid who competed with the Leo in every way. The cousin eventually began to make better grades as well. When the cousin visited the little Leo, they got along. However, the Leo youngster was not allowed to visit the white side of the mixed child's family. Leo became resentful and told his cousin that he liked his white family better. In this case the parents should have offered the children some explanation for the treatment.

As toddlers, they are either lovable little tykes who master potty training, walking and talking easily or late-bloomers who have to be painstakingly prodded every step of the way. They are generally sweet, adoring children who are devoted to their parents. Try to avoid overusing confining playpens, swings and cribs. Overuse can sometimes have an adverse affect on the little cubs because they need continous contact.

Leo children need to be needed. Allow them to help in the kitchen. Let them make the Kool-Aid. Cracking the eggs, pouring in the milk and stirring the corn bread batter is a big deal for them. Oh, I know that many times the egg will land on the floor, not the bowl, and the table will be wet with water and Kool-Aid from their efforts, but Leos love responsible chores.

Constant yelling and screaming at Leo children will do more harm than good. Although strict and consistent discipline is needed, their egos are very fragile; they will take constant criticism to heart and may begin to feel that they're not worthy enough to try again.

Leo children are well liked and popular with playmates but will definitely run the show if given an opportunity. They don't merely want some of the attention; they want it all. For example, while you're engaged in a serious conversation with a friend or relative, the Leo child may come to you and suddenly put her arms around your waist to make sure you notice the small scratch on her elbow. She'll also expect to be noticed by the friend as well. She must have your undivided attention, you know. The Leo child has to be acknowlegded at least every hour on the hour.

During adolescence, you need to start the birds-and-bees talks as soon as humanly possible. These children are very inquisitive about most things; they need little encouragement to venture into sexual explorations and the rest will be history. As children or teen-agers they become aware very early of the stereotypical comments about the perceived sexual prowess of African Americans. Parents must dispel these concepts early so that the little lion king won't become a teenage parent. As early as first grade, they will want to know about the feminine hygiene products in your bathroom, how females get pregnant and why boys are different from girls. So when they demand answers to questions, please explain. "Because I said so," won't be sufficient.

For example, the mother of a six-year-old Leo confessed that there wasn't a Santa Claus after her little cub demanded an explana-tion as to why his playmate received Nintendo, an elaborate video game, and he didn't. A few months later, the Leo child announced to his mother that she, not the Tooth Fairy, had placed the money under his pillow and there was no Easter Bunny either.

The teenage years will be another exercise in extremes. During their high school years, they will fall out of love as quickly as they fall in, averaging one courtship per semester. They will be very popular with the students and teachers. Leos are the class presidents, football queens, cheerleaders, majorettes, and drama students, en-joying center stage. Academics will be secondary if too many extra-curricular activities are allowed. Leo children, although smart and creative with lots of vitality, can also be lazy. They are also capable of faking illness to solicit your sympathy and get out of doing chores and homework.

Leo children grasp the whole concept of skin color and how racism affects them as children in America. They also usually under-stand the prejudices of African Americans about skin tones, for example, the perception that lighter-complexioned people are more accepted and "privileged." But Leos are smart enough to adapt to most sticky situations and won't allow it to get next to them. One Leo teenager was constantly harassed by his peers because not only was he smart, he was also fair-complexioned and wore glasses. After being constantly picked on, he abandoned plans to continue making good grades and opted instead to join a gang. He knew that he would have to be one of the toughest members to compensate for his physical features. Although later he became an accomplished professional photographer, during his childhood, he felt that he had no other choice. "I did what I had to do to survive," he said.

The Leo Employee

Leos can handle whatever jobs they find themselves in. However, they don't particularly enjoy routine jobs that are repetitive in nature and provide no real challenge. The key to maximizing a Leo's performance level is to allow him or her to be in charge of something, even if it's the water cooler. Leos function their best when they know that their contribution has challenge and some significance to the overall good of the company.

They are born leaders, and they want you as the boss to recognize all their many talents—their organizational skills and their ability to motivate people and bring projects to closure. And you have to have a clear understanding of why you absolutely cannot get along without them. Once you as the boss understand that the Leo has more vitality than other employees and is willing to make great sacrifices, your labor with the Leo will be most rewarding. If Leos are appreciated, they will go around the bend and back again to do the best job imaginable.

For example, a Leo nurse worked for thirteen years as the recovery room supervisor of a major hospital. She was often on call for twenty-four-hour stretches and only took a less demanding job when she adopted a baby. Had she not decided to adopt, she would have been perfectly satisfied to continue her heavy workload.

Most Leos function best in a job with significant public contact. They are people persons, and they know how to charm an audience, a classroom full of eager students or a potential business client. Leos are at their best as teachers, entertainers, actors, politicians or public relations managers—in jobs where their adoring audiences await them.

Like Aquarians, Leos love challenging jobs with a unique twist, so they find themselves in international business, investment banking, commodities trading and even national politics—places where blacks are just beginning to join the ranks in significant numbers. Therefore, Leos are usually undaunted by curious whites who take it upon themselves to intimidate and interrogate them on controversial topics like gangs, welfare reform, violence, the teenage pregnancy rate and other topics for which some whites think blacks should be held accountable. Leos never shy away from a juicy confrontation. They're usually well read and know the statistics on subjects of this nature. So beware.

The coworkers or boss who shows a bigoted or racist attitude toward the Leo will be met with the same disdain that's spewed out in the lion's direction. Lions and lionesses have a diginified manner overall, but when provoked, they roar so loudly that even the most formidable opponent will be cowed. They generally won't start any confrontations of a black-versus-white nature, but they can certainly end them with the last word.

Leos make better supervisors than employees. They get a kick out of not only drawing up the plans but bringing the project to closure. They can do it all. The only problem is, as the boss, you might find yourself taking orders instead of giving them. They are the go-getters, and they aren't afraid of hard work or making the necessary sacrifices to achieve their goals. They probably have more confidence in their own ability than in yours.

Don't become overly concerned about the Leo's tardiness; even though they may take an extra fifteen minutes for lunch occasionally, in a crunch or a pinch, it's the Leo you want on your team.

Warning: Don't put your Leo employee in charge of the operating budget. Facts they can deal with effectively; figures are another story. Leos love lavish surroundings, so squeezing a dollar until it hollers has no meaning for this fire sign. When they do go over budget you can bet, your lion will be able to tell you the cost of the boss's new oak desk, artwork and stereo system and argue that the new clients enjoy the music while they wait. The clients will also be able to relax while enjoying coffee or tea poured from the new sterling silver tea set. Image is everything, you know!

Health Matters

Regular excercise, a high-protein, low-fat diet and plenty of rest is the formula to help Leos cope with the rigorous demands of their jobs, their bulging social calendar and the daily unexpected challenges this lion must face.

One point that most Leos won't address is, yes, they too can run out of steam. They may be the last in the crowd to do so, but when fatigue takes over, so should the voice of reason. Get some rest before it gets to the stage of being hospitalized!

Leo people won't sit still long enough for any serious illness to take hold. Being sick signifies weakness, something they rarely tolerate. But if you find this fire sign bedridden, there's a serious problem. There's rarely a middle ground with health-related matters: The Leo either exudes energy and vitality or is listless and sickly.

The Sun, their ruling body, is associated with energy and vitality. Leos have energy to burn in both work and play. Long after the cleanup crew comes in, the energetic Leo will be among those still in "da house" ready to move on to the next phase of the program.

The sign of Leo rules the heart, back and spine. Leos are susceptible to heart disease, high fevers, backaches, aneurysms and rheumatic fever. The career-minded Leo is a hard worker and sometimes won't stop long enough to get the needed rest that is essential for peace of mind and overall well-being.

Failure to acknowledge fatigue could also result in heart disease or heart attacks during the twilight years. Cigarette smoking should be terminated immediately, as it only facilitates heart attacks. And because Leos are prone to heart disease, fatty foods and foods high in cholesterol should be eliminated from the diet. Instead, a diet high in protein, like fish and turkey, along with lots of plums, oranges and other fruits will support your around-the-clock marathon-type life.

Keeping your weight under control can be easy for you because you must be the centerpiece at most social functions. And you definitely enjoy being all that. When weight gain occurs, it's usually because you have wined and dined too much. Of course, with the Leo, it's first class, which means the fanciest restaurants and the priciest wines.

Leos' vanity won't allow weight gain to get out of control. They will merely look in the mirror and catch a glimpse of the bulges, and the diet will commence. (Leo will notice added pounds before anyone else.)

They love to eat out and rarely take time to do any serious cooking. Although they can cook, their hectic schedules, especially if they're single, don't leave much room for hanging out in the kitchen.

As for grocery shopping, you're into the visual display of the product and not the product itself. If the display is colorful and appealing, you'll absentmindedly retrieve it from the shelves. That doesn't mean that you need the product and it'll be useful; it simply catches your eye. As with the Aries, grocery shopping is something you'd like to leave to the underlings. You simply feel that something as trivial as grocery shopping doesn't warrant your attention and you don't have the patience to wait in long lines. Here are two other points to remember for your mental and physical well-being. Leos must have peaceful, orderly surroundings in which to function. A wounded ego or lack of appreciation, either on the job or in family situations, can cause mental stress that invariably leads to physical ailments.

Famous African American Leos

Molefi Kete Asante
Patti Austin
James Baldwin
Halle Berry
Tempestt Bledsoe
Vida Blue
Barry Bonds
Carol Moseley Braun
Ron Brown
Ralph Bunche
Wilt Chamberlain
Joycelyn Elders
Larry Ewing

Laurence Fishburne
Marcus Garvey
William Gray III
Kadeem Hardison
Dorian Harewood
Isaac Hayes
Anita Hill
Whitney Houston
Iman
Magic Johnson
Malcolm Jamal-Warner
Vernon Jordan
Dawnn Lewis

Leo

Abbey Lincoln
Karl Malone
Oscar Peterson
David Robinson
Carl T. Rowan
Wilma G. Rudolph
Deion L. Sanders

Haile Selassie (Africa)
Wesley Snipes
Emmett Till
Melvin Van Peebles
Maxine Waters
Whitney Young

VIRGO
August 23 to September 22

Symbol: The Virgin

Positive traits: Practical, analytical, industrious, conscientious, neat, hypercritical, meticulous, perfectionist

Negative traits: Hypercritical, fussy, a worrier, cranky, pessimistic, prudish, workaholic, grouchy

Ruling planet: Mercury is associated with intelligence, reason and a high-strung temperament.

Virgo people are highly intelligent, precise and as close to perfect as anyone can get. They usually have an overabundance of nervous energy with a somewhat grouchy temperament. But with all of their traits, you can't help but notice the Virgo brother's creased jeans and starched white shirt or the Virgo sister's beige linen double-vested dress fresh out of the cleaners with her matching shoes and squeaky-clean appearance. They stand out in a crowd because of their attractive faces, removed demeanor and strikingly neat appearance. But be advised, don't run right over and strike up a conversation; you may or may not get a warm response. They must first determine if it's feasible to respond, weighing the pros and cons. I know you're not proposing marriage, but the Virgo analyzes everything. Virgos are definitely not people who react based on emotion. Any decision made by a Virgo will be determined by factual information that can stand up to the close scrutiny of the eagle-eyed virgin. If the matter can pass the Virgo test, then it's ready to roll.

Virgo

Virgo is the sign of the virgin, which represents purity, perfection, chastity and all that they imply. In short, even if there's no criticism verbally, Virgos' constant drive for perfection, will have them mentally criticizing whatever they see. They also feel that everyone is as critical as they are. One Virgo man I know, who's now in his forties, has never worn sandals because he didn't like the way his toes or feet looked. He had bunions and his children would tease him, calling his tennis shoes Air Dads (like Air Jordans) after the outline of a bunion protruded through the worn shoes. He also felt his toes were too close together and on top of each other. His wife, who recently bought him a pair of sandals for the first time, pointed out that normal people don't go around staring down at the ground commenting on the ugliness of people's toes. Only Virgos do that, she reminded him. Virgo people are the critics of the zodiac. A Virgo can criticize everything from how his son makes a bed to the snug-fitting dress worn by the pastor's wife. The Virgo brother will be the one who will invariably straighten the picture on your wall or empty the ashtrays at a friend's house.

These earth signs are definitely not social butterflies. They would be the friend to help with the dishes while others are relaxing because they're usually more comfortable cleaning up during the party than enjoying it. In fact, they shy away from crowds and large-scale events. Instead, they enjoy dining out in a quiet, intimate setting or attending a play, an art exhibit, a movie or a sports event of any type. A couple considering marriage, asked me what I thought of a two-Virgo pairing. I told them that if they didn't bore each other to death, everything would be fine. Their idea of an enticing evening is to sit at home watching movies and pigging out on popcorn.

Virgos are so analytical and practical that it can drive a person crazy. Being frugal is a main point with them. And along with the frugal philosophy will be the point-by-point analysis. For example, a Virgo physician changed a patient's surgical dressing, told the patient that the $15 dressing package would be charged to her bill, and then left the remaining bandages and gauze, telling the woman she should keep the pack because she had paid for it.

Virgo is an earth sign whose ruling planet is Mercury, which is associated with intelligence, strong analytical powers and a high-strung temperament. Virgos are usually running around trying to dot every *i* and cross every *t*. You'll find these practical people constantly straightening the covers on the bed, (even if you're in the bed asleep) or following their children around as they're getting ready for school making sure that they pick up their clothes, make their beds and rinse off their plates. The house must be perfect before everyone leaves, you know. (If you're lucky, the cleanup doesn't include backing out of the house with the vacuum cleaner in use so that there aren't any footprints on the carpet. Pu-leeze!) These earth signs are neatness freaks. The aforementioned toe-watching Virgo father worried so much about whether his son's room was clean that he would forget to ask his son about his homework.

Although Virgos will drive even a Vulcan crazy with all of their flying around the room, hand-wringing and needless worrying, you have to feel some sympathy for them. Just think how frustrated *you* would feel if you could never actually relax and stop worrying. You would probably make the person closest to you nuts, too. And don't try to analyze why they worry so much. They will simply respond with the kind of look that says that they are no different from anybody else. They probably feel that everybody flies around the room. That may be true sometimes, but with Virgos it's constant.

For example, Virgos will forego grabbing a bite to eat in the car because they don't want to mess up the upholstery. There's also a possibility of getting some sort of mortifying stain on their shirt or blouse. If that happened, it would ruin their whole day.

Physically, Virgo people are generally slim in build, wiry yet muscular. Both men and women have pleasant yet striking faces. They usually have bright, alert eyes that rarely miss a thing. The women generally like their hair cut short. The hairdo can range from a short 'fro to braids to a bobbed haircut that promotes the pixie look.

When contemplating a relationship with a Virgo, think snail, turtle, or even inchworm. In other words, it's going to be slow going, so slow that you'll feel like like giving up sometimes. This man or woman may never notice you, let alone consider a relationship! They are going to take their own sweet time about getting knee-deep in an uptight, out-of-sight love affair. This is how the relationship with a Virgo will go. They're not going to be rushed, pushed or coerced into any relationship without weighing the situation from all angles and assessing *all* the players—the children from a previous marriage, a meddling mother, overbearing, nosey neighbors. For, you see, their peace of mind is also at stake here. For example, if they're approached by an overbearing female in a social setting, here's the scenario: They're at a class reunion. A sister spots the Virgo and whispers to her girlfriend, "I like him, I really want to get with him." As soon as the whispers are verbalized openly to the Virgo, he will do one of two things. Either he'll get real loud on the woman, saying, "You want to get with me?!" Or he'll completely ignore the situation. Any leanings, musings, or advances absolutely must be subtle!

There are probably more bachelors born under the sign of Virgo than under any other sign. Both the men and women are very comfortable being single. The Virgo brothers can cook, clean, sew on buttons and run a household as well as or better than most women. The Virgo sister will want to understand the innerworkings of her car. She's frugal, you know, so knowing about what's under the hood is an advantage for her pocketbook. If Virgos don't get married very young, it's usually very late or not at all. And that's okay with them. When they do marry, however, both the men and women of the sign are stern disciplinarians, and they will also demand perfection from their children. Virgos could take a lesson or two from the laid-back Taurus parent and learn to relax, enjoy their children and ease up a bit. Virgo, this is not the military!

The Virgo Man

You won't find this man picking up women at the local honky-tonk. In fact, he wouldn't be caught dead in one. He's too cautious and reserved for that scene. If by chance you persuaded him to go to a bar, and a favorite blues song—"My baby don't have to work. She don't have to rob and steal"—is playing on the jukebox, the Virgo would no doubt be the only person paying attention to the words. He would probably also wonder why the song with the crude words was written in the first place. Virgos are so intellectual sometimes they fail to consider the source of what they're analyzing. In the case of the song, it was probably an old bluesman born in the Mississippi Delta who had never seen an English book. There will be constant questions that he'll want answers to, when sometimes there are none.

You will usually meet this brother in a controlled setting such as church, through a mutual friend or on the job. They don't play that one-night-stand stuff. They know that the dating game is too risky or too deadly. If he is propositioned by a female, he will more than likely inform her of the perils of AIDS and herpes and provide a detailed explanation of other sexually transmitted diseases. In short, you need to have your health card handy with this brother, and you may *still* be looked at with suspicion. These brothers function best in long-term relationships. They simply want to keep the dating game to a minimum.

You will find this brother hard at work, owning his own business, directing the church choir, cutting his mother's grass or safely tucked away at home, where he functions best and feels safest. He may also be the scoutmaster, the neighborhood watch organizer and a single parent, all at the same time.

The Virgo man is loyal and faithful. Usually, they are well liked by most and devoted to their friendships. You can always count on the Virgo at crunch time. The Virgo brother will be the one you can call on in a crisis. He will accompany you to the emergency room and stay all night if need be. Or he'll remain in the college dorm staying by the phone to send word to your parents after any accident.

Virgos are the no-nonsense types of the zodiac. There are several lists of "you shoulds" (be neater, be on time, etc.) that the Virgo wants his potential companion to aspire to. Once he meets the woman who fits his long list of criteria (church-going, God-fearin', doesn't pick her teeth in public, isn't always out partying), he's content and the fever-pitch search will be over. You better get your hair done regularly and dress neatly, and not with a lot of flash or flare either, but with the sort of dress that reminds you of a librarian. Virgo men like the shirtwaist dress look, the sheaths and clothing where an overabundance of cleavage, kneecaps or butts are not apparent. He doesn't like a woman who has to be on display. Tight-fitting spandex dresses or tube tops that are worn for skirts are not his idea of proper attire for anyone, except maybe a stripper or prostitute. Don't misunderstand, he's not made of stone. He enjoys what he sees. This brother just doesn't want his woman to let it all hang out—not in public, at least.

He's more interested in the damsel-in-distress type than the prima donna type. This brother has to be needed and he must be the one to render service. He doesn't go in for a lot of drama, intrigue or mystery. He wants a woman who is straightforward, down-to-earth and from a "good family." He really wants a woman with a clean slate. The Virgo brother doesn't ever want to be pulled to the side and given information like, "Your woman ain't nothing, man. I knew her in high school and college and she dated several members of the football team and my fraternity." If this happened, the Virgo will be gone in the blink of an eye. She doesn't have to be a virgin, but close to it.

By this time, I'm sure you're thinking, "Why bother? This brother has so many do's and don'ts, how in the world does he ever enjoy life?" Although this brother's checklists are long and varied, he's much harder on himself than he will be on a mate. He requires a lot of himself and has plenty of self-discipline.

Virgo brothers are good listeners, but the problem is, they don't have the ability to examine or expose themselves. He'll be glad to listen to all the gory details of your life, but he won't openly share any of his secrets, misgivings and concerns.

As husbands, they are also good providers. Most Virgos work two jobs, a full-time job and a part-time one. The part-time job may consist of deejay gigs on the weekends, playing for a church on Sunday, working part-time in retail or the military reserve.

They will also be able to do housework readily and efficiently. A Virgo man will iron his shirts himself, for he simply feels that he can do a better job. He probably can. If you're married to or dating a Virgo, don't try to flex your domestic muscles, because you'll be embarrassed. When it comes to domestic affairs, their perfectionist attitude carries over in that arena as well. The house will be squeaky clean, everything orderly—a place for everything and everything in its place, including the closets. The dress shirts will all be hung up in the closet with the buttons and collar points all facing in the same direction. I know it's weird, but this is the life of the Virgo man, so get over it!

Image is everything to these brothers. They simply can't stand to be looked at unfavorably on any level. For example, the mother of a Virgo's girlfriend inadvertently picked up her daughter's pictures at the drugstore. The pictures showed the couple scantily clad and in suggestive positions. The mother gave the Virgo the pictures, saying the clerk at the drugstore had given her the pictures by mistake since she and her daughter had the same surname. The Virgo brother was so mortified that, for several months, whenever he called and the mother answered the phone, he would hang up the telephone without saying a word.

The Virgo Woman

The Virgo sister is very complex and introspective, a worrywart neatness freak with a good heart. When you first meet this sister, you won't be able to pick up many signals of her interest in you or in anything else for that matter. Your only vibrations from this sister will be caution. This Virgo female is so preoccupied with all of her responsibilities and worries that she will probably be pondering how soon she can get to her safe haven—home, sweet home.

Probably the only thing you'll pick up is indifference, at first anyway. These Virgo sisters are not going to fall for the first man they meet. But when they've determined that the liaison is what they perceive to be true love, their logical assessment of whether it's workable goes out the window and determination and sacrifice take over. This earth sign will sometimes stay in a relationship for several years, being the devoted mate and sacrificing her own career to help her companion. Such was the case with one Virgo who was smart, focused and knew what she wanted out of life. She was an accountant, fresh out of college. Homeboy, a Scorpio, walked into her office with his clean-cut Mr. Peabody looks and the rest was history. He had dreams of owning his own business and she became his chief executive officer. The first dream was a construction business. It fell through. The trouble was, he was an architectural engineering major and math minor. He could design the structure, but that was it. The next dream was an ice cream franchise, but the company folded after the city constructed an additional leg of the expressway that obstructed the view of the ice cream parlor from the street and the flow of traffic stopped. Then there was the pooper-scooper business—but that didn't work either after the couple moved to a small town and there wasn't a high demand for such contraptions. I'm not sure what the new venture is, but the Virgo is still hanging in there.

Virgo sisters long for a strong man who's smart and has integrity. Although she doesn't necessarily like the idea of living with a man, she's not above it either, as long as the ultimate goal—namely, marriage—is kept in mind.

As with most areas of their lives, Virgo women can be the backbone of most families. Like the men, the women are perfectionists with all things, including you. These sisters are precise and systematic and will give you advice on every topic, from your finances to why it's important for a man's shoes to be shined. They're hard workers, they pride themselves on doing all the right things and they're pleasant people most of the time. On the flip side, they are the critics of the zodiac—but that doesn't mean that they can be criticized. They find it almost impossible to be wrong. If, by chance, you show them that they are wrong in black and white, they will usually brood about it for weeks, as if to say, "How could I have made a mistake?"

Even though they may also have careers (and they usually do), they will cook the meals, sew on the buttons, bake oatmeal cookies for the booster club meeting and give you a little TLC, provided they don't fall asleep in the chair during the nightly news program. Finding time to relax, not to mention actually relaxing, is a luxury for the Virgo woman. She is not happy unless she's working, piddlin' around the house, or even picking lint off a white dress.

When the Virgo female is not cooking, running the household or working on community grants to help young African American children by volunteering the little precious time she does have, she's gabbing on the telephone with friends. She doesn't have a whole boatload of friends, but for the few that she has, she's there lending support, giving advice on love relationships or simply declaring that she needs to stop working so hard. The working-less conversation is an exercise in futility: She can't stop. She wouldn't know what to do with herself if she had a lot of time on her hands. That extra time would merely be spent on another volunteer effort or worrying about the outcome of an upcoming project.

Although Virgos are nonthreatening types, you don't want to make the Virgo woman angry, because that lovable, smiling and sweet Virgo can become a raging shrew. When this happens, most people do a double take; they simply cannot believe that this polished, classy lady is cuttin' up sideways! She'll hurl a flowerpot (ceramic) at her husband in the middle of an argument or chastise a rude salesclerk and follow it up with a tersely written letter to the manager.

But usually these sisters have the patience of Job, particularly in love relationships. And they're not going to settle for just any companion simply to be able to say, "I got a man!" If they can't have who they want, they are willing to wait. One sister met her husband at a wedding. She was a bridesmaid and he was her escort. She knew right then that she wanted this Piscean as a lifetime companion. It took eight years to get the relationship moving, in part, because she was in Los Angeles and he was in Washington, D.C. But the Virgo refused to settle for anyone else; they've been in a relationship for eleven years and are now married.

Virgo sisters are also the caretakers of the zodiac. The detailed dedication with which they perform most tasks is legendary. A patient was brought to the hospital to die. A Virgo nurse singlehandedly saved his life. The patient had developed gangrene in the stomach area. Three times a day, the Virgo nurse bathed the patient, submerging him in water, cleaned out the openings in his stomach to allow drainage, inserted antibiotic fluid and then packed them with gauze. The task went on for several weeks until the drainage cleared up.

However, this same caring Virgo sister can raise a ruckus when racist taunts are directed at her. When she asked a nursing assistant if she had measured a patient's urine output, the assistant retorted that she didn't need a "nigger" nurse asking her anything. The Virgo reported the incident and insisted that some action be taken that very day. When several days passed and no action was taken, the Virgo didn't let the incident rest. Eventually, the assistant's work performance was investigated. Racial slurs toward black patients were recorded, a poor work record was uncovered, and the woman was eventually fired.

Love Connection

Virgo people are quite entertaining once they feel comfortable in their surroundings and with their associates. They will keep you doubled over in laughter with their dry sense of humor and critical insights. And they can even fly by the seat of their pants on occasion. However, timing is everything. They're not quick to initiate hotter-than-July sexual encounters, but if you catch them in the right place at the right time, it's a sure bet. With a Virgo, the wild and kinky stuff usually comes much later in a long-term relationship or marriage. But the encounter won't ever get *too* kinky: Their prudish nature tames any would-be reckless romps around the bedroom.

The conditions for any love connection with Virgos could have you feeling like you're applying for acceptance into a religious order. They're picky about everything, from the food they eat to the men and women they meet. They usually have a long list of requirements that they expect from any potential companion. You'll definitely know what's included on the checklist before any area that's remotely associated with love gets underway.

With the Virgo woman, friendship is more important than a good sex partner. In order for this lady of the zodiac to get involved sexually, she must first trust you completely. She moves slowly and cautiously, so gaining her trust is the essential first step in a rewarding relationship. These women are not apt to swoon over the Mr. Look-So-Good types. You may wonder, why bother. Here's why. Virgos are loyal, steadfast, and faithful to any relationship in which they are involved. They have no interest in having two or three mates. They're too preoccupied with all the worries of life in general to have to guess which one of their companions is on the telephone. This earth sign is the consummate "do-right woman." Besides, Virgo women have a tendency to downplay their qualities. They're so critical of themselves and the world around them that they simply don't see what others find attractive in them. A Virgo reporter with light brown eyes and sandy hair simply couldn't understand why she was constantly getting compliments about her eyes from men. "What's this fascination with my eyes?" she would respond with annoyance, unable to see what others saw. Her hypercritical analysis only allowed her to see her eyes when they were red and tired, without makeup or behind her glasses. Therefore, she wasn't all that impressed.

Most women find Virgo men curiously attractive and interesting. Virgo brothers rarely have to initiate any interaction with sisters because Virgo men are usually propositioned first. It's something about their nonthreatening nature. They're usually immaculately dressed, shoes shined, not a strand of hair out of place and moving in a hurry but very deliberately. They're slow as molasses, however, when it's time to come on to a woman. On second thought, don't even use terms like "come on to," because he probably won't know what they mean.

When it comes to women, his turtlelike moves are due in part to his low confidence level. And because he's so busy analyzing the situation, by the time he musters any courage, the woman has usually given up hope. If the women waited on this earth sign to make his move without any prodding, the poor "chile" might be beyond the child-bearing age, say the late forties maybe.

For example, a young Virgo brother, age twenty, developed a relationship with a Piscean woman who was three years older. Both were on the fast track: college, career and definite goals with marriage plans on the back burner. However, after the Pisces companion got out of graduate school, she wanted to get married right away. The Virgo was willing to be engaged, but the marriage, he felt, wouldn't take place for another four years. The couple broke up and this sister was engaged six months later. (Hmm.) In short, Virgos will never be pushed into situations that they are not ready for and feel doubtful about.

If you want these virgins to throw away their chastity belts, stroke their stomach and lower chest area in a light, feathery manner and watch the sparks fly. You may also get a rise out of Virgo by massaging or stroking the upper groin area. These areas are the erogenous zones of this earth sign. Using these little tips will transform your controlled, quiet, cautious Virgo into an eager, imaginative bedmate. Many times they may not initiate new activities in the bedroom, but most of the time they'll go along, adding their own creative twist. Virgos also enjoy watching the undressing process—they may pretend like they're not looking, but believe me, they are. They don't miss much, not unless they're asleep.

Virgo is usually more compatible with the other two earth signs, Taurus and Capricorn. These signs are all predictable, stable and steadfast. Virgos are also in sync with Cancers and Scorpios. With water signs, the emotions are usually in high gear, but that's okay, because Virgos' even-keel personalities will support all the emotional baggage that water signs bring to the table. Pisces is the opposite sign of Virgo. Out of all of the opposites in the horoscope, the Pisces-Virgo combination is probably the only coupling that could work. Both are easygoing types that complement each other nicely. But bear in mind that they *are* opposites and there could be trouble ahead.

How to Get Next to a Virgo

• Neatness is very important to the Virgo so you need to check your teeth for leftover broccoli and look your best.
• This Mercury-ruled sign is very smart and equally impressed with the intellect of others. So keep the idle chatter to a minimum, and have some knowledge of current events.
• Understated elegance is what gets this brother's attention. A simple black dress and a string of pearls will make him stand up and take notice. And the sisters love a man in a crisply starched white shirt and slacks.
• Most Virgos are sticklers for punctuality. Running in on CPT to pick up your date will put a damper on the whole evening. They want to be at the movie or theater when the houselights are still on.
• Loud, boisterous behavior is a definite no-no. Virgos enjoy companions who have home training and who are not prone to outbursts or an unbecoming demeanor.

• Stay away from booty bars, gambling halls and honky-tonks if at all possible.

• Spontaneity is not a virtue that Virgos want to claim. If you're planning an outing, the Virgo must be in on your plans. They want to know where they're going, when, how, what kind of place and if they have to meet and greet strangers. They must be prepared.

• Toupees and dreadlocks on men are a turnoff for the women, and hair weave and wigs are better left off, according to the Virgo men. The philosophy here is, Less is more, because they will be preoccupied by what's underneath the hair enhancements.

• Also the colored contacts could be replaced by regular eyeglasses in traditional colors of brown, black, steel and gold rims, thank you.

The Virgo Child

Virgo children are a joy to have around. Raising a Virgo child will be a pleasant experience and present very few problems. Early in their lives, they want to please mommy, daddy and their teachers. They're great little helpers around the house and will learn at a very early age the art of doing any task correctly. Being looked upon in a favorable light and doing tasks in a precise manner are all-important to them.

They are also neat freaks at a young age. As early as grade school they will want to decide what to wear to school. Don't worry, they won't request combat boots and a lace dress or baggy pants and a midriff top. They'll be pretty conservative when it comes to clothing. If they have their own room, it will be neat: The dolls will be lined up in a row, the trucks will be in the toy box and the books will be in orderly fashion on the bookshelf.

As babies, Virgos require more attention than most children because of their innate fear of everything and everyone in the first months of their lives. They won't readily lie in their cribs, but will usually fall asleep quickly when being cradled in mommy's arms. Like the big Virgos, the little Virgos can be very cranky, crying frequently even though nothing is apparently wrong. When Virgo babies want mommy or daddy, there's nothing the baby-sitter, sibling or neighbor can do but allow them to cry themselves to sleep or wait until the parents finally come home. Don't bother trying to placate them with soothing baby talk or a warm bottle of milk. They want mommy and will not be pleased, no matter what you do.

As toddlers, they usually pick up developmental skills like potty training, walking and talking without much effort. Speaking clearly will come easy to the little one, but when company is around your chatterbox will become quiet and withdrawn.

Virgo youngsters must have plenty of positive reinforcement to offset low self-esteem, which if not addressed, will follow them through life. Hugs, kisses and words of encouragement should be expressed frequently. Virgos feel that they don't quite measure up, no matter what the deal is. One Virgo woman in her late fifties said she never wanted to get married because of the antagonistic relationship her father had toward her mother. Her father constantly accused her mother of infidelity, even though the mother simply had no time for love matters, what with taking care of her five children and being the dressmaker for the local neighborhood. According to the Virgo, her mother never left the house unless accompanied by her father. Two Virgos remember every detail of a particularly traumatic family incident. Their older sister had taken her father's anatomy book to school without permission. Each time her father demanded to know where the book was, the girl refused to respond and the father became angrier. The girls' younger siblings, both Virgos, yelled, "Tell him, Gwendolyn! Tell him where it is!" Then the father slapped her. The two Virgo children were so upset by the incident that day they couldn't eat their favorite breakfast of grits, sausage and homemade biscuits. Peaceful surroundings with very little bickering is very important to Virgo children.

Virgo children don't grasp the ramifications of being black in today's society right away. You see, to their way of thinking, they have too much other trauma to worry about—homework, making A's, being liked and doing chores at home. Virgo children place a lot of added pressure on themselves because they are constantly striving for perfection. So the dynamics of racism don't hit them until much later, unless there is some overt incident. When the subject of racism comes up, a detailed explanation from you as a parent should commence immediately. By the way, the explanation doesn't have to be after the incident. Virgos need to be guided and informed about the ways of the world on an ongoing basis. They can't handle being uninformed.

Virgos usually have very few discipline problems at school, and they're usually well liked by teachers and students. You only need to tell them once about an error or problem pertaining to discipline. Virgo children are perfectionists, sometimes as soon as they can walk. They will always be compelled to do the right thing. Constant yelling and ridiculing will not be needed. They're hard workers and work more effectively and comfortably behind the scenes. Although they could definitely become the class president, being the statistician for the athletic department or the student choir director in high school would be more suitable.

Virgos generally have a conservative nature. The birds-and-bees talk could take place around adolescence. Although this sign is popular with the opposite sex, Virgos are not gullible starry-eyed teens. They have a practical approach to most things, including sex. And no one, I repeat, no one, will be able to talk them into doing anything they don't want to do. That's not to say they may not want to experiment early with sex, but a discussion of AIDS, other sexually transmitted diseases, and teenage pregnancy should satisfy their curiosity about the matter.

Also, siblings of Virgo children, beware. Little Virgos want to be left alone by siblings, friends and family. They're good, well-mannered children and they expect others to treat them with respect. If they don't get respect, they don't usually give it. For example, a nine-year-old Virgo youngster, who grew tired of being picked on by his brother, a Sagittarian and four years his senior, decided to retaliate. The older brother pushed the Virgo to the ground and happily ran off. The little Virgo picked up a Ping-Pong size rock and threw it directly at his older brother, hitting him in the mouth as he held his head back laughing. Needless to say, he broke his brother's front tooth. I know this may sound grim, but the Virgo very quietly explained what happened and he didn't get punished for the deed.

The Virgo Employee

If you have a Virgo employee in the workplace be assured that they are doing the job and doing it well. Virgo employees are the people you won't have to worry about because they take care of business! Virgos are at their best working meticulously behind the scenes and probing into the inner workings of problems to find solutions. They are the accountants, financial analysts, police officers, physicians, secretaries, food service people, writers and nurses.

Virgos are perfectionists, so part of the time they're looking for ways to improve and hone their skills for greater on-the-job efficiency, which can drive any laid-back boss a little batty. Virgos will make their bosses feel as though they need to be working harder. Don't worry about it. Move out of the way and let your trusty Virgo go to it—the job, that is. Virgos invariably go beyond the call of duty. They are the kind of employees who make less driven workers seem incompetent.

They'll always be on time, or thirty minutes early. As one Virgo commented, "If I'm late, it's not my fault." They must prepare, you know, making coffee, returning phone calls, putting away files in an effort to keep their work areas immaculate or simply meeting with the boss. When it's time to go to work, the Virgos are on it and they have finished all of the preliminaries.

The Virgo's keen eye for detail makes him more than suitable for tedious work. If you have a Virgo for an assistant, you will definitely be spoiled. And when your conscientious Virgo is not there to anticipate your every move, you will definitely feel vulnerable and somewhat helpless. For example, a medical secretary found that her Scorpio pediatrician boss couldn't function without her. She had spoiled him to the point of even reading medical journals for him to determine the relevant pediatric articles. This Scorpio went into a tizzy every time she was out, which was rarely. The doctor wanted to know in advance when she would be out of the office so that he could mentally prepare.

When it comes to racism in the workplace, Virgos are so hard at work that many times they miss the subliminal messages on the job. Virgos have a strong sense of fairness in the workplace. Often when they witness unfairness on the job, they feel compelled to let their feelings be known, either verbally or by overt action. A Virgo biology teacher who finally grew tired of the white teachers segregating themselves by crowding together at one table during lunch decided to put the two lunch tables in the teacher's lounge together. She also made a point of telling those white teachers who wouldn't speak to black teachers that they neither had sense nor manners. Of course, this declaration made its way back to the other white teachers, who began speaking to the Virgo.

Being in a supervisory role is not really a Virgo's forte. If they didn't have to worry about all of the minor details of life, Virgos would probably make good supervisors. They simply don't want the responsibility of having to worry about employees as well as all their daily problems—like how to fix the leaky toilet, whether he'll have to accompany his wife to the company picnic or if she left the coffeemaker on all day. All these things will get done, and done well, but Virgos simply worry about what they think they should be worrying about. Huh!

Many times Virgos find themselves between a rock and a hard place when performing duties on the job. If you want a task done well and in a timely manner, give it to a Virgo. But many coworkers see the Virgo's actions as trying to take charge or take over. Others don't choose to be as conscientious but will resent a Virgo for doing the work without hesitation. Virgos simply cannot just sit back when work needs to be done. For example, a teacher in Los Angeles worked with community-based black-oriented projects to help interested students in pursuing teaching careers. She took over a floundering black executives exchange program in which corporate executives were supposed to visit high schools to talk to business students. Instead of passing the buck, like her predecessor, she set up a system to contact the executives directly. The executives were more than happy to accommodate the students.

Health Matters

Virgo people are very conscious of eating right, getting needed rest and regular exercise and consuming alcohol in moderation, and for this reason, their health is generally better than most. Early on, they approach good health as a significant area of their lives that they must continually address.

But they are workaholics by nature, which means, as with most addictions, they have very little control over trying not to work so hard. They see nothing wrong in their all-encompassing approach to the job. They are at their best when they are working in a controlled environment and rendering some sort of service. In fact, they're more comfortable working than "playing."

But because they're worriers, and I do mean worriers, their digestive systems and stomachs rarely get a rest. Seemingly, the more minute the problem, the more they worry. Virgo rules the intestines and abdominal area, so worrying doesn't help. These areas are prone to ailments, and supersensitivities to which Virgos should pay particular attention. Nervous tension and the inability to totally relax could be the catalyst for serious problems later. Some of the diseases that Virgos are prone to are damage to the digestive systems, nervous breakdowns, hypoglycemia, ulcers and weak intestines.

Additional problems surface for Virgo people because they are perfectionists, and everything they seek to do must be done again and again until it's satisfactory to them and others. Of course, if you're on the receiving end of the assignments, you'll no doubt be pulling your hair out. But if the situation is satisfactory to the Virgo, it's more than satisfactory to the eleven other Sun signs of the zodiac.

Workaholic plus worrier plus perfectionist equals one-sided Virgos who must achieve some balance in their life to avoid being hospitalized for mental and physical exhaustion. Therefore, yoga or meditation and aerobics can offer this uptight earth sign a few relaxing moments before he dashes off to his part-time job or choir rehearsal (he's probably the minister of music).

Virgos should steer clear of spicy or fried foods and red meat. Eat more fiber-rich foods, such as whole wheat bread, fruits, bran cereal and almonds. Don't forget the green vegetables (all kinds of greens—turnip, mustard, collards—but use smoked turkey parts instead of ham hocks). Virgos are also finicky eaters. If the food doesn't look appealing and there is no logical explanation for the ingredient, Virgos will not touch it with a ten-foot pole. They also don't care for foods that are messy to eat. One Virgo man never ate corn on the cob because he didn't like the biting motion, which he said resembled a typewriter gone wild. The food must be prepared in almost sterile surroundings. They view eating food like most everything else; the endeavor must be analyzed and examined before it goes into the body. Grocery shopping is no different. The trip to the store is planned with a grocery list along with food coupons. The coupons will be organized according to food categories. The food items on the list will more than likely have an asterisk to indicate those foods that the Virgo has coupons for. If you're in a hurry, I suggest you not go to the store with a Virgo. They are a part of the label-reading, produce-thumping crew, which means you'll probably be there for at least an hour or two if there's family shopping to be done.

But overall, if you can convince Virgos that everything is going to work out whether they worry about it or not, you'll have mastered a major hurdle.

Famous African American Virgos

Gerald Albright	Jesse Owens
Carl Banks	Robert Parish
Elgin Baylor	Charlie Parker
Wilfredo Benitez	Pebbles
Marva Collins	Billy Preston
John Coltrane	Otis Redding
Camille Cosby	Frank Robinson
Nikki D	Roxie Roker
Rita Dove	Sonia Sanchez
Lola Falana	Isabel Sanford
Henry Louis Gates, Jr.	Valerie Simpson
Althea Gibson	Wyomia Tyus
Robin Harris	Blair Underwood
Michael Jackson	Barry White
B. B. King	Roy Wilkins
Mark McEwen	George C. Wolfe
Reggie Miller	Richard Wright
Edwin Moses	Frank Yerby
Jessye Norman	

LIBRA

September 23 to October 22

Symbol: The Scales

Positive traits: Diplomatic, refined, charming, romantic, easy-going, seeker of harmony, idealistic, orderly

Negative traits: Indecisive, gullible, changeable, frivolous, resentful, flirtatious, extravagant, vacillates between two extremes

Ruling planet: Venus is associated with love and beauty.

The song entitled "Back and Forth" by Aaliyah probably sums up the personality of the Libra. Getting to know the sum of all this air sign's parts will be a real challenge. When you meet the Libra, you'll be intrigued by the female or enjoy the cut-up antics of the male. Libras love to be in the mix. And they're extremely popular with members of the opposite sex. They're charming, engaging conversationalists, and of course, they'll be tastefully dressed for any occasion. And they're usually easy on the eyes and someone who you'll be thoroughly entertained by as well. This is the up side of Libra.

However, this same calm, easygoing charmer can become, within a twenty-four-hour period or less, argumentative, stubborn, mean and tactless. You will be utterly flabbergasted and be certain that this person must have an identical twin, for this couldn't possibly be the same individual. But there are no twins here; that's the sign of Libra. The symbol is the scales, typifying his lifelong quest to maintain perfect balance in his life. They vacillate from one extreme to the other, and only during intervals are they able to reach that perfect balance where peace and harmony are at the pinnacle.

So if you're dealing with a Libra, there will never be a dull moment, that's for sure. And don't ask them why they have such a contradictory personality because they don't know any more than you do.

The sign of the scales has this Venus-ruled person in a quandary over any decision, which can sometimes take an eternity. If you're a part of the decision, and you're about to go ballistic, it's best to make the decision for the Libra. In most cases, he'll be glad you did. Then again, he might challenge your reasons, with a list of opposing ideas. See, here we go again! The air sign will take thirty minutes to determine how he wants his eggs cooked in the morning. One of the reasons for the indecisiveness is that the Libra is able to examine both sides of the problem with clarity. Consequently, it's easier to straddle the fence. For example, when asked if he was indecisive, a Libran brother replied that he couldn't decide if he was or wasn't. Whew! In another case, a Libran sister constantly complained to her Aquarius boyfriend that they didn't go out to enough interesting places. But when this brother asked his girlfriend where she wanted to go, her reply was, "I don't know!!"

One of the things that's hard for Librans to accept is that everyone cannot live up to their expectations. Librans feel everyone should be like them—kind, generous and diplomatic. Libra is the sign of partnerships, and as a consequence, marriage is very important to them. Libras will sometimes get married right out of high school or in college. If the Libra finds herself in a marriage that's abusive or just not clicking, this sister is the first to sever the ties.

After the marriage is over, the Libra will forever search for that all-important mate. For Libras, it's always greener on the other side of the fence. One Libra woman I know, who married in her early twenties and divorced after three short years, longed for that soul mate, that husband with whom she could make a life. However, each time Mr. Wonderful came a callin' and the relationship appeared to blossom, the Libra would pull back, saying she wasn't sure that this was what she wanted. This is the norm for the Libra. For all practical purposes, there's seldom, if ever, any certainty about any facet of life with a Libra. If I were you, I'd get in a go-with-the-flow mode. What can I say? There's no emphatic way of letting you down easy with this human roller coaster.

They make very considerate mates, but remember, the scales of a Libra's life won't always be balanced. Marital bliss will come in spurts. As parents, Librans want their children to have good manners and look and act "appropriately." If the girls enjoy basketball instead of dolls, undue stress will set in. Children will take advantage of Libra parents' good nature because most of the time they won't follow through with punishment. When money problems arise from the Libra's must-have spending or when there's trouble on the job or with the kids, the marriage will suffer just like everything else in the Libra's life. This air sign acts on impulse, and many times, both men and women will rush into a relationship prematurely without thinking things through. And because Librans want peace and harmony, and will do anything to maintain it, companions will take full advantage of the situation, causing early disappointments in the union.

Because of their natural curiosity about all aspects of life, Librans are in interracial relationships more than other Sun signs. If they're interested in someone, race is secondary to getting to know the person. For example, a young Libran brother in the military, stationed in Alaska for over a year, met and married an Italian woman ten years his senior. He was warned by family members that his judgment could be clouded because he was several thousand miles away from home and extremely lonely. She, a Gemini, had lived in Alaska for several years and wanted out. They believed at the time that they were in love. But three years after the couple moved back home, the marriage dissolved because neither could stand the pressures of the interracial marriage.

Libra's ruling planet is Venus, which is associated with love and beauty. Need I say more? They love beautiful surroundings, clothing, art and all of the amenities of life, including the BMW, Benz or Lexus. And they will order the very best that the ol' checkbook can stand.

Generally, if there are other siblings in the family, the Libra child is the sibling that stands out in terms of good looks and overall natural beauty. Physically, the only discernible feature of the black Libra is their big butts. This is the case no matter how skinny or tiny the Libra. In both men and women, the booties are substantial and well rounded. The women are neither top- nor bottom-heavy and usually have neat waistlines with rounded hips—not too big, not too small but just right. Usually, both men and women are of average size. Even when they're heavy, their bodies will be well proportioned. Weight gain occurs in later years or when the Libra is depressed or in the depths of despair. Don't try to coax them out of the depression. It's something they must work out for themselves. Being around them when the scales are out of balance is a headache you definitely don't need. So a word of warning: Stay away until they contact you, which will mean they're ready to be civil human beings. It's a Libra thang!

Both men and women of the sign have a natural, irresistible charm, and with their keen intelligence, they can use these traits very effectively to get what they want. The generally easy nature of Librans finds them acting as mediators in family and relationship squabbles all too often. In order to maintain the balance they seek, they must think of their needs first sometimes and put off the tendency to please someone else all in the name of keeping the peace. The one primary lesson that Librans must learn is that they can't be all things to all people. Librans are so hell-bent on being liked or loved that people take advantage of their kindness. But as one Libran brother put it, individuals have a tendency to take his kindness for weakness. And let me tell you, Librans aren't weak!

The Libra Man

Girlfriend, this brother is something else! If you're looking for romance to the max, I'm telling you, this is the brother you need to find! They have the fine art of pampering a woman down to the last detail. Falling in love with a Libra man will be easy. They're totally laid-back, receptive and nonthreatening cutie pies. Their dress is impeccable. They are neat and clean and pride themselves on knowing how to please a woman (in and out of the bedroom). They function best when they're in a relationship, as opposed to going it alone. But, remember, just as you found them attractive, others will too. And he's a flirt. I'm not saying that he's going to drive off into the sunset with another sister—he may only wink at her or make idle small talk when the two of you are in a crowded restaurant waiting to be seated. Don't sweat it. The best thing to do is talk to someone as well or join in the conversation and not with an attitude! Jealousy is a flaw with which they have little patience.

Just as they like beautiful surroundings, they like beautiful companions. Good looks are definitely a plus, but that will only get you to first base. There has to be something in your pretty little head. You must know about current events and what's going on in the world. They want you to have your own life because their livelihood cannot be yours. In other words, get a life. They're not going to be around to hold your hand—not constantly, anyway. Librans are air signs, meaning, their thoughts are far out in the stratosphere. They won't be controlled, contained, manipulated or constantly told what to do but, like air itself, they will simply vanish. They must have balance in their lives. Balance for the Libra means a pleasant work environment, nice surroundings and a rewarding relationship with very few arguments. Screaming, cussing, spitting and flailing your arms will get you to stage left and out the door quicker than you can say "My Libran man." And when things that are important to them don't gel, they are miserable.

For example, a Libra man moved in with a divorced Scorpio and her two children, and they eventually decided to get married; the Libran also had a son, and the couple decided to rear the three children together. But during an incident in which the Libran was disciplining the woman's son, the child wouldn't comply, saying his mother told him he didn't have to obey the Libran. The point here is the Libran brother thought that he and the Scorpio had an agreement that all three children would be reared as the children of their cohesive family unit. But when the Libran learned that his efforts at child rearing were being undermined by the Scorpio, it became clear to the Libra that, however minute to some, this was a situation he couldn't forget or forgive. Well, since the incident, the relationship has been damaged almost beyond repair.

Don't ask the Libra brother why your pictures are no longer on his dresser. There may be a feasible explanation. He may have sent the pictures out to be matted and framed. Don't always assume that there's competition looming on the horizon. But if you find pictures of another woman, keep the accusations to a minimum because you'll be the loser. They don't take too kindly to being backed in a corner. In situations like that, they usually retreat.

A Libra politician decided to celebrate his election without his wife. As members of his political party gathered at a popular night-spot for a surprise party for the politician in the capital city of his Southern state, in walks Libra with Ms. 1-900-FUNTIME wrapped around him like Saran Wrap. It didn't help that she wore a black miniskirt about the size of a bandana. When he spotted his col-leagues, he exited through the side door without a word. His com-panion tossed a glance of curiosity at the gallery of friends waiting to congratulate him.

Long after the relationship is over this brother will be a linger-ing and haunting memory, pleasantly so. When the girlfriends are invited over and the hen sessions kick off, your Libran will come up again and again. As you testify over and over about how good he was in bed, how he could cook and brought you roses, how he tried the latest sexual gadgets on you and what an overall nice guy he was, you'll wonder, "Why did I let this brother go?" You'll constantly compare him with other men in your life. And most of the time, your present mate won't measure up.

During the 1970s, one Libra brother, a writer, had a long-distance relationship with a woman that ended after four years. When the woman died recently, her daughter contacted the Libran to inform him that after twenty years and three husbands, the woman had kept every one of his love letters tucked away in a box. He was initially mortified because the daughter had read about the intimate details of their relationship. He never entertained the idea that he had a special place in his former lover's heart after all those years. The situation was like a page out of *The Bridges of Madison County*.

Welcome to the world of the balancing act or the tightrope walk. Libra men are very fair-minded people—that's the problem.

They will always weigh all of the elements of the relationship. He may wine and dine you until you finally say yes, then just when you think the courtship will commence, you'll find that he's reluctant to act on it. He's pretty intuitive as well, so don't think any secret motives on your part will not be picked up on. Just be patient. He's worth the wait.

If by chance you fall in love with this brother, patience is a virtue and, let me tell you, you'll need plenty. They can definitely be hard to deal with, with nitpickin' elements that will constantly amaze. When you're dressed to the nines to go out for the evening, Libras will let you know about any pet peeve that most people will probably perceive as a bit ridiculous. For example, one Libra brother said if a woman is dressed from head to toe, chipped nail polish is a definite no-no. Or if a woman is dressed and her child isn't, that's a turnoff. And ladies, good manners is a plus with them, so don't drink beer from the bottle. While the nagging may be difficult, there are more serious issues that the Libra brother can be indecisive about. For example, one Aquarian sister, who had a fifteen-year up-and-down relationship with a Libra, has never gotten over a devastating decision she made. The Aquarian had been married previously and had two children. The Libran had on several occasions talked of the two getting married and having a baby. When the Aquarian sister became pregnant, the Libran brother went ballistic and demanded she have an abortion. After she complied, he constantly blamed her for not having the baby, saying, "You should have had the baby, no matter what I said."

The Libra Woman

This sister must be the apple of your eye, the big cheese or the pick of the litter. Like Leo, she'll expect to be complimented when she astonishes you with her melodramatic antics. When you're invited to her house for dinner, more than likely the meal will be catered— she simply doesn't have time to make a big fuss in the kitchen. She's got to have her nails, toes and hair done, you know. All of the trappings will definitely be in place—the best champagne, the most seductive music, the candles and thou. The point to all of this will be to amaze you with her ability to offer an enchanting evening that you won't forget. It's not necessarily for you. It's for her, as well, so that she can enjoy your reaction to her creative abilities. Once she has your attention, she might lose interest in keeping the relationship at its current level. The point is the romance of it all, not necessarily the actual courtship.

Such was the case with a Libra student who attended a private Catholic college. After meeting and dating a brother at a neighboring college, Libra lost interest as the courtship moved to phase two, meaning a more serious relationship. Unbeknownst to the brother, the Libra coed had started dating someone else—the brother's roommate. After the inevitable confrontation, the roommates asked her to decide on one of them, so guess who took an eternity to do so. Roommate number two eventually won out, but this romance didn't last long, either.

The Libra woman can be very lazy when it comes to nurturing a relationship. But she'll demand a lot from *you* and expect you to know what she wants even before she realizes it herself. She expects the world and then some from her mate—a tall order, indeed. Does this sound like a person who's self-centered? Well, if you're not up for pampering her, she'll do it for herself. For example, one Libran woman I know decided she would leave the country every year on vacation during her birthday week. The first year she went to enjoy the Caribbean, the second year she went to Acapulco and the following year to west Africa. She went on these trips for purely hedonistic reasons, (hedonism being the doctrine that pleasure is the principal good and should be the aim of action). She found that she was treated like a queen in these places because she learned that, unlike black men, professional black women are not seen too often in these places.

The Libra sister will spend money like it's going out of style—and it doesn't matter whose it is. She's the consummate prima donna. She believes that lavish possessions and personal pampering are what she deserves. And if you happen to be along for the ride, you'll be pampered, too. One Libra sister, a manager with the phone company in the Midwest, found that over the years her associates who made less money became habitual freeloaders. Many of her friends expected this air sign to just set "it" out. If there was a concert or ball game, guess who was expected to put up the money or pay for the tickets? During happy hour guess who paid for most of the drinks? When the Libra sister pointed out the imbalance in the situation, several of her so-called friends dropped from sight.

Libras are devoted wives. Her husband will be the focal point around which everything functions. She won't necessarily be the great cook that he wants, and that's okay, because as long as there are plenty of restaurants around, the husband will be happy. Librans have excellent taste, and home furnishings will be semilavish with soft blues, roses and turquoise, whatever the couple's pocketbook can stand. Librans function better in a partnership rather than going it alone. But once the children arrive, the relationship will evolve into a whole different story. The key word for Libras is marriage, so raising the children will be a real challenge for them, and one where two parents are needed. Libras simply have a difficult time balancing both husband and children effectively.

If you're married to a Libra, don't leave the task of balancing a checkbook to her—you'll be sorry. They simply don't have the patience for such detail work, and besides, money is for spending, not hoarding.

The Libra sister is a lesson in contradictions. She is attracted to intelligent men, but at the same time she likes the strong silent types. She admires a man who has the guts to boss her around, yet she's really her own person and more than likely won't be controlled.

Straddling the fence is her forte, as a young Libran made clear regarding the prochoice-prolife debate. The conversation went like this: "I can't say that I'm all the way prochoice or all the way prolife. I feel like a person should have the right to end an unwanted pregnancy. I would want that option for myself, but I probably wouldn't choose it if I were in that situation because I believe the baby should live." Hello?!

Intelligence is a big plus with this Venus-ruled sign. They cannot tolerate people who are not well versed in a variety of subjects. Intellectual stimulation is second only to sex for this air sign, and you simply must know what's going on in the world. The Libra sister is also a people person. She enjoys a variety of outings, including a

Prince concert, an NBA basketball game, an art exhibit and even a baby shower. She usually has lots of friends and her social calendar is crowded. She simply must try to be the center of attention no matter where she goes. She's the standout in the crowd. She will get her share of attention if it kills her. This charmer will be the sister wearing the most intriguing outfit in a social setting—a backless dress, a skirt with the provocative split or even a micro-mini.

Sometimes when there's a serious imbalance of the scales, Libras will resort to extreme measures to get what they want. For example, in her determination to snag a particular brother, a Libra sister went to a phony psychic. The psychic told her to tell her lover that she and the brother were getting married. The psychic also told her that she would have a job soon. Six months later and $300 poorer, she had neither lover nor job.

Love Connection

Libras are easy to fall in love with, and they love to be in love. In an effort to have a strong emotional and loving attachment, they often blindly fall head over heels in love with a person who is not right for them. And because of their eagerness to please a companion in every way they are sometimes left holding the bag when potential mates take advantage of their trusting nature.

Both men and women of this sign love the romance portion of courtship. For them, that's the best. The Libra woman prefers to be taken to out-of-the-way restaurants or villas with roving musicians and soft lights. She'll be elegantly dressed, with soft accents of mellow perfume, holding one of the roses you sent. Even if you're not inclined to accommodate the Libra with this fantasy date, you need to fake it. Their expectations of potential companions are high. If you don't put forth a valiant effort, you'll notice an abrupt change in what you thought was a budding relationship.

A romantic interlude with the Libra brother, will have all the trappings—champagne, wonderful cuisine and, of course, plenty of atmosphere, with scented candles and mellow mood music. Nothing will be overlooked. A Leo telephone operator I know told me her Libran man would have her bath drawn and dinner ready when she got home. He would greet her at the door with a kiss, a rose or both. If she was particularly tense, he would give her a back rub after the bath.

By the time the adventure reaches the bedroom, you'll be delightfully surprised to discover that the Libran brother is eager to please between the sheets. He has the art of making love down to a science—and like any science, research can't be rushed. I'm talking an all-day treat here. Both men and women of this sign take sex seriously. It's as important to them as air and food. Both sexes are in the no-holds-barred category, and both will try anything once. Once may be enough! And if you want the sparks to fly immediately with the goddess or god of love, stroke them on the small of the back or butt, erogenous zones for this air sign. Any touches to those areas will put this air sign in overdrive.

These air signs can sometimes be too eager to please. A Libran man sent his dates flowers and cards, just because. . . . But he found that the objects of his pursuits were often unappreciative, and the relationships would end with the woman saying that the Libran man was "too nice" to them.

Aquarius and Gemini, the two other air signs, are compatible with Libra. Librans thrive with mates who will allow them to have their freedom while at the same time support them in their many endeavors. Sagittarius and Leo, both fire signs, are also compatible with Libra. Air and fire mix well together. Both have plenty of self-confidence and won't be intimidated by Libra's charm, good looks and outgoing, flirtatious nature.

If you're a Libra, you've probably had plenty of contact with Aries, your opposite sign. The two of you can vibe so completely —Aries is so taken with Libra's charm and Libra hangs onto the knowledgeable Aries' every word. And as with any satisfying encounter, couples have the mistaken notion that because the intimate relationship is oh, so mutually satisfying, the rest can be worked out. The trouble is, in order for the liaison to work you must spend all your time in the bedroom! Most people have to come up for air sometime. In other words, opposites don't work out over the long term because the duo is not compatible, except sexually, and there are too many other differences to be overcome.

How to Get Next to a Libra

• Don't ever take a Libran on a date to a juke joint or a bar that looks like a hole-in-the-wall with beer. That date will be your last.

• Librans pride themselves on being very classy, and they will expect the same from you. A nice restaurant, not necessarily the most expensive, with dim lighting and soft music will score "cool" points with them.

• Be complimentary. But don't go on and on with comments to the Libran as if she's an angel from heaven or too fine for words. They will only be turned off.

• You need to read the newspaper and know about current events. Librans definitely know what's going on in the world and if you expect to accompany them, you'd better at least know who the current president is and some of today's burning issues.

• Don't be too aggressive or pushy. Although Librans love attention, they don't like overly aggressive suitors. Librans must maintain a balance of what's acceptable and what's not.

• The know-it-alls of life turn Librans off. Librans won't shy away from a good argument because they want to consider both sides, but peace and harmony is more important to them than winning an argument or major verbal battles.

• Taking a small gift on a first date such as a delicate piece of jewelry or flowers is always a plus with the females. And giving your male date a small bottle of cologne will delight him.

• Don't be a slob when it comes to dressing. Even though you don't have to wear designer clothing, you must be dressed neatly and tastefully. When in doubt about what to wear, ask the Libra. He or she will be more than happy to tell you.

• Carrying your portable phone around to restaurants and other public places will only infuriate Librans. They aren't impressed with gadgets like phones and beepers. They only serve as a distraction when out on a date.

• Stay away from the 1976 Buicks with the fuzzy dice dangling from the rearview mirror and the fur on the dashboard. This sends the wrong message to the lady Libras.

The Libra Child

Libra children need plenty of attention, love and overt affection in abundance. Hugs, hugs and more hugs is what they require. And your hugs will be met with eager hugs in return. So once the hugs and affection begin in their early years, these children will want and expect it to continue. These children are easygoing and will present parents with very few problems.

These beautiful little ones are the winners of the baby contests. Whenever friends and relatives are around these babies can charm. They're so adorable and cute with a smile that lights the world, all you can do is coo at them.

As toddlers, they will find walking and talking easy. Even as young as age two, Libra children can talk intelligently to adults. But the potty training may be another story, especially for the boys. A calm, logical, step-by-step approach to potty training will go much further than spankings for this little air sign.

Parents, keep the yelling and screaming to a minimum because Libra children will do whatever you ask to keep from being yelled at. The yelling will make matters worse, with the Libran child crying uncontrollably. Like the big Libras, the little Libras must have peace and harmony in their lives too. No matter how old this child gets, he or she will need the reassurance that hugs provide.

Libra children are also indecisive and it's important to push these children to make some of their decisions for themselves. Honesty and long talks on problems that concern them will keep their little lives in balance, which is key for any Libra. One Libra child, who was a doted-on only child and never knew her father, felt a missing link in her life. Her mother's refusal to even discuss the matter caused instability in the mother-daughter relationship. Instead of an open discussion, the mother overindulged the Libra child to make up for the lack of a father. The Libra said her mother created a handicapped child, because at age twenty-four, she didn't how to wash her own clothes. A wedge has been driven between these two that may never be withdrawn.

Libra children are pretty punctual, but if you want these children to be on time for school, don't allow them to decide what to wear, especially in early adolescence. This process will take all day. The mother of a Libra had to coax her child daily to put on her socks. The youngster simply couldn't decide which to put on first and would sit as the clock moved closer to schooltime. But please be advised that you must try to get them to their recitals, bowling tournaments, swim meets or spelling bees on time. It drives them crazy when they're late, especially if it's the parent's fault.

This soft-spoken youngster won't be the high school jock. He's the concerned boy-next-door type; he may not get the girl, but he'll be there to listen as his female classmates go on and on about the high school jock. These children are very intelligent. Making good grades shouldn't be a problem unless there's strife at home; it will definitely affect their schoolwork.

Generally, you'll find these children in the band, speech, drama or writing poetry or short stories. They're usually more interested in the arts and the softer side of schoolwork than woodworking, home economics or auto mechanics.

In integrated school systems the Libran child will sometimes have an identity crisis. One Libra boy, age six, came home from school and announced to his mother that he wanted to be white because he wanted his hair to blow in the wind like his white schoolmates during recess. The little Libra also felt that if he were white, his fellow classmates would like him more and not pick on him as much. If this occurs, a long talk about cultural diversity and being proud to be African American is in order. But again, the talk should be in a conversational tone.

Libra children may be picked on in school because they may be perceived as pushovers and because they're well liked by both teachers and students. The Libran will try to avoid confrontation at all costs, so joining a gang won't be in the cards for this child.

Both sexes are very popular with the opposite sex. The lecture on the facts of life should be presented early. Their natural curiosity can spill over into experimenting with sex at a young age. (For the parents, no matter what age, it'll always be too early.) And in the case of Libras, the members of the opposite sex could be black, white, striped—whatever.

The Libra Employee

A pleasant environment in which to work is the key to getting the maximum effort from the Libra employee. Soft music and a decor of pale colors (blue, rose, beige) will make the Libra happy and life a little easier for the boss and other employees. You see, the Libra goes from one extreme to another in terms of behavior. You may want to check out their mood for the day before you utter the words "good morning" because if you don't, you might get your head bitten off. Libra, the sign of the scales, must have balance on the job as well. And the lovely, refined, pleasant person you met the day before will not be the same person all the time.

Libras function best on jobs in which their artistic side can be used. They are extremely intelligent and creative and can do anything they put their minds to. That is, if they want to do it, which is the key. Libras' work efforts come in spurts. This sign will work tirelessly and diligently on putting out a report on time; and then the lazy, listless individual will resurface after the mad rush is over.

Libras couldn't ever get used to jobs such as dishwasher or factory, sanitation or construction worker; they can't tolerate unpleasant job surroundings. Libras function best as union reps, beauticians, actors, social workers, receptionists, writers, literary agents, judges, or in jobs where they feel they can make a difference. A Libran brother once worked for a white mortgage company. During his tenure as a loan officer, he saw how whites constantly received preferential treatment over blacks. In many cases, the credit ratings of the African Americans were better than those of the whites. He started his own mortgage business and fights to secure home financing for blacks. Although the work is harder, he doesn't mind because, as he put it, "I'm helping my people."

On the job, Libras can keep strife to a minimum. When racial tension occurs, many times they will be able to successfully mediate the situation because they have the uncanny knack of looking at both sides of a situation fairly. Librans are the voice of reason. However, this air sign is not going to tolerate being put down racially. For instance, a Libra counselor whose white coworker put on a pair of sunglasses and told the Libra that she couldn't see her immediately reported the incident to the woman's supervisor and voiced her displeasure with the situation.

These air signs can definitely hold their own in a good argument. But they're also good listeners and sympathetic supporters of any problems of their friends or foes. If Librans feel that an injustice has been dealt a fellow employee, they will rush to the victim's defense, whether he's asked or not. For example, a white male state employee gave a black woman a white dildo as a birthday present. When she unwrapped the "gift" as a small crowd looked on, the white coworker played it off as a joke. A Libra brother stepped forward and explained to the white guy the inappropriateness of the gesture and advised that there was no room for jokes of that nature. He also asked the white guy if the situation had been reversed—if a white female employee was given a black dildo—would that situation have been a joke to him?

Although Librans have a gentle nature, don't be mistaken, because they're not pushovers. They demand respect and can also be effective leaders. If you're the boss, put them in a role of responsibility and watch them thrive. Her analytical powers give her a keen sense for business, and his ability to see all sides of a situation will find bosses reluctant to give others more duties, eager to give her additional responsibility. The Libra employee will be well dressed, organized and punctual. The work area or office will be neat with files and information easily accessible.

For over twenty-five years one Libra sister worked for a major telephone company, first as an operator and later in various other capacities. A few years ago, the company downsized and several thousand people were laid off. This sister was the only one of her coworkers who had earned a college degree during her years with the company. When her fellow coworkers were let go, she was offered a job as a supervisor for the department because she was punctual, had a good work record and took advantage of the tuition reimbursement program the company offered.

Part of the reason for the achievement is that Libras feel that they must be well thought of and project a positive image. But the image they project isn't positive all the time. Librans can also be very inconsistent and lazy, performing whatever the task is on a last-minute basis. And you need to expect an attitude if the timeliness of the finished project is in question.

Whatever the job, Librans will do it effectively and then some. But the scales of her life must be balanced. When there are problems in the Libra's life, there will be problems on the job.

Health Matters

Libra, the sign of the scales, must maintain a happy medium between work and play and avoid overindulging in alcohol, sweets and rich foods.

When one of the aforementioned is out of whack, it wreaks havoc on the psyche of any Libra. Peace and harmony in the life of a Libra is so important for a happy and healthy existence that if one element is off balance, physical ailments and depression may result and this air sign could go into seclusion in some cases. Don't freak out; these are the worst-case scenarios.

Librans are generally pretty healthy people. Their vanity won't allow them to become obese or struggle with the battle of the bulge over long periods. They pretty much have a handle on maintaining and controlling their weight because they want to look their best at all times.

But overindulgence in alcohol is one of the potential health risks, causing possible problems with the kidneys and bladder, parts of the body ruled by Libra. Other possible ailments for Libras are diabetes, liver disease, and injuries to the lower back and abscesses.

Librans are so obsessed with maintaining balance in their lives that they have a tendency to swing back and forth from one extreme to another. On the job, they are either workaholics or incredibly slow. Being the former only serves to promote excess fatigue in their lives, which must be offset by lots of rest and relaxation. That doesn't mean resting with a brandy or champagne, either. Being the latter points up their indecision. They put off completing a particular project until the cows come home, and this gives the impression of laziness.

In either case the mental as well as the physical strain takes its toll. In addition to problems in the workplace, a bad relationship can also cause health problems, possibly migraine headaches and listlessness. With all the stress in their lives, eating well-balanced meals is essential for this air sign and problems that cause strife and disharmony should be eliminated.

The greatest antidote for job or relationship stresses is rest and relaxation. Chillin' at home in a bubble bath with soothing music will sometimes tranquilize their frazzled nerves. This will also eliminate the inclination to overindulge in alcohol when depression sets in.

The second approach for the Libran who's constantly on the go is to eat meals that are high in protein, but low in fat. Lots and lots of water (eight glasses a day) will help flush the kidneys. Try to avoid sweets, especially mama's German chocolate cake. I realize that this request is next to impossible, but if you're going to indulge, settle for the lesser of the two evils, sweets, and cut out the alcohol. Libra, it shouldn't be your life goal to sample every chocolate chip cookie recipe under the sun, either.

Like Virgos, Librans can also shop for groceries for hours. But their problem is that they cannot decide on what foods they want to buy. Just leave them alone. When nightfall comes and the clerk announces the store is closing in fifteen minutes, the Libra will get it together—or come back the next day.

Libras are happiest when they have a partner, as opposed to being alone. Libra is the sign of partnership. Having a healthy, happy, give-and-take relationship with someone you trust will promote your overall well-being.

Famous African American Librans

Samil Abdullah Al-Amin
  (formerly H. Rap Brown)
Debbie Allen
Amiri Baraka
  (formerly LeRoi Jones)
Lerone Bennett
Chuck Berry
Art Blakey

Toni Braxton
Shirley Caesar
Tisha Campbell
Ray Charles
Chubby Checker
Don Cornelius
Clifton Davis
Dizzy Gillespie

Dick Gregory
Bryant Gumbel
Fannie Lou Hamer
Tramaine Hawkins
Tommy Hearns
Evander Holyfield
Cissy Houston
Jesse Jackson
Tito Jackson
Mae Jemison
Patrick Kelly
Joseph E. Lowery
MC Lyte
Wynton Marsalis
Johnny Mathis
Marilyn McCoo
Terry McMillan

Ronald McNair
Thelonious Monk
Elijah Muhammad
Karyn Parsons
Scottie Pippen
Jerry Rice
Howard Rollins Jr.
Patrice Rushen
Nipsey Russell
Bobby Seale
Ntozake Shange
Will Smith
Koko Taylor
Reggie Theus
Ben Vereen
Demond Wilson
Dave Winfield

SCORPIO
October 23 to November 21

Symbol: The Scorpion

Positive traits: Passionate, emotional, independent, energetic, determined, creative, persistent, intuitive

Negative traits: Jealous, stubborn, secretive, vengeful, manipulative, violent

Ruling planet: Pluto is associated with regeneration and obsession.

Scorpio is the most powerful sign of the twelve Sun signs of the zodiac. This is the powerhouse of the zodiac: What the Scorpio wants, the Scorpio generally gets. Perseverance, determination and downright stubbornness play a significant role.

Scorpio is also the sign of extremes. There's rarely, if ever, any middle ground with Scorpio people, whose emotional passions run deep about most things. With most things, it's feast or famine. They're either ranting and raving about some perceived injustice or they're as docile as a lamb. For example, a Scorpio brother whose cake was purposely taken off the table in a college cafeteria by some visiting Frenchmen at a college screamed, pounded on the table, waltzed around waving his arms like he was conducting an orchestra and spoke whatever high school French he could muster, demanding the return of his cake. Of course, the cake was returned and the "we were only kidding" attitude prevailed, but I am sure the Frenchmen had no idea that they were messing with a Scorpio.

Scorpio

Scorpios are fun-loving and have a good sense of humor. They need these traits to offset the intensity and drive with which they pursue most things in life. They simply must find an outlet like laughter to create a balance. When you meet this water sign, you will be automatically drawn to this person, not romantically at first, but out of curiosity. They present a calm, nonthreatening outward appearance. They're usually overly friendly or totally distant. But the inner struggle of Scorpios is effectively masked by their facade.

Their ruling planet is Pluto, which is associated with regeneration and obsession. Not only can they bounce back from traumatic situations in their lives, but they are usually intrigued by the challenge. They're also obsessive when it comes to protecting loved ones, family and friends. They can be very protective of persons whom they perceive as weaker. Both men and women are very ambitious, with brilliant minds. Scorpio people have definite goals regarding careers, marriage and children.

But they are also willing to make supreme sacrifices in order to achieve their goals. For example, a former teacher, who lived in a small town in Arkansas, decided to become a lawyer. This brother kept his day job to support his wife and two children and commuted two hundred miles a day to Little Rock to attend law school at night part-time. He sacrificed six years of a normal daily routine, a comfortable life and probably a car to boot, but he obtained his law degree.

People born under the sign of Scorpio are highly emotional and intuitive. They can spot a phony or insincerity a mile away, so if you're interested in getting to know this sign, be genuine, straightforward and direct. Scorpions are about as subtle as gangsta rap. If you don't want to hear the "painful truth," then don't ask. For example, if you need to lose weight, don't ask the Scorpion to assess a new outfit. What you will hear is a lecture on the cost of clothing; why you didn't need the outfit, and a final comment: "My God, there's enough material there to cover your queen-size bed!" The point here is they simply don't feel the necessity to spend money needlessly or make a comment they don't mean. If you're given a compliment by a Scorpion, take it to the bank; they don't waste words or money.

When the Scorpio brother enters a room, he won't be the one

dressed to the max. Ladies, this brother may even have on polyester or a green three-piece suit from the 1970s. But, don't be fooled by appearances. He's a master of deception. He probably has more money in the bank than everyone else in the room. He's very frugal about money and saves it readily. His sixth sense also carries over in his ability to invest money wisely. On the other hand, the Scorpio women love to dress up. They won't spend their whole paycheck on an expensive outfit, but they may spend *your* paycheck on one. These women are always tastefully dressed, with subtle hints of their high-powered sexuality peeking through.

Scorpions must win, no matter what the consequences. Everything they say or do is for a specific reason. Every innuendo, gesture, look, movement and inference has an ulterior motive, whether significant or trite. They may sacrifice a relationship with you if they're running for public office and you've been divorced twice. The widowed Scorpio woman may marry a man she doesn't love so that her children can have financial security or a stable family life. The situations may sound extreme, but to the Scorpio, whatever the situation is, the end results must benefit them directly or indirectly.

But don't forget about the Scorpion's sting. If provoked, their calm demeanor may change to cold, calculating manipulation. Don't let them catch you looking at or flirting with a member of the opposite sex or suddenly trying to end the relationship without a valid reason. (Actually, there isn't a valid reason to end a relationship with a Scorpio!) The Scorpion probably originated the expression, "Break your face." Remember the old *Rocky and Bullwinkle* cartoons, when the villain would yell, "It's curtains!" This meant that the damsel in distress would be tied to the railroad tracks, and saved with only two seconds to spare. If the hero had been an angry Scorpion . . . well, you get the picture.

You'll find Scorpios at card parties, camping, at the beaches, clubbing, on the city council or any place where there are lots of people. Scorpios love to read because it helps them to relax, and at the same time, it's mentally stimulating. By the way, they'll read you like an open book, but hold their own cards close to their vests.

The Scorpio Man

There is an odd intensity about this brother that's dangerously exciting. The feeling is similar to staying out late at one of those blue-light basement parties when you were a teenager. You knew you'd be in trouble when you arrived home, but you stayed anyway, hugged up, slow-dancing to the same Smokey Robinson song over and over again in a "heavenly" headlock with a guy whose deodorant faded like your carefully constructed hairdo as the night wore on. (And you loved every minute of it!) So goes the dance with the Scorpio. You may know that the relationship is potentially troublesome, but you continue to see this man, or begin a relationship with the brother, (in spite of yourself) knowing that you shouldn't.

One Scorpio told me that on his best days, there's not any sister he would meet who wouldn't think that he was a fine catch. "She may not give me her phone number, because she's married or seeing someone else, but she would be impressed," he said. Applause, applause. Ladies and gentlemen, the words of a true Scorpio.

Most Scorpions feel that they can do most things. Their egotism propels them to test themselves far beyond the realm of most possibilities. If the Scorpion feels that he can play football, he'll try out for the pros. If you're the coach of a high school or college basketball team, your Scorpio player will coach you and the team too. If he feels that he can sing, he'll try to obtain a major deal with a record company. Last but not least, if he feels or knows that he's attractive, he's going to have women.

Girlfriends, now don't get bent out of shape over the thought of more than one woman. That's not to say he can't be faithful, because he can. Granted, a woman will notice the magnetic attraction between the two of them. Of course, he will be flirtatious, accommodating and attentive, but that doesn't mean he'll trade you in for a new model, not right away at least. (Just kidding!) Actually, he would never trade true love just to knock the boots. It just means women will find him attractive, passionate, sexy, confident and presumably the kind of man women dream about.

But, hold it! The dream could become a nightmare if you're not careful. The sign of Scorpio is the sign of extremes. There is rarely any middle ground or position. They either love or despise. They're either at the top of their game in terms of career success or in the depths of despair, brooding over the one that got away, not being properly appreciated and feeling like the world owes them something.

He's fiercely loyal to his friends and family. He won't ever forget a favor, but on the other hand, they never forget any indiscretion on your part either. They are very vengeful. Once they latch on to some perceived wrong, they don't let go until they've gotten "justice." They can be your best friend or your worst enemy.

For example, one Scorpion landlord got into a knock-down, drag-out fight with one of his tenants. The tenant had been giving the landlord the runaround about the rent for the past three months. After the fourth attempt to collect failed, the landlord tried to change the locks on the doors and the tenant tried to stop him. A fight ensued and both were arrested, but the tenant had to be taken to the hospital first. This Scorpion landlord was also a lawyer and his behavior could've had a direct bearing on his job, but he couldn't control his rage over the tenant's indifference in that moment.

When you meet this brother, initially, his outward appearance will appear to be very calm, controlled and placid. But inside this passionate person rages an eternal flame that will warm the hearts of many, including you. That flame also burns with the desire to conquer and cure the ills of the world—racism, child abuse, teen violence and wars.

Okay, let's consider the relationship with this brother, who could possibly take you to heights you never thought possible. He will expect total loyalty from you at all times. The courtship will be as unique as his personality because every date will seem as though it's your last. This man makes the most of every moment.

If marriage is in the future, you may plan to be the black Brady Bunch because Scorpions are breeders. Many Scorpio men may be teenager fathers or dads in their early twenties. You and your Scorpio will probably have at least three children, maybe four or five. (That number may also include the two children he had out of wedlock.) He loves children and will be a demanding but effective father.

He is a true renegade who is not concerned about keeping up

with the Joneses, and further, he probably doesn't know the Joneses. He's going to do things his way. "Don't you realize that this is the best way?" So let me make this perfectly clear. This brother is "tuff," and he knows it, and is definitely not going to be controlled by any female, job or anything else for that matter. When the term "male chauvinist pig" was created, the creator probably had the Scorpion in mind. Having a relationship with this sign is going to be a real challenge. Being in a relationship with this Pluto man will feel like you've "died" and gone to Heaven. But he *is* a chauvinist, and the first to admit it.

One sister told me that a Scorpion has sex as if he's going to die in the electric chair in a few hours, and this encounter will be his last (and yours too, in terms of the best you've ever had, unless, of course, another Scorpio eases his way into your life). Most folks can't explain the whys and wherefores of the Scorpio's magnetism; they merely comment, "It's like that." When another woman was asked to rate the first sexual encounter with her Scorpion companion on a scale of 1 to 10, she commented, "Twenty-five!" Another tried to explain the attraction as she shook her head slowly from side to side saying, "The brother is just passionate!" Any questions?!!?

The Scorpio man is passionate about everything in his life—his job, his companion, his family, special causes and even his recreation. He's very smart and creative, in the bed and out. Know this, if you're squeamish, girlfriend, I suggest you not play with the "big boys" (no pun intended).

The Scorpio Woman

The Scorpio sister is the ultimate as far as what it means to be a woman. They are classy sisters who always dress appropriately, are up on current events such as the ramifications of the O.J. Simpson murder case, the state of the economy, the educational system and all the other burning issues. If you're at a party in a crowded room and she sets her sights on you, you're history, buddy. All she needs is a few minutes to get your attention, and her hypnotic and magnetic appeal will draw you right to her.

If the low-cut dress and pendant with the single diamond that dangles seductively between her adequate breasts don't get you, her penetrating eyes with the long, long lashes will. Both the men and the women have a penetrating look, and when their eyes are on the prize, their stare does not waiver. Eye contact is very important to them.

The Scorpio sister's emotions run deep. She expects a lot from her mate, but she gives 120 percent in return. She cannot stand a man who is a pushover, but at the same time, she won't be told what to do either. The brothers will have to walk a fine line with this sister, but from all accounts of those who are in relationships with Scorpio women, there are very few complaints. I suppose there is some merit to being totally possessed. (Just kidding!) A man usually gets a clear sense that this sexy creature is genuinely interested in his welfare.

In addition to a satisfying relationship, her home is another important element in her life. The Scorpio woman must have beautiful and comfortable surroundings in which to dwell. One Scorpio called it the "poetics of space." After she's been "on" all day long in meeting after meeting, where she has been, more than likely, the only black female, this water sign must retreat to her beautiful floral surroundings and ocean colors of coral, blue and turquoise to calm the raging seas that dwell deep within her. The house will be neat, and because she loves her home, the surroundings will reflect her unusual taste and will be as comfortable as possible. The bedroom, the most provocative, is where much of her time is spent. I wonder why?

The Scorpio sister is passionate about the causes that she believes in or that have touched her life in some way. For example, if a Scorpion was a teenage mother, she will devote her time to the Girl Scouts. If the lady Scorpio grew up in an abusive household, she may become a foster parent. She may even start a mentoring program at her church if she was touched by someone's guidance along the way.

But be careful. If her temper flares, move out of the way. I wouldn't come within a twenty-mile radius of this woman's wrath. A Scorpio woman, whose own mother died when she was twelve, ended up having to take care of her abusive alcoholic father during the twilight years of his life. Even after he moved in with his daughter he continued to drink and cut up, but learned to be docile and quiet around his Scorpio daughter, who matched his initial outbursts with a few screams, punches and threats of her own.

Scorpio women have lots of friends who confide their secrets. Lady Scorpio rarely reciprocates. Unlike the Aquarian, her life is not an open book. She's a very private person and you'll only know what she's wants you to know. Unlike the men, Scorpio women don't readily coddle other women. In fact, they're usually very suspicious of them. Remember, the Aretha Franklin song "Dr. Feelgood"? The first line is "I don't want nobody sittin' around me and my man!" Well that song could be the theme for a Scorpio sister. Her female friendships are few, and those that she has are usually friends from high school, college or even grade school—people whose loyalty she's tested through the years. She's a loyal friend herself, but she discourages current or new acquaintances. Everyone can't be worthy of the Scorpio's trust and admiration.

As parents, most Scorpios can be very demanding of their children, and want them to succeed. A Scorpio mother who was also a teacher in Chicago was very supportive and sometimes overindulged her children. But she had had to work her way through college and made it clear to her two daughters that they were to go to college and make careers for themselves. And she let it be known that there wouldn't be any "professional" children or "professional" students, said her Capricorn daughter. The Scorpio mother won't tolerate laziness in her child.

This Pluto-ruled sign has a very daring streak. They will try just about anything once. One Scorpio woman I know, a college professor, decided to go out alone to a local spot in a very unsavory part of town to see the Temptations. How's that for daring? Upon entering the club in her long-sleeved black leather minidress, she found that patrons were searched and required to walk through a metal detector. Three hours later, the owner announced that the Temptations probably wouldn't perform and he didn't know if any money would be refunded. The crowd grew restless, and a fight ensued. The professor ducked into an alley and caught a ride with some friends back to her safe abode.

One Piscean husband describes his Scorpio wife's approach to life: "She walks back and forth to the edge of the cliff, looks over and then pulls back at the last minute."

Love Connection

If you're reading this section of the book, you're probably a Scorpio, in a relationship with one, thinking about taking the plunge, or trying to recover from one. Well, are you ready to fly by the seat of your pants without a net? Okay, boys and girls, hang on to your hat.

Let's talk about the recovery first. It's kind of a never-ending story because Scorpios will forever want to pop back into your life whenever the mood hits this water sign. They are so relentless in whatever they do, they figure that although the relationship is over, they will eventually wear down your resistance. And more than likely they will!

In short, if this man or woman wants to be in your life for the rest of your life, you might as well resign yourself to these facts: You will open your heart in spite of yourself, and they will tiptoe back in before you have time to plan a counterattack. Not that you'll really want to plan a counterattack in the first place. You may wonder to yourself, "Why am I accepting this brother's phone calls and giggling and going on the phone? This boy dogged me out and I'm tickled that he called. Seems like I needed to play hard to get or something." He already knew before he dialed the number that you would be glad to hear from him. He can anticipate and see through your every move, thought and innuendo. There's no escaping the magnetic attraction of Scorpio people.

If you're in love with a Scorpio, the relationship will be carefree, fun and exciting, with an "Eat, drink and be merry, for tomorrow we die," approach. Listen up: Once you've been to the mountaintop, it's really hard to settle for the molehills of the world. You'll marvel at the Scorpio's determination and daring spirit. She'll want to be the first deacon at her church. You'll love his fearless nature. You'll always feel safe when you're around him. He'll be the one who'll take charge, adding, "Leave it to me, let me handle it."

Scorpios drip sex appeal, and they know it. As they are getting dressed for a party in front of the mirror, they already know what the reaction to them will be. They have eyes, too. They dress for success.

When you initially meet this brother or sister, you will more than likely think to yourself, "Good Lord, isn't he fine!" "Is this sister a cutie pie, or what!" This reaction is exactly what they expect. Honey, they *know* they look good! And rarely will they leave the house without having all the details in place. Even if the lady Scorpio is dashing out to the store, she'll stop to put on her earrings or lipstick. So at this point, you might want to consider the "or what!"

But remember, the Scorpion's bite can be fatal. Scorpio people are very jealous and vengeful. A Scorpio can make life miserable for anyone who they feel dealt them an injustice, including and especially you. So while you're all enthralled in the relationship, or in the potential for one, consider all facets of the Scorpio personality.

Yes, they are sexy. And yes, they are good conversationalists, attentive, successful. And yes, the sex will be out of this world. And yes, and yes, and yes . . . the beat goes on and on. But while you're enjoying the music, consider both sides of the situation.

Sexually, Scorpios need very few maneuvers to get them aroused. Their erogenous zone is the genitalia. Any move in that direction will transform them into insatiable tigers. They are very effective in the bedroom. And with Scorpios, anything goes. The women love to wear sexy lingerie and the men, well, the men won't be wearing much of anything. Both men and women of this sign are at their most passionate when they fall in love. *Warning:* You can't take this relationship lightly because they won't let you. They want and expect your undivided attention twenty-four, seven. (24 hours a day, seven days a week.)

Not that they'll give you all of *their* attention. They won't have the time because of their bulging schedules, which may include volunteer work at the rape crisis center or halfway house, storytelling at the local library or just plain kickin' it with the boys. But whenever there is time for play, they expect you to be ready, with no questions asked. So if you don't plan to be there for the long haul, you'd better run now. Just put this book down and get the hell out of Dodge City!

Scorpio is compatible with the other two water signs, Pisces and Cancer. All three signs are highly emotional and can lend each other emotional and physical support. All three water signs can be highly jealous; this could cause problems. A Scorpio is also compatible with two of the earth signs, Virgo and Capricorn. These down-to-earth, practical, cautious people can benefit from the passion, emotion and determination of Scorpio.

Scorpio's opposite is Taurus, the third earth sign. You talk about hot to trot in the bedroom. Whew! But opposite combinations are usually only that, purely physical, and a long-term relationship between these two is not on the horizon. They do a lot of kissing and making up, though.

How to Get Next to a Scorpio

• Be honest. They are very hard to deceive because they are highly intuitive.

• Be attentive. Laugh at their jokes and be at their beck and call most of the time.

• Be sexy. Accentuate the positive. For example, if you have great legs, wear miniskirts. If you have a massive chest and protruding pecs, wear fitted shirts.

• Be versatile. Don't complain about their being late. Just be eager and willing whenever they arrive.

• Remember, a Scorpio is his own biggest fan. You must have style and a sense of self-confidence to warrant his attention in the first place.

• Don't be complacent or content to only be her companion. Have a thirst for knowledge. She will respect you for it. And please have some knowledge of current events. For example, Bosnia is not a chocolate drink!

• Wear black, white or both. The colors together drive them wild! Also, sea green, ocean blue, coral and turquoise get the attention of Scorpios.

• Another pet peeve of the Scorpio is the failure of individuals to speak correct English. Don't say "nawfin' " when it's supposed to be "nothing."

• When you're on a date with a Scorpio, I suggest you not flirt with others. You may live to regret it.

• Replacement parts are somewhat of a turnoff for Scorpios. Keep the hair weave and blue contacts to a minimum. And to the men, having your hair lightly texturized is okay, but the Ike Turner look and Jheri curls are out!

The Scorpio Child

Creative recreation for these miniature adults is crucial to the little peace of mind that you will be able to salvage while they're "rearing" you. Several areas must be addressed here if you don't want them running the household.

The Scorpio child will need constant supervision and strict discipline. This is not to say that as the parent, there are not any gray areas or compromises, but this child needs to know from the beginning who the boss is. For example, if he's been grounded for two weeks, don't give in after one week. Scorpion children have an uncanny resilience and a week's grounding won't get their attention. Forbidding him to attend a party, where he hopes to get a date with the new kid on the block, will. Part of the Scorpio child's strategy is to wear you down so you'll give in. But you must be consistent with your punishment with this child. He is smart and intuitive and will learn early on what's off-limits. Parents, once control of this child is lost, there's no regaining it.

Little Scorpios should also be taught integrity and respect for others, fairness with classmates and forgiveness. These are not virtues that a Scorpio child will readily accept. This little water child will need more attention than most and will not accept anything less. Your patience will be tested to the limit. You must constantly supervise schoolwork and even sit with the child to ensure that the work is being done. They must be helped every step of the way. Everything must be explained including why doing math homework is important and how it relates to everyday life. Explain that the world is laid out mathematically from the width of the streets to how tall buildings will be. Once they fully grasp the big picture, they won't oppose the learning.

Most Scorpio children can't just be left alone with a good book. Their creative minds will wander into something a little more daring, such as playing with matches. Most Scorpios have a fascination with fire, and the children are no exception.

Parents, you will need plenty of creative outlets for this "busy-body" in the house. This child is a water sign, and water has a very calming affect on her. Enrolling her early in swimming lessons, as early as five years old, is a good idea. She will also like to solve puzzles and explore what's beneath the surface of things. A magic set, mystery books and any toy that can be dismantled always piques and sustains the Scorpio child's interest.

Remember that cute little toddler with the penetrating eyes and stern look? That is the big Scorpio, waiting to grow up, be in control and have everything exactly the way he wants it. Even as toddlers, Scorpio children can sense when something is wrong in the family. A mother gave her four-month-old Scorpio child to her own mother to care for temporarily. The baby stopped eating and, after two days, had to be hospitalized. Since the doctors couldn't find any medical problems, they attributed the baby's problem to the mother's absence.

As toddlers, Scorpios will develop very early. As to discipline, scoldings may work temporarily, but they will eventually figure out a way around any restriction. For instance, he may stop banging his bottle on the glass-topped end table in the living room, but when the baby-sitter comes, he'll start up as soon as her back is turned for thirty seconds. Even as early as the first two years of his life, he knows how to get what he wants.

These children are also able to sense when problems and changes occur within the family. For example, don't keep information about the arrival of a new baby away from the Scorpio child until right before the birth. This can cause extreme trauma that may result in violence toward the new baby if the child feels that she's being replaced. Instead, include her in the planning and give her some responsibility as it relates to the new baby. The results will be rewarding for all concerned.

Sex education on some level should begin as early as five years of age. These little ones are energetic, curious and ready to try anything new, including playing house, doctor or any other games that involve exploring. Don't be shocked if one day you look in the backyard and find your Scorpion laying on top of the neighbor's child. These children develop early and usually look older than their years. Giving them pertinent information of a sexual nature will save you from being early grandparents. They are so secretive that by the time you find out a Scorpio's girlfriend is pregnant, she may already be in labor.

By the time they reach the teenage years, they're already running the show in school—as class president, student council president, band leader or all of the above. In terms of career goals and the pleasures of life, Scorpios are capable of soaring to heights not even considered by most. But the critical foundation of love, attention, supervision and discipline must be laid first. They must have a sense of security within the family structure to function effectively, for without parental guidance, the Scorpio child can and will sink into the depths of despair. This could translate to involvement in gangs, criminal activity, drugs and even violence. They must be monitored closely!

Scorpio children intuitively know that they will grow up to be bigger and stronger than their parents, but they are fiercely loyal to friends and family. Their respect for their parents will be evident, and the child won't ever cross that line.

The Scorpio Employee

If there is a sign that overindulges in work, it is the Scorpio. Scorpio is the sign of extremes—either working like a dog or being incredibly lazy, but most of the time it's the former. They set goals early in a career; hard work is just part of the process. Scorpions have a self-confidence that knows no limitations. They can do any job effectively if they put their minds to it. As long as they feel that the work that they're doing has a purpose, they go beyond the call of duty. Scorpions won't participate in office gossip or idle chatter—they simply don't have time. Because they are so secretive and mysterious themselves, they usually are the ones being discussed. Because of Scorpios' dedication to and passion about the job, other employees may feel resentful, feeling that Scorpios are trying to make them look less effective. This water sign could care less about what coworkers think, or anyone else except maybe the boss.

If you're the boss, you won't have to stand over this employee to make sure she's doing her job. She has a strong sense of loyalty to the boss and the job. A Scorpio sister, who was assisting her boss in personnel matters, including layoffs and firings, never discussed the matters with her coworkers, who were concerned for their own fate. Although she was only helping in a temporary capacity, she wouldn't divulge the pertinent information that pertained to her friends.

If Scorpios are in a rewarding job with the possibility of moving up through the ranks, the motivation to work hard is there. As supervisors, they can sense your moods and your effectiveness on the job. You won't be able to hide much from them. Their genuine concern and emotional connections to all aspects of life in general will have you baring all. They're good listeners and won't divulge secrets.

Scorpions are smart and highly intuitive about most things, including the job. They instantly know when something is not going according to plan. And they can usually spring into action with a solution before most of the coworkers know there's a problem. For example, a Scorpio manager realized the night before that there would be a problem with the water system in the building where she worked, and she began making mental notes of whether to allow individuals to leave early. Of course, when she arrived at work the next day, the water system was out everywhere except on the third floor.

They are also well respected by the employees, both black and white, because they're fair-minded and don't indulge in idle chatter or gossip. A Scorpio sister, who was assistant personnel director for a major city in the South, learned that her new white boss consulted with the white support staff regarding any policy matters and generally undermined her efforts to be effective. Each time the new personnel director approached the support staff to verify any information given to him by the Scorpio, the staff simply referred him back to the Scorpio, saying that she was the person to consult. She eventually left the position and many of the support staff followed her lead, saying that they no longer felt they had a voice or any support.

Scorpions are mostly interested in careers that provide the ultimate mental challenge and tax their abilities. The more difficult the job, the better they like it. Generally, Scorpios excel as psychiatrists, psychologists, detectives, police officers, undertakers, soldiers and even criminals.

Scorpios work better in occupations that they feel are important and have far-reaching effects. They are at their best on jobs that involve troubleshooting, analysis or uncovering mysteries. Scorpions also make good soldiers. If they're bored on the job, they have no trouble or insecurity about changing career goals in midstream.

In a racially uneven work setting where blacks are in the minority, the Scorpio comes alive. Because of his self-confidence, he is never intimidated by other employees, and he knows that he will succeed. However, don't cross this Scorpio with any snide remarks or efforts to discredit him. He will seek revenge, and you'll definitely be the loser. Although they have no real ambition to be president of the company, if they're promoted to the position, they can handle the job. A Scorpio brother from Tennessee, one of the few brothers to own an oil company, took over the reins of the company as its assets plummeted. He kept the company out of the red for several years. When the oil market took a nosedive in the 1980s, he sacrificed his own money and assets to keep the company afloat and continued to pay his employees until the money ran out.

Health Matters

Scorpios must be very aware of their excesses, be it overeating, drinking too much, not getting enough rest or the emotional rollercoaster ride they find themselves on because everything doesn't go the way they planned. All of these can have a devastating effect on the body over time.

Scorpios are usually extreme and compulsive about most things. There is rarely, if ever, any middle ground with this sign. This theme is carried throughout most of their lives, and health is no exception. Many Scorpios have the potential to become obese. As with most things, eating can be a passion in which they overindulge. Sometimes their eating habits take a backseat to liquor consumption, and consequently they are slim and puny-looking because of an overindulgence in alcohol.

Scorpio rules the lower middle area of the body, including the genitalia, reproductive organs, rectum and colon. As a consequence, these areas are vulnerable to health problems. They may have lower back problems, strained groin areas, persistent gynecological infections or venereal diseases. Generally, both sexes have strong bodies. The men are usually robust in appearance, with broad shoulders and adequate "buns," the kind you just want to reach out and touch. The women are voluptuous with big butts (the black woman's trademark, no matter how small in stature she is), large breasts or legs, or all of the above. Both men and women have strong constitutions and can withstand long work days. But problems surface with Scorpios when they constantly eat on the run and don't get the necessary rest.

Although Scorpios have amazing powers of recuperation, the best remedy for recovery is rest. Usually, if a Scorpio is hospitalized, it's pretty serious. This water sign will need to follow the doctor's orders and not try to instruct the medical personnel on the best treatment. They may be well versed on a variety of subjects, but they can't cure or treat themselves.

Persons born under this sign should eat foods high in protein, such as seafood, and food containing large amounts of calcium, such as milk, cheese and yogurt, to provide energy for their constant movement. Eat fresh fruits and vegetables, and avoid fatty foods such as pizza, fried chicken, hamburgers and hot dogs, which you have a tendency to overindulge in. Scorpios also love Mexican, Italian and soul food and foods that are spicy-hot, but these aren't easy on the digestive system.

Shopping for the right foods is an exercise for which Scorpios have no tolerance. Once they're in the store, they barrel down the aisles, constantly looking at their watch and wondering if they're going to be able to make their next appointment. They may buy a lot of junk if they don't take the time. Remember, haste makes waste. Scorpio, since you don't like spending money needlessly, you should shop carefully and prudently, and not when you're hungry.

Scorpio

For relaxation, instead of drinking alcohol, Scorpios should get regular exercise, along with long and frequent visits to the sauna and hot tub. This water sign loves to be near water, so swimming, fishing and boating are additional ways to relax. Many times when Scorpios get upset, they will turn to drugs or alcohol for solace. Exercise will help relieve tension when they want to ram their fist through a wall or through the boss's head. In either case, a good workout will substitute sufficiently.

Scorpios work hard and play hard. When they finally realize they must slow down, it's usually in the later years of their lives. The rabble-rousing, all-night poker games and fraternity and sorority parties take their toll. The key to better health with this sign is moderation.

Famous African American Scorpions

Benjamin Banneker
Lisa Bonet
Roy Campanella
Dorothy Dandridge
Tommy Davidson
Ruby Dee
Shirley Graham Dubois
Zina Garrison
Bob Gibson
Robert "Hoot" Gibson
Whoopi Goldberg
Alex Haley
W. C. Handy
Larry Holmes
Telma Hopkins

Mahalia Jackson
Yolanda King
Yaphet Kotto
Kweisi Mfume
Warren Moon
Melba Moore
Norma Quarles
Minnie Ripperton
Esther Rolle
Michael A. Schultz
Attallah Shabazz
Sinbad
Sippie Wallace
Ethel Waters
Alfre Woodard

SAGITTARIUS
November 22 to December 21

Symbol: The Archer

Positive traits: Energetic, free-spirited, ambitious, generous, optimistic, sincere, frank, dependable

Negative traits: Tactless, irresponsible, restless, careless, erratic, prone to exaggeration, frivolous, undisciplined

Ruling planet: Jupiter is associated with good fortune, optimism, expansion and abundance.

Sagittarius people are the perplexing sign of the zodiac and the most optimistic. There are many aspects to this fire sign's personality that you won't understand. If you're interacting with this blunt person or (to put it a little more bluntly) this tactless person, you might as well put your feelings in your back pocket. There's no place for getting your feelings hurt when a Sag is around. The symbol for Sagittarius is the archer—and the arrow is pointed straight at its target. The Sagittarian pulls no punches and basically tells it like it is. And there is no sense in trying to figure out why they say a certain thing; they couldn't tell you if their lives depended on it.

For example, a Sag woman was attending a black-tie reception with her companion. She was beautifully attired in a most alluring manner, her conversation was stimulating and her date was the envy of most of the men in the room. The only trouble was, after noticing a seriously overweight person, who happened to be the boss's wife, what popped out of the Sagittarian's mouth during a lull in the conversation was, "I need to go on a diet." You could have cut the silence with a knife, but it never occurred to this Sag sister that anything was wrong.

The ruling planet of Sagittarius is Jupiter, which is associated with expansion, good luck and optimism. Therefore, luck, as well as their thirst for knowledge, plays a major role in the success of a Sagittarian. They don't have the finesse, suave or cool attitude of other signs. They're straightforward and unpretentious, and they don't care who knows it. They're like the proverbial bull in the china closet. They're forgetful and clumsy and may even belch in public without so much as an "Excuse me." But they're kindhearted, down-to-earth, genuine people. For example, a Sag sister had just walked in the door from a long day at work, when she got a frantic call from her nephew asking for help in finding his dog. Without a word, she drove her nephew to the animal shelter, selected a wounded collie to substitute for the missing chow and promised the boy the collie would be his if his own dog was never found. In addition, she put up flyers in the neighborhood, placed classified ads in the local newspapers and took the collie to a veterinarian. The chow was later found but the Sagittarian allowed her nephew to keep the collie anyway.

Both the men and the women of the sign are flirtatious by nature. And when and if they decide to get married, they will have to send video copies of the announcement to all of their past, present and potential loves. The comments from the dumbfounded may go like this: "Girl, I don't believe boyfriend is gettin' married; you know he's got a child by his next-door neighbor." Or in the case of the female Sag: "I don't know why girlfriend is getting married, she's nothing but a flirt. Have you seen her work a room?" The Sag sister can step in the door of a small gathering, assess who's married, who's looking and who's taken in about as much time as it takes to order her first drink. Talk or not, they're usually undaunted by what others say, because they're seekers of the truth. And no matter what is speculated about them, they feel that they've acted honorably and done what they feel was best. So, save the platitudes for others who may be paying attention. You're wasting your time in this case.

Physically, Sagittarians are at two extremes. The men are either short with broad shoulders or tall and willowy, even athletic-looking. The women are either thin or making significant strides toward obesity. Some Sagittarian females who are thin don't stay that way, however, especially if they get married and live a sedentary lifestyle. If the Sag female is heavy, she'll still want to dress in the latest styles—leggings, tight-fitting clothing and all the leather outfits that her pocketbook can stand. Sagittarians have nice oval faces and well-shaped heads. The men of this sign could probably wear the bald look without stares of disbelief. Their foreheads are usually high. The women like a short haircut so that if they need to wear a wig, the extra hair won't be cumbersome underneath. But with either a short cut or long hair, the Sag sister enjoys a variety of hairstyles, including braids, perms, wave nouveau, wraps or the curly look. Hairstyles for the men run the gamut: permed, texturized, bald, dreads or a fade—you just never know.

This fire sign loves the great outdoors. Family reunions, horseback riding, camping or relaxing under the moon are all appealing outings for the adventuresome Sagittarian. The Sag dad will take his son fishing, and his daughter too. Dad will show the kids how to survive in the great outdoors as well as in life. You'll need a motorbike to keep up—but then he'll convince you that a motorbike is environmentally detrimental and convince you to purchase a bike or a horse or both. The bike for traveling in the city and the horse for trips in the country. And if they grew up in the country, get ready for plenty of horseback riding and good food. She'll cook ten sweet potato pies at a time. The new neighbor must have one, and the paperboy, the postman and anybody else who may look hungry. The Sag man will have you riding a horse through woods, down by the creek and into town to meet and greet the locals of his hometown, population 7,200.

Sagittarians are restless and need constant mental stimulation. They are very much interested in higher learning and exploring new territories. The challenge of solving a problem piques their interest more than the problem itself, just as the chase in the relationship is more important and challenging than the capture. Here's the poop: keep the Sagittarian on a string, playfully teasing and flirting, but not surrendering totally. They will be there for the mere challenge of trying to get you into their clutches. Sagittarius people may stray if home and hearth are staid and boring. These fire signs have a secret fear of dying from "terminal" boredom, so keep things lively. They love surprises. Planning a surprise trip to a place they've never been is a big turn-on. The big question with any Sagittarian is whether they'll be interested enough in the liaison to stay in it for long. As one Sag brother put it, he was pretty happy with his wife, but he determined during the marriage that he might be happier somewhere else, say, with a new "main squeeze."

The Sagittarius Man

The Sagittarian brother is his own person. You may as well just get used to it. Instead of an intimate date at a restaurant by candlelight, you may be taken over to his female friend's house to watch them play a heated game of Scrabble. This will be a test, of course: first, to see how you'll react in the situation, and second, to allow his best friend a chance to assess you as a potential companion.

The Sagittarian male is always cheerful and in a good mood. They love to laugh, and you'll laugh too when you're with them. Sometimes there may be some moodiness, but most of the time, he has a sunny disposition. This brother is also a free spirit. Let me give you a glimpse of what this all means. When you meet this brother, he'll be full of conversation, appreciative eyes with a look that you may feel is only for you. And yes, you'll probably be absolutely right for the moment. But when the next lovely creature enters the room, those eyes of appreciation will settle on her with the same intensity. Now don't go getting your feelings hurt—it's simply the Sag's personality. He doesn't play games. He would never hide the fact that he was just as intrigued by another woman. And better yet, he might have a pregnant wife at home. But when you meet this brother, he will be very interested in you. The fact that he's also interested in "Miss Thang" across the room has little to do with his interest in you.

The Sagittarius brother will forever be on the prowl. Not that he's going to have multiple affairs, but he'll want to test his charm to determine if he's still got the touch. As one Sag brother put it, "It's fun." The chase for this brother is more significant than the actual relationship. A Sagittarius brother may take you on as a friend and become your biggest ally by listening to your gripes about "your" man. He may even encourage you to go back to college or consider some sort of financial planning. This brother will be as encouraging as possible. He may even talk you into leaving the man you've been in the unfulfilling relationship with for the last five years. But please don't consider this to be the beginning of a budding relationship between the two of you. He's just trying to be supportive. He simply doesn't have the time for another relationship, what with the two he may have going already. Besides, he's the headmaster for the neighborhood scout troop, has a day job as a policeman, and a part-time job delivering pizza. There's probably another female just like you who's admiring him from afar. He's simply spreading his charm around. He wants to be your friend and confidant. When the two of you first met, he had already weighed the pros and cons of the relationship and ruled out the possibility.

A true intellectual, the Sag brother is smarter than most. But looks can be deceiving. At first glance, you'll think of him as the absentminded professor with soup stains on his tie. But if you're looking for the man who's so down in his black T-shirt and his double-breasted suit or in the two-piece linen baggy look, the Sagittarian is not the one. If he's dressed in this manner, he was probably coached by a friend or companion. In order to please his Virgo companion, a Sagittarian brother allowed his mate to make him over completely. A tailor fitted him for several suits and upscale casual clothing. He even grew a beard at her urging for a more sophisticated look. But a year after the relationship ended, so did the Sag's quest to dress for success. This brother is not at all that interested in the total look. He's more interested in the total checkbook. And the latter includes investing money wisely, sacrificing and being scrupulous about overspending. So dressing like he's on his way to the nearest runway (and I don't mean at the airport) is simply not his style. But he's smart enough to know what works in terms of attracting women and what his appearance says about him.

Sagittarius men don't have a problem with spending money on a date or on you. But these brothers don't like to be badgered. That leather coat that you want for your birthday, that you've bugged him about since you first saw it a month ago, won't end up in your closet. Instead of the coat, you might end up with a sweater or an answering machine. Sagittarians don't like to be told what to do or given an ultimatum. You'll be the loser. Another Sag brother who recently met a single mom with three children realized that this sister was constantly asking him for money to help pay her rent. At the first request he complied, but after it became an apparent monthly occurrence, the relationship ended rather abruptly.

If and when he finally decides to tie the knot, which will take a good ten years longer than most (just kidding!), don't expect him to ask you in the traditional manner. He might ask, "What do you think about getting married?" Or he might say, "If you want some (insurance) benefits, we need to go and get married." Huh? This Sag will want to know because if you don't think much about it, it'll be okay if you don't accept his hand in marriage. He'll probably be relieved.

The Sagittarius brother isn't overly concerned with his companions' looks or weight, even wigs, dentures and other replacement parts are okay. And this makes him extremely popular with women, both young and old. As a Sag brother sees it, if a woman doesn't have hair, she needs a wig or something. They usually don't have preconceived ideas about the matter. Intellect carries more weight than looks and all the other amenities. Most Sagittarians feel that the initial attraction is physical, but a pretty face and an empty head is a combination that won't work. For example, at a party the Sagittarius will be the ringleader in the group of adoring suitors around a woman whose neckline plunges past the limits of decency or whose dress is so short, there's nothing left to the imagination. He'll gawk with the best of them. But after the party's over, and he determines that this sister's brain power is shorter than her skirt, well, the Sag will make it very plain, saying "You need to go to school." He'll waste no time telling you what a good lover he is. But I wouldn't take it at face value. Don't write him off yet. With the Sag brother, it's his way of letting you know what he's been told. And he wants you to know up front. He likes to know the details of things immediately, so he figures you would too.

As the Sagittarian brother gets older, he forgets about the amenities such as flowers and vacations that keep the relationship ignited in the first place. For example, although travel is his key word, a weight problem that is usually inevitable may keep him from wanting to travel. Oftentimes, he will want to substitute a card with money inside instead of the gift that he used to put some thought into. After a hard day's work, he's into retiring for the evening with a six-pack and the remote control in the easy chair that resembles a mold of their bodies. There they recline until bedtime. Sorry.

The Sagittarius Woman

The Sagittarian woman, although fun-loving and good-natured, is going to be a real challenge for anyone to get close to or develop a relationship with. First and foremost, this independent sister has her own life and her own way of doing things, so get used to it. If you're married to a Sagittarian sister, you should hire a housekeeper if you can afford it. Being a loving housewife isn't a goal to which she aspires. Of course, like many black women, she grew up in her mother's kitchen, but long hours doing the domestic scene don't quite do it for her. If she's married, she will want to have a career even if it's part-time. She has no time for thumb twiddling. There's too much to explore.

She's loving enough with her husband and family and will sacrifice her career, if need be, to raise the children or support her husband in a budding career. The Sag wife will be the first to tell her reluctant husband that he needs to relocate for the regional manager's position of an electronics company. She's the eternal optimist, and she knows in her heart of hearts that her husband will excel in his job. Her role in this instance is convincing him.

Like the Gemini, this sister is a charmer; she can and will charm the pants right off you if she chooses to do so. But don't get too enthusiastic. The Sagittarian's erratic and impulsive nature will have you in a cold sweat trying to keep up with her mood changes.

The Sagittarian woman usually has plenty of friends, but in the process of friendship, there's lots of hurt feelings along the way. Remember, none of this behavior is intentional. Her intentions are honorable all the time. She has a code of ethics that she adheres to, and she's sometimes naive enough to think that she can change the world by being forthright and honest. If you don't want the painful truth, don't ask the Sag girl. That's not to say that she can take what she dishes out. For she feels it's a matter of intent. She feels her intentions are not to hurt, but your response in retaliation to her words are. Don't ask for an explanation; she doesn't know and you'll never know either.

For the sheer challenge of it, Sagittarians never shy away from a good argument, either. They generally face any challenge head on. For example, a Sagittarian sister had the last laugh at her twenty-year class reunion when a former classmate introduced his wife to her, saying the Sagittarian was the only girl who had ever whipped him in a fight. Seems that when they were both in junior high school, this Sag sister had made a model airplane out of popsicle sticks and used pop bottle tops for the wheels. Intrigued by the project, the classmate kept messing with the airplane despite repeated warnings by the Sag. He eventually knocked it off of the table and broke it. Well, the rest, as they say, is history.

As parents, Sagittarians will be very protective of their children. One Sag mother's nineteen-year-old became involved with a twenty-four-year-old librarian. The Sag mom carefully monitored his involvement with the women he came in contact with, even at church. A church member made a comment that the young man looked like Denzel Washington, to which the Sag mother replied, "He's still a baby!" Sag parents are like buddies with their children. These parents make learning fun and will impart a wealth of knowledge through games that teach, extensive travel and long philosophical discussions with their children without the kids realizing what is happening.

Flying by the seat of her pants is something she's used to. She simply wouldn't have it any other way. But what this Sag dreamer, who throws caution to the wind, doesn't realize is that her practical down-to-earth husband or boyfriend (hopefully, a Taurus or a Virgo) will be there to pick up the pieces. For example, a Virgo companion warned his Sag girlfriend of the pitfalls of starting a catering business without enough capital to last at least a year. This Sag sister's comments were that everything would turn out all right. And it did—for about six months until some unexpected obstacles came up, like plumbing problems and a new heating system. The Virgo ended up getting a second mortgage on his twenty-year-old house to bail out the Sag. However, the magnitude of what the Virgo had done was never acknowledged, not to his satisfaction, anyway. But the Sag woman expects nothing less. This woman wants a man she can respect and look up to. She wants someone who's smart and has drive and initiative so that when she flies by the seat of her pants, the safety net of that all-important man will be there to catch her. She's not interested in how it's done. Just do it!

Love Connection

Sagittarians know how to enjoy life. They love to travel and try new adventures, and they will constantly be looking for the next challenge, which might be you! But never think you can totally possess a Sagittarian. They are adventuresome and free-spirited and that also includes bedroom matters. Bedroom matters have always been a source of curiosity for the Sag even as early as adolescence. So brace yourself.

When you meet these people, you'll laugh a lot, because Sagittarians are fun to be around. The women of the sign are intriguing, intelligent creatures who will keep you guessing about whether they will even consider a conversation with you, not to mention a date. She may make a comment such as, "I don't usually date men with children." Or she may ask, "Why on earth are you still living at home? Don't you make enough money to live on your own?" By the time you retreat with your tail between your legs like a wounded puppy, you'll get a backhanded compliment from her; "You know, I really admire a man who supports his mother. That says a lot for how he will treat his woman." As far as the dating game goes, this woman will be an excellent hostess if she invites you over to her house for dinner. The meal may be mediocre or she may order food in—she's not the type to slave over a hot stove, not on a regular basis at least—but you'll be thoroughly entertained. She'll be witty, clever, and attentive. You'll be amazed by her intellect and general knowledge about most things, including sports. The Sagittarius man won't mind an expensive restaurant every now and then, but don't make it a habit. He's not the type to be a tightwad, but he doesn't want you going buck-wild either.

Sagittarius is generally more compatible with the two other fire signs, Aries and Leo, because persons born under these signs share many characteristics of Sagittarians. They are bold, aggressive, spontaneous, not easily intimidated by most and can give Sags a run for their money. Anyway, Sag people are interested in someone who can stand toe-to-toe intellectually, spiritually and even physically with them. If you're the timid type, this fire sign will leave you in the dust wondering what happened. The main ingredient needed to offset the whirlwind behavior of the archer is to be a whirlwind yourself. The two air signs that Sags will possibly gel with are Aquarius and Libra: They are independent and successful and have good self-images, and they certainly won't be intimidated by a Sag's antics.

Gemini, the third air sign, is the Sag's opposite, directly across from the Sagittarius on the horoscope. When these two signs meet, they will find themselves in the most stimulating conversation they ever thought possible. Gemini will be charming and the Sag will flirt. They will both wonder how they got so lucky. I hate to sound like a broken record, but opposites won't fly—not past the bedroom anyway, although that's where you'll spend most of your time. Once out of the alluring haven of the boudoir, the attention span of both will be tested. The breakup will be inevitable, for it's time to move on to the next phase of the program or the next part of the ever-exciting life of the Sag and the Gemini. Most of the time the two will remain friends with few hard feelings.

Don't ever worry about breaking off with a Sagittarius. They are probably more relieved than you are. Both the men and the women are prone to erratic behavior. The companion that the lady archer thought she was madly in love with and was about to marry can suddenly become an afterthought. If the lady Sagittarian finds that her mate is jealous and begins questioning her about anyone she says hello to, then the old what-ifs will kick in. "What if I marry him and he acts worse? What if I marry him and I meet somebody else I like better?" If the engagement is broken, don't fret; in the long run, you'll be glad it happened. Sag people are very impulsive—in agreeing to marry you and in reversing the agreement. They simply don't want to feel that they're tied down.

As far as bedroom matters are concerned, don't be surprised if you find yourself in an interview before any physical contact begins. He may ask you what you like sexually. He may even ask, "You do have orgasms, don't you?" Now for some women, the questions may be an invasion of privacy. But for the Sag, he's merely assessing the companion's attitude about sex. And from a practical standpoint, he doesn't want to work overtime in an attempt to make the "big one" happen if there's no chance. They are free spirits of the zodiac—do I need to spell it out for you, boys and girls? Sagittarians are into trying new things, so battery-operated contraptions, videos or any other enhancements to get you there are fine with them. The point is this: If you get there sooner, you can get there more often.

The Sagittarian woman will want to make it perfectly clear that just because you and she are about to consummate the relationship doesn't mean that she'll be interested in the relationship on a long-term basis. And she'll remind you again about the original agreement to take things one step at a time. Lady Sags like the great outdoors, so invite her on a picnic, hiking or river rafting. The end result may be a sexual encounter you've never had before—outdoors!

The erogenous zones for the Sag are the hips, thighs and all areas in between. Most Sagittarians may not even realized it, because when it comes to foreplay they're usually so impatient to get to the actual play, they may simply bypass those vulnerable areas. Once the archer is aroused, there's no turning back.

How to Get Next to a Sagittarius

• There aren't any serious requirements to get a Sag man or woman to notice you, but be flexible and responsive.
• Sagittarians have diarrhea of the mouth. They are constantly talking about a variety of subjects. Don't stare in amazement; just try to jump into the conversation with something pertinent to say.
• Take your Sagittarius to outdoor events like a fair, carnival, picnic or outdoor concert. Sag people love the outdoors.
• This fire sign loves simplicity and casual clothing. They don't care for a lot of fanfare and pomp and circumstance on a date. They're more interested in the person than the ambiance.

Sagittarius

- Having a good sense of humor or appreciating the Sag's dry humor will help the relationship along.
- Sagittarians are constantly on the go with all of their many projects, so if you're stood up a few times, charge it to their heads, not their hearts.
- Intelligence rates about a 7 on a scale of 1 to 10. If you're not an intellectual, you're gonna have problems because they are well versed on a variety of subjects.
- Sag people are free spirits. They simply will not stand for being told what to do and when. If you try to control them, it will never work.
- Save the nose-in-the-air routine for the monarchy. Sag people are down-to-earth, honest and direct. They don't like to be coy or play games; they won't be around long enough for you to reap the benefits.
- Wigs are okay and so are toupees, because as they see it, if you're bald, you need it.
- Sag people are very blunt—some would say tactless—but it's never an attempt to hurt feelings. They're very honest and simply feel that a person should be told the truth. As you know, the truth sometimes hurts.

The Sagittarius Child

Sagittarian children are lovable and playful little tykes who must have constant stimulation. Even as infants, these children will have a constant curiosity about the world around them. If you're the parent of a Sag child, you need to buy plenty of books and read to them constantly. Also, toddler games must provide some sort of challenge. Building blocks or games that teach are recommended for Sag children, who need constant mental stimulation.

The baby archer will be good-natured and smile at whoever is looking on. These youngsters are rarely crybabies because they are simply too busy finding all of the forbidden areas and things in the house, such as the closets, the contact lenses on the vanity in the bathroom, the shaving cream on the dresser and the space underneath the kitchen sink.

They're inquisitive little rascals. You need to monitor them closely. Sag children will also question the existence of Santa, the Tooth Fairy, the Easter Bunny and all that business at a very early age. And you better have some valid, reasonable explanation for these phenomena, because they won't be beyond alerting all of the kids on the block that it's all a hoax.

The Sagittarius teenager will forever want to be in the great outdoors. Scouting, baseball or any outside activity will be to this teenager's liking. As teenagers they will question your authority, and they will definitely have a rebellious streak. For example, a sixteen-year-old teenager, who was 6 feet, 4 inches tall and easily taller than his older brother, couldn't understand why his curfew was two hours earlier. He felt that he had just as much right to be out late as the other boys who weren't nearly as tall as he. This parent's best tactic was to tell him the truth in a logical manner. The "because I said so" approach did not work with this child. They even found their Sagittarian teenager sleeping on the back steps after he missed curfew. He had attended a party, drunk too much, been escorted to the back door by his friends and then they jetted. Of course, the parents were going to put out an all-points bulletin. After the child was discovered, he had a foolproof excuse for why he didn't come into the house, something like, "I lost my key, and I didn't want to wake anybody up, so I just slept on the steps."

As parents, early discussions of sex may not be necessary. Sag children are somewhat immature late bloomers. Their playful attitude and naive personalities don't promote a lot of serious involvement with members of the opposite sex. The boys like to agitate the girls by pulling their braids or hitting them playfully. The girls are busy competing with the boys in baseball, wrestling or basketball. They're usually the tomboys. For example, a Sag girl living on a farm could pick and chop cotton better than her brothers. She would pride herself on being able to arm wrestle with her brothers and intercede for them during fights. In the case of these tomboys, affairs of the heart don't normally kick in until much later in college or even until the early twenties.

Sag children will undoubtedly do well in school. They have an insatiable thirst for knowledge. Although these children will have very few problems with schoolwork, they nevertheless are playful and will cut up in class, or even cut class. Teachers will have to control the Sag's need to talk out in class. The Sag child won't have a problem grasping what's going in class but will, nevertheless, talk to a fellow student who needs to pay attention. Sag children are usually involved in a variety of activities at school. Teachers who aren't encouraging to Sag children and who try to stifle their insatiable thirst for knowledge may do damage in their early years.

The Sagittarius Employee

If you don't provide mental stimulation and a challenge for the Sag employee, you may find yourself with one less person to handle the day-to-day operations of the company. And believe me, they will be sorely missed and may even provide you with some stiff competition when they start their own business. Sag people, like Arians, are enterprising folk, and will always take a situation and try to improve on it.

Your Sag employee may determine that the advertising company you own could save a lot of money by buying a computer software package that would meet all the graphic needs in-house. The measure would save money in the long run. Of course, the Sag would volunteer to take the software class. Everything will be rosy until this brother announces that he's taking his show on the road and quitting his job to start his own computer graphics business.

As for starting their own businesses and possibly becoming supervisor themselves, well, that's a horse of a different color. Sags are as effective as the people around them. As supervisors, they're too preoccupied with all the unfinished business, unrealized dreams and traveling to parts unknown to really be confined to a supervisory role. Being stuck in a routine job, checking the nuts and bolts, will never do for the Sagittarian.

If you have a Sagittarius for an employee, one of the first items for business will be the daily appointment calendar. Sag people, although keenly intelligent, will forget appointments, birthdays, anniversaries and any other important dates unless they're reminded. When he asks you to call him and remind him about the morning meeting, you need to do just that because if not, you'll be keeping company with yourself.

For example, a Sag communications director for a major hospital chain invariably had her own lists of things to do, but didn't always check with her secretary about additional appointments. She found that she missed a few important meetings and a very significant one with her immediate boss. After those blunders, her secretary began putting the daily planner on her chair to remind the Sag executive to look at it even before sitting down to plan her usually busy days. So I suggest you try and come up with some way of reminding your preoccupied Sag employees of their many obligations. Before their tenure is over, they will come up with a foolproof idea for making money that will have you, the boss, wondering why you hadn't thought of it.

These outspoken people are very much into their African American heritage and lean toward doing their own thing. They're their own persons and they don't take orders too well without a struggle, so for the most part, Sag people usually own their own businesses or they're on jobs with a lot of autonomy. A word of advice: Leave the Sagittarian alone to soak up the latest technology and theories related to your company and watch your company thrive. One Sagittarian dentist living in the New York area used the latest in technological procedures and equipment. He was a voracious reader and readily kept abreast of the lastest techniques, so much so that he found attendance of national conventions to learn of new procedures was unnecessary because he was already using them.

With Sag employees, you won't have to worry about moodiness or feelings of inadequacies; they are always upbeat. They are genuine, generous and helpful in every way—the bright spot of the office. However, the archer won't take too kindly to her secretary gabbing on the telephone all day or his assistants not getting the work out. Yes, she's clumsy, forgetful and blunt. And yes he's tactless, asks pointed questions and brags. (In terms of what the average person sees, the Sag looks at it as pure truth.)

Sag employees do extremely well in jobs where traveling is involved. They're also intellectual and have a keen interest in higher learning. You'll find the Sag sister working as a college professor, or the Sag brother as a lecturer or a motivational speaker. They also make good veterinarians, sportswriters, travel agents, lawyers and teachers. Basically, however, Sagittarians can do anything they put their mind to.

The only time you'll see Sags get angry is when their integrity is questioned or when blatant racism is involved. A Sag person will face a racist comment or act head on. When racially motivated problems occur, the boss will have a real problem keeping the peace because the Sag won't hold back. It's simply not in their nature. For example, a Sag brother, who worked as an environmentalist in the health department, confronted his white coworker in a meeting when the coworker implied that people living in predominately black areas in the city didn't know their own addresses. When the Sag's supervisor didn't take issue with the negative comments, the Sag felt it necessary to speak up.

Health Matters

The restless and free-spirited Sagittarians must eat healthy food and avoid tobacco and excessive amounts of alcohol if they want their bodies to keep up with their finely tuned mental capacities. Sag people are the thinkers of the zodiac. They're constantly thinking about their next business venture, new hobby or how they're going to make their first million. They are also eternal optimists, so advising them to eat properly, get rest and have annual checkups will fall on deaf ears because they feel that everything is going to work out for them anyway.

The biggest threat to their overall well-being is themselves. They are accident-prone. They will try anything once, including bungee cord jumping, riding a bike across the country, hang gliding or motorcycle riding. If they set their sights on doing something, they'll usually throw caution to the wind. They rarely consider the risks. If they don't kill themselves in the process, their health usually holds up over time. Life's a beach for the Sag person. Sagittarians are one of the few Sun signs who don't internalize a lot of mental and emotional stress. They're happy-go-lucky people who rarely allow life's twists and turns to get them down. Although they're constantly on the run and will grab a bite to eat here and there, Sag people have a tendency to gain weight as they get older. They rarely listen to early warnings, and they won't address the weight problem until it's gotten out of control.

Sagittarians must eat properly if they want their energy level to keep pace with all their many projects, ideas and inventions. It would help if they had someone to prepare these meals, for they feel there is simply too much to be accomplished in their lives. And they don't or won't take the time to plan a week-long regimen of healthy food. Their erratic eating habits are also a reflection of their erratic lifestyles. They're constantly running from pillar to post with very little order in their lives. They're not the most organized people in the zodiac. Therefore, the time that they spend always on the run could be managed better, allowing more time for rest and relaxation.

Sag people should avoid fatty foods while loading up on fruits and vegetables and drinking lots of water—also ample amounts of protein like fish and chicken, which should be broiled. The Sag is already getting lots of fatty food from the frequent pit stops they make at the local burger joint en route to a meeting or their second job.

Sagittarius rules the liver, hips and thighs, and these areas are definitely more vulnerable and prone to problems. Alcohol consumption for the Sag spells trouble. A little wine or a beer won't hurt, but the hard stuff must be avoided. They have their sensitive livers to consider. Also, cigarette smoking only aggravates respiratory systems and promotes bronchitis. Some of the health problems Sag people suffer from are hepatitis, bronchitis, diabetes and accident-related injuries such as broken bones.

The lesson for a Sagittarius is, if you won't listen to reason, listen to your body. Take the time to notice any physical changes. Sag people are moving so quickly, both physically and mentally, that they won't entertain the thought of being sick. If by chance they get that way, they have the resilience and positive attitude to recover from most illnesses quickly, but they should have annual checkups and rest and meditate. And any form of exercise on any level is better than none at all. For the Sag, there'll always be new hills to climb and other challenges ahead but they should take the time to smell the roses and keep regular doctor's appointments.

Famous African American Sagittarians

Erika Alexander
Anita Baker
Guion Steward Bluford, Jr.
Shirley Chisholm
Olivia Cole
Benjamin O. Davis
Ossie Davis
Sammy Davis Jr.
Ronald Dellums
Bo Diddley
Mike Epsy
Redd Foxx
Robin Givens
Berry Gordy
Robert Guillaume
Jimi Hendrix
Bo Jackson
Jermaine Jackson
John E. Jacob
Scott Joplin
Shawn Kemp
Jayne Kennedy
Don King

Mickey Leland
Reginald Lewis
Art Monk
Archie Moore
Gordon Parks
June Pointer
Adam Clayton Powell Jr.
Richard Pryor
Lou Rawls
Little Richard
Oscar Robertson
Kurt Schmoke
Art Shell
Carole Simpson
Cicely Tyson
Tina Turner
Paul Warfield
Dionne Warwick
Reggie White
Joe Williams
Flip Wilson

CAPRICORN
December 22 to January 19

Symbol: The Goat

Positive traits: Prudent, reserved, patient, determined, reliable, ambitious, organized, has a sense of humor

Negative traits: Opportunistic, mean, rigid, overly conventional, won't leave well enough alone, miserly, social climber

Ruling planet: Saturn is associated with limitation, restriction, obstacles and discipline.

Ask anyone about the overall personality of a Capricorn and the following adjectives come to their lips: serious, ambitious, reserved, organized, rigid and calculating. However, we've heard other terms, like "users" or "pimps of the zodiac." Now all of you Capricorns reading this section are thinking, "How can a term this unflattering be used to describe me? I'm not a pimp!" Well, in the literal sense that's true. You would never, ever send a man or woman out to sell their bodies for money. I hope. On the other hand, if the pimp wanted to help finance the business venture you needed capital for, well. . . . In other words, you use the experience and knowledge of others to succeed.

And to succeed, these earth signs know without a doubt that hard work must be in the plan. But aside from the hard work, Capricorns don't mind using the experience of others and a little kissin' up here and there. They're not above marrying for money, social standing or career enhancement. For the most part, Capricorns are definitely decent human beings, but their analytical and strategic minds propel them a little further than most when it comes to jockeying for position. And they have been known to step on a few toes as they tiptoe to the top of the game.

And I know it's lonely at the top because having meaningful contact with a Capricorn is a tall order. There won't be much contact because they're loners and essentially they're very hard to know. They find it very hard to show any vulnerable side to their character. Capricorns may not realize it, but they need people, and if they would ease up a bit, a person would really enjoy their company.

Capricorns are friendly and above all else polite. But the friendships that they hold dear are sometimes those relationships that have evolved and developed over time such as the ones from college, the neighborhood or the initial job. Trust, respect and honesty are the common denominators for all of the relationships Capricorns have, whether they're platonic or love interests. They will absolutely not open up unless they trust the person. And even if they completely trust the person, there are areas in the lives of Capricorns that only they know about. Capricorns are definitely not your social butterflies. Most of the time, if or when you meet this earth sign, it'll be in a controlled setting such as work, church, health club or maybe at the fundraiser for the local boys or girls club. But they enjoy a variety of activities such as outdoor sports or anything where strategy is involved, such as tennis, chess and basketball. Capricorns also love African art, plays, jazz concerts and kickin' back with a good book. The events that they usually attend have some good-deed overtones to them. If by chance you notice a man dressed in a navy blue suit or a woman in a black suit with silk blouse buttoned to the neck, the image of reserve, the Al Gore type, stiff and wooden and intermittently looking at their watch, it's probably a Capricorn.

But the contradiction is that the men of the sign exude masculinity and the women are the ultrafeminine cutie pies. When they're in a room, you'll first notice that they're dressed in a way that reeks of perfection. Their bodies will be toned and their outfits will offer just the right degree of subtlety. These earth signs generally have to be dragged most places biting, scratching and pulling. (Just kidding! Caps wouldn't be caught dead demonstrating unbecoming behavior.) For example, if you spot a Capricorn at a piano bar or club in the heart of downtown, this sister is usually taking out someone from out of town. But they wouldn't ever be caught dead dancing on top of the table, or even be *seen* with the person who's dancing on top of the table, either. Capricorns must be careful, you know; the boss may be out on the town as well.

These earth signs are far too serious for their own good. They secretly want to be footloose and fancy-free, but they simply don't know how. For example, if you invite a Capricorn out, saying, "Let's go and throw down," they may think you're talking about participating in a wrestling match and would probably question why being dressed up was necessary. That statement might be oversimplified, but you get the picture.

Capricorn's symbol is the goat. The ruling planet of Capricorn is Saturn, which is associated with discipline and hard work. These mountain goats will work as hard as they need to, to reach the top in a career or any other areas in their lives.

The physical makeup of a black Capricorn won't include too many distinguishing features. Capricorns are usually slim and athletic-looking, but physical size can run the gamut. Most of the time, Capricorns look quite a few years younger than they actually are. The jawbone is prominent, and they will sometimes have a habit of biting down in a clenched-toothed manner. If the Cap man is bald, he won't try to wear a toupee. He feels that he should be man enough to show the real person. Capricorn women generally like a variety of hairstyles, but most of them will be conservative in nature —a short cut, braids or a perm will do just fine. Capricorns generally have an intense look as if they're contemplating the solution to a problem in world affairs.

This sign thrives on competition of any kind, even when they're relaxing at home with all the adult toys (computers and other electronic equipment) their apartments can hold. They are constantly consumed by some mental strategy. These earth signs are systematic in everything they attempt. Even in affairs of the heart, their dates and outings will be planned, scheduled and orderly, just like their lives. And you won't have to worry about these earth signs playing the field. They don't see the need and they don't want to be caught in an embarrassing situation, with two dates showing up at the same time. For example, a Capricorn was invited to her boyfriend's house for the weekend. Her boyfriend's parents made a surprise visit to their son's house. Rather than give the parents any inkling that she was spending the night with their son, she woke each morning before anyone got up and left the house. At night she went to bed after his parents. Of course, she and her companion laughed about it later. Having a sense of humor puts a lighter touch on the Cap's otherwise overly serious nature.

The children of Capricorns feel that their parents are far too serious as well. As parents, Caps have a tendency to dominate their children. These parents can definitely be stern taskmasters. Because Capricorns in general are so serious-minded, their children tend to suffer; most children won't be able to live up to the unreasonably high standards the Capricorn places on the child. Capricorns must remember that children should be given affection, attention, quality time and flexibility. Children shouldn't ever be treated absentmindedly, like employees that the Capricorn may supervise.

The Capricorn Man

This brother is very good at pretending. He pretends that he doesn't know that all eyes are on him as he enters the room. His dress will be impeccable right down to his manicured nails. When you approach this brother, you better be careful—he can also pretend that he's not aware that you're making eyes at him. If you don't meet his long list of criteria as he's sizing you up, the fat lady has already sung and the hot pursuit is over. You don't have much of a chance. He'll notice your nails, the missing button on your clothing, your eyes, your mouth. And by the way, please try to speak correctly. A few slang words are okay, but no profanity in mixed company. I know you're probably thinking, Who needs this stuffed shirt? Well, he's got a great sense of humor and a pleasing personality once you get pass all the stuffiness. This all sounds like what a friend says when she's trying to coax you into going on a blind date with Mr. Geek of America, but it's true. For him, he believes beyond a reasonable doubt that he must "come correct." Who knows, someone may be watching!

At a party, the Capricorn will strategically place himself in the background. He's a master at the game of chess, so making a determination of how the real-life pieces all fit together in the scheme of things will be easy. He wants to be in the mix, moving up the social ladder, where he feels his rightful place is. If you're in a casual discussion with a Capricorn, you'll find yourself in an interview, sort of. He won't be able to help himself. He'll question you about your background and your employment and will know most of your pertinent info before the night is over. That is, if he's interested.

On the other hand, if he's ill at ease at the social gathering, the conversation may go like this: "Hello, it's good to meet you, my name is Roosevelt Jones. I'm new in town and I don't know anybody here. I was invited by my boss to this party. . . . No, I better not drink anything tonight because I don't want to get stopped on the way home. Besides that, I need to go to the office tomorrow [Saturday] to look at my desk and sort through some things. . . . Well, I know, no one will be there, but I need to go to work and get organized. Well, good meeting you, I better go." His appearance at the party, for the sake of the boss, lasted all of about forty-five minutes. You as the conversationalist just happened to enter the picture during the last ten minutes. Don't take it personally. It's the serious side of the Capricorn that the outside world sees.

Those persons privileged enough to see the other side—the sensitive, strong, caring side of this earth sign—probably have known this brother for years. Or you may be in a long relationship with him, and by now you know all you want to know. Capricorns prefer long relationships. They don't relish the thought of playing the dating game and the cat-and-mouse maneuvers that go with it, so once they find a good, safe, comfortable relationship, you may have to ask him to marry you instead of vice versa. It won't be a turnoff, especially if you're five years into the relationship. You've earned it!

A scorned companion of a Capricorn confessed she hung with this brother for four years hoping and praying that he would eventually settle down and marry her. She thought he was so exciting and smart and knew exactly what he wanted out of life. The only thing was, he didn't want her—permanently that is. But again, as one Cap said, "My girlfriend and I broke up because she didn't mature as I had hoped." What was he doing, raising cattle?

Capricorn

If you're married to this Capricorn man, you were probably handpicked. The selection of a mate for the Capricorn is a slow and tedious process because your main job as the wife is to enhance his image and make him look good. It'll be okay for you to have a career, but your job cannot interfere with your husband's. Capricorns will trade in emotion and passion in a mate for a companion who, they feel, will be more of an asset to them as they move ever so carefully and methodically up the mountain of success.

Such was the case with a Capricorn couple who met as coworkers in the military and eventually married. The two worked together, but the Capricorn brother didn't like his companion "shootin' the breeze and jivin' around" with the other military men. Of course, there weren't any flirtatious overtures, but the Cap brother wanted to be in control. After the two were married, the Cap brother wanted the social encounters to end entirely. His companion objected and said he was trying to change her personality. He later admitted, after the marriage ended, that he picked her to marry him because he wanted more control over her activities.

In the Capricorn man's quest for prestige and success, he may marry for money and status instead of love and happiness. For example, a long-distance tractor-trailer driver married his second wife for what he called the "colors of success"—her nice car, clothes and job. But all she really had was a bunch of bills from all her trappings. I'm sure the wife had some motives of her own. The marriage lasted only eight months after the two discovered that love, or the pretense of love, could not conquer the mounting bills and obligations of the marriage.

If the Cap's a college student, more than likely he'll have a job, which means going out to eat on dates and movies. But the problem is, he'll be involved in so many activities—band, fraternity, intramural basketball, and of course, hangin' with his boys—that you'll have to fight for his attention. So get out the boxing gloves. Of course, the boxing gloves are strictly figurative, because real scenes are definitely a turnoff with this earth sign. For example, when a scene broke out in a restaurant between a Capricorn's current girlfriend and his ex, the Cap brother was so embarrassed by the incident that the present girlfriend soon became an ex-mate too.

If you're with this brother, you may notice his understated, reserved GQ dress. Quality is important and looking his best is, too. But this brother won't be spending money frivolously. He's got his investments and savings, along with his goal of owning his business. He's not a tightwad. Let's just say he's prudent, judicious and frugal about spending. Those adjectives would be more to the Capricorn's liking.

The Capricorn Woman

Don't take anything for granted with this woman. When planning any event, you'd better check with her first. If you're lucky enough to be invited into the hallowed walls of this dynamo of prissiness, you will be thoroughly impressed. If the invitation is officially from her and not finagled by you, this is a sure sign that she's interested. The lady goats are all about serious business. They won't waste their invitations if they are doubtful about the potential for a budding relationship. In other words, you've got to have potential. You need to have the basics such as employment (hopefully, a *good* job); you have to know what a resume is and how to speak English, not slang. When you greet her at her door, you need to be on time, freshly shaved, bathed and smelling good. *Note:* Don't go to the local drugstore and pick up the cologne that's on special this week or that was popular back in the 1960s, like High Karate or Jade East. She also keeps up with the latest fragrances, and anything that has a country-and-western ring to it, like Tumbleweed or Ranch Hand, is out!

To get the evening off on the right foot, bring flowers or a small gift of some kind, like scented candles or bubble bath. A box of candy would not be to her liking because Capricorns are diet-conscious and are usually engaged in an exercise program and trying to eat healthy. At the lady Cap's abode, there will be amenities galore. The apartment or house will be squeaky clean. You may even feel compelled to take off your shoes. Everything will be color-coordinated in earth tones of beige, soft green or mauve. Original artwork, prints and artifacts from frequent traveling will rubber stamp this sister's unmistakable eye for quality and style.

And don't forget that she invited you over; that's saying a whole lot. So step right up, loosen your tie, enjoy yourself. The meal will be exquisite, with after-dinner brandy as the two of you sink back on the couch to listen to Luther Vandross's soothing voice on the stereo. This sister will be done up from head to toe, hair down her back, either permed or braided, big booty, shapely figure and, yes, stimulating chitchat. Hello!

Although things are off to a rousing start, you won't be able to guess what your next move will be. So a suggestion would be to follow her lead, because if you make your move too soon, you'll be out of the door. Any man that can stand up to the independence, aggressiveness and assertiveness of a Capricorn sister deserves a medal for simply being able to hold up under such scrutiny. Probably from the above description, you'll be thinking that you are about to date a drill sergeant. It won't be quite that bad. But, her overall persona can be intimidating. Granted, she won't tell you immediately how she feels, but that doesn't mean she doesn't care. This careful Capricorn simply cannot put herself out there unless she's sure that she likes you, that you have potential or that you care about her. There aren't any easy answers here. She must feel secure and trust you without reservation if you plan to get to the reckless-abandon stage, where the sex act may be performed anywhere in the house. But once you've gained her trust, which may seem to take forever, she can be an attentive and loving companion.

The women of the sign enjoy shopping for and collecting antiques, art, books or any item of value. Secondhand stores particularly pique her interest because she can slowly prod through stacks of "stuff" to find the right treasure. This pastime is very relaxing to the Cap sister because she can bargain-hunt and find items of value simultaneously.

Capricorn sisters are proud people and have a sense of who they are and what they expect from a mate. Even though love for them is important, a Cap sister cannot tolerate any impropriety on any level. For example, a lady goat working for an international air freight packaging company met her husband-to-be, a pilot working for the same company, on a vacation flight to London. As romantic as the meeting and eventual marriage sounded, the two separated because she couldn't tolerate watching him undress other women with his eyes when he looked at them.

When the Capricorn female ends up in a traumatic situation (which is, for the most part, rare), she can generally bounce back and learn from the experience. For example, a Capricorn sister, married a Virgo who constantly dissed her and slowly chiseled away her self-esteem. Eventually, she divorced her husband of twenty years, but before she left he told her that she wouldn't ever amount to anything and she certainly wouldn't succeed. The determined Capricorn started cleaning houses and eventually opened a cleaning business. She later sold that business and opened another, lecturing on meditation and spirituality and conducting self-help seminars à la Oprah Winfrey. You showed him, girlfriend!

Capricorn sisters have plenty of causes they believe in. But worthy causes with a focus on children, particularly boys, get those creative juices flowing. For example, one of the most effective ways for this sister to work is in the church. She's usually in charge of Vacation Bible School, directing the choir or teaching Sunday school. And additionally, being the planner that she is, she'll be constantly looking for ways for her church's youth program to bring in speakers, orchestrate career days, and set up scholarship programs to teach and encourage black children to achieve.

Love Connection

After going over all of the do's and don'ts, you're probably wondering what's up with these quiet, serious-minded people. And you're also wondering if they're really all that. Yes, they are, because they're not trying too hard to impress. They know they are a class act and that's what they expect from you: class—not underclass. They conduct themselves like ladies and gentlemen, and they expect nothing less than near perfection from you. I know this may sound like a lot of nonsense, but for Caps it's not.

If you're planning a date with a Cap brother, he'll probably show up early. *Warning:* I would suggest that you have your place in some sort of order. Please don't have nylons hanging from the shower curtain or dirty dishes stacked up to the ceiling or the cat sitting in the middle of the kitchen table. These kinds of things will freak him out. Everything must be in order, or there should be an appearance of order, even if you have to shove all of the clothes, newspapers and pets in the closet. On this date understated elegance is what this brother will look for. A red rubber jumpsuit with a Goodyear tag in the back of the collar is not what this brother expects. Hopefully, you'll be in a conservative outfit, perhaps a tasteful pantsuit or knit or silk dress, plain, not too tight, and maybe a scarf.

As for a date with the lady Cap, most of the same rules apply. She will want her date to be neatly dressed and have some knowledge of current events and what's going on in the world. Initially, you may get the impression that she's a snob or social climber, and that impression could be accurate. But to this earth sign, image is all-important. And the total package, who you are and what you do, is a consideration.

I'm telling you now, Capricorns don't like country behavior. You're not going to impress a Cap, male or female, with a beeper or a cellular phone (unless you're a physician and on call). Please, please, please don't bring these contraptions to the restaurant or sit up in the bar and talk on the phone just to impress. It won't work! Your date won't ever utter a word of displeasure, but the annoyance will definitely show on his or her face. You'll be written off before you can order the appetizer.

Most people who meet Capricorns perceive them as stuffed shirts. Others say that they try to project a perfect image and are too demanding and critical. These statements may be true, but Caps also set high standards for themselves. Nevertheless, as driven as they may be, they need friends and people who care about them unconditionally. They sincerely want to be warm, friendly and revealed. Capricorns must learn how to truly relax and go with the flow.

Capricorn rules the knees, joints and bones. Any strokes or touches to the knees or in and around these areas will wake up the flavor in this lukewarm person. The back of the knees are especially vulnerable. Once things start heating up in the bedroom, your long anticipation will be rewarded. The Capricorn's sex life is essential to their overall well-being. Like everything else in their lives, it's going to be a scheduled happening. And you'll be notified in advance (hopefully not by memo or e-mail!). Be prepared because you'll be in for a long night. When Capricorns want information, they'll usually buy a book on the subject. So if you see any books like *The Joy of Sex* or *Erotique Noire* around the apartment, underline the pertinent parts. They'll pay attention, and it will keep them from any intimate discussions on the matter that they feel should be left for marriage. Capricorns are very adept at bedroom skills, but all of the passion-laden emotional displays won't be evident at first. In fact they may never be. But you'll definitely enjoy yourself in the bedroom.

As far as compatibility, here's how it goes: Capricorns get along with the two other earth signs, Virgo and Taurus. Earth signs are the stable, practical types; all three get along and complement each other. Water signs, Pisces and Scorpio, govern the emotions so these two will provide the serious Capricorn with a little emotional balance.

If you're a Capricorn, Cancer, your opposite sign, is the person that you'll have an instant attraction to. When you meet, the conversation will be stimulating and you'll laugh a lot. You and your Cancer won't want to leave each other's side, not even for a minute. If you're asking yourself, "How will I know this person?" you'll know. There will be a strong magnetic attraction between the two of you. However, very few relationships of opposites work. Cancer's moodiness and emotional eruptions will drive a controlled, quiet Capricorn batty. The "here we go again" look on Capricorn's face will only make matters worse for teary-eyed Cancer. Caps are usually unemotional and aloof and will find Cancer's behavior to be unsettling and burdensome.

How to Get Next to a Capricorn

• If you're into the natural look, that's okay. But don't let a Capricorn spot you in your nappy-headed state. The hairdo needs to be permed or natural, but not half and half (permed on top and nappy underneath). The men certainly don't like their companions to be between hairdos.
• Being impeccably dressed will most certainly catch the Capricorn's eye. And don't forget the fingernail polish.

• Having a sense of humor will always help to break the ice. Capricorns, both men and women, are very serious-minded. They can always use a good laugh.

• Loud and boisterous behavior is a definite no-no. You must act like a lady or gentleman even if it's a put-on.

• Coaxing Capricorns to talk candidly about the intimate and private details of their life is an exercise in futility. Your best approach here is to talk about yourself, but not incessantly. Later, after they feel you are worthy of trust, you'll be allowed a small glimpse into their life.

• For the first date, please be ready on time—not CP time. First impressions are lasting ones. Oftentimes with a Cap, you won't have a second chance to make a first impression.

• If you're into Spandex, boa constrictor–type clothing, save it to be part of your Halloween costume. The Capricorn brother will be turned off and you may even be asked to change. (If you weren't "his" date, the outfit would probably be okay. He enjoys girl watching.)

• Men who are taking Capricorn sisters out should leave all the gold chains at home—one will do. If you have gold teeth, I suppose there's nothing you can do about it, but try not to grin too much.

• Capricorns are far too serious for their own good. If you give them a present, make it something practical like books or mentally stimulating gadgets such as puzzles or games that teach.

The Capricorn Child

As a parent, you'll have very little trouble from your little goat. From the earliest stages of development, the Capricorn child will appear to be much more mature than his or her chronological age suggests. As toddlers, Cap babies will lie quietly in the crib as long as they are dry and fed. There will be very little squawking or bawling. Music is very soothing and provides a quiet way to lull this baby to sleep. One six-month-old Cap baby would squeal with delight when his parents played "Make Yours a Happy Home," by Gladys Knight and the Pips. When the Pips sang the chorus of the song—"doot . . . doot, doot, doot . . . doot, doot, doot, doot"—the baby would listen intently, grin his toothless smile, and then kick his feet in the air with enjoyment.

From the toddler stage on up, the little Caps are serious about everything they do to a fault. Potty training, walking, talking and all of the preliminaries to preschool are mastered with ease by Capricorns. These children do not like to be scolded for any reason. A reminder in the form of a verbal reprimand of disappointment will have your Capricorn youngster scrambling to get back in your good graces. When they're young, you'll simply marvel at their ability to remember the lines to nursery rhymes and children's stories. They love getting your approval for these achievements.

As early as kindergarten and first grade, Capricorn children will take it upon themselves to keep the other students quiet in class and volunteer to be the hall monitor, along with performing any other service, including teacher's pet.

These children love to excel. Homework and keeping up with school projects won't be a problem. In fact, they will constantly remind you that you need to take them to pick up poster board or paints for the project. Never underestimate a Capricorn's slow, methodical way of plodding along. Sometimes a class or science project may take them longer than most, but give them time, because they will win in the end. For example, a Capricorn child in a sixth-grade class won first place for the science project she presented on areas of the human brain. Instead of a diagram of the brain on a poster, the Capricorn child used cream cheese and made a three-dimensional replica of the brain, using a variety of food colorings to denote areas of the brain. After the in-depth presentation, the Capricorn youngster retrieved a box of crackers from her backpack and later the class enjoyed an afternoon snack.

If by chance you grew up in a household with a Capricorn, no matter where this earth sign was in the birth order, it was an unforgettable experience. You learned very quickly to leave the belongings of the Capricorn sibling alone. Maybe it was you who took her fingernail file out of her manicure case or borrowed his basketball and left it in the yard for the dog to gnaw on or took her pet turtle to school for show and tell. If by chance this happened, chances are it didn't happen again. Capricorns, both adult and child, go ballistic when their belongings are misplaced. If you wanted peace in the house, it was best not to touch Capricorn's belongings for safety reasons—your own.

Although Capricorn children are mature and serious most of the time, puppy love and affairs of the heart should be handled carefully. Your Capricorn child is shy, introverted and awkward when it comes to the opposite sex. Don't force the issue, but let the child know you're there if there are any major hurdles such as what to wear on a date, how long to stay out and what the conversations should be like.

Now for the other burning issue—the birds-and-bees discussion. There's no doubt about it, you'll feel like your life is passing before you with all of the curious and probing questions that your thorough Capricorn youngster will ask you about the facts of life, including the origins of the expression "birds and bees." I would advise you to be prepared with diagrams and literature and to be as open and honest as you can be. You're in for a long evening.

Capricorn children have a tendency to stay indoors with family, where they feel the safest. These youngsters should be encouraged to get involved in outdoor activities such as scouting, a paper route or sports. If you put a basketball hoop up over the garage, your house will become the new community center and your Capricorn its director. He will attempt to bring water out to the troops, and food too, if you'll let him. As teenagers, Capricorns ease up a little bit and can actually enjoy themselves some. The children will be popular with the other students, but most Capricorns will be serious-minded students—president of the student council or captain of the debate team or both.

They will be receptive to white children as well as to children of all nationalities—it won't matter much to the Capricorn. This child's basic philosophy is, Live and let live. This child will be mature enough to put race aside. Capricorns love a challenge and will compete with you no matter what color you are—unless, of course, confrontation is directed toward him. In that case, your Cap youngster will try to resolve the matter by going to the principal or facing the adversary head on.

As children, Capricorns will feel compelled to address adult issues. Such was the case when a twelve-year-old child found letters from her father to her mother. The letters revealed his undying love for his wife and begged her to allow him to return home. The Capricorn daughter, feeling she could act as a go-between, even at age twelve, confronted her mother and wanted an explanation. She never learned until years later the real dynamics and reasons that her mother didn't reconcile with her father. But early in her life she felt justified in her action.

The Capricorn Employee

Ambition is the key word here. Capricorns' careers are second only to their family. From a very early age, their minds are set on being successful and having power, position and promise—the promise of ascension to the top of the profession.

If you're the boss, the Capricorn employee will be an asset to your company. He or she is overly conscientious and organized and rarely wastes time engaging in idle chatter or office gossip. In fact, the Capricorn would just as soon avoid the water cooler or the coffee maker altogether at peak periods during the morning and afternoon. More than likely the Cap employee arrived about thirty minutes early and took care of coffee, water or whatever. This workaholic was ready to begin work at the stroke of nine o'clock. Time is money, you know. And speaking of money, they plan to have plenty of it one day.

Capricorns are born leaders. Therefore, putting them in charge of a project, temporarily or permanently, is a good idea. If you're the boss and need to travel, the best approach is to allow your Capricorn employee to hold the fort while you're gone. Capricorns are dependable and determined to make good on the job and impress the boss. They don't actually care who or what they lead. The motive here is to learn all facets of the business because Capricorns function on any job as if they'll be in charge or own the company one day.

If you're the boss and don't readily realize this earth sign's potential, they will simply take their show on the road and pitch a tent somewhere else. Such was the case of a jewelry designer living in Chicago who worked in the production department of a major newspaper. After almost falling through an elevator opening that wasn't supposed to be there, the Capricorn employee found out that her supervisor at the newspaper minimized the incident. After surgery on her arm, physical, and a little mental, therapy, the Capricorn sister left the newspaper and set up her own business making jewelry.

Most of the time, Capricorns will be fully immersed in a full-time job, but they will also take on part-time work selling real estate, being an umpire for the Little League baseball team or teaching adult education courses. The money from the second job will be the nest egg, the children's education, savings for the all-important trip to Africa or making significant contributions to the church's building fund.

Capricorns make excellent teachers, scientists, architects, dentists, engineers, politicians and supervisors or administrators on any level. Jobs where there is stability are positions that Capricorns seek.

Racism can have a devastating effect on most employees, and the Capricorn is no exception. But this goat also views racism as a challenge. They won't have blinders on, by any means, but this goat, plodding slowly up the mountain, won't allow racism to be a hindrance, either. They will simply work harder to prove to the boss or the racists that they are wrong. For example, a Capricorn in a management position of an international food service company made a formal request that January 15, Martin Luther King, Jr.'s birthday, be observed by the company as a holiday. Although she was very organized in her reasoning, management tried to hem and haw, saying it would be too costly to include the King holiday in the company calendar. The Capricorn pointed out that the King holiday could be substituted for one of already existing floating holidays. The company now observes Martin Luther King, Jr.'s birthday as an official holiday.

Capricorns are far too serious and organized for their own good sometimes. For example, during a fire drill, a female Capricorn employee grabbed her purse—and her electronic calendar, explaining that her life depended on it. This Cap sister couldn't be without the calendar, even during a fire drill. Whew!!

Health Matters

Capricorn, the sign of the fountain of youth, is on top of the diet, eating right and avoiding excessive amounts of alcohol. The Capricorn is the one you'll meet on the stairwell at work, taking the stairs instead of the elevator. Or else, he'll be cycling instead of driving his car. They're far too serious as youngsters, but they seem to get better with age because, early on, the Caps were doing all the right things to preserve their looks and longevity.

Both the men and the women have lots of energy and vitality. They are also capable of handling stress in the various areas in their lives and in the workplace because they want to move up the corporate ladder. And any opportunity to show the boss how they handle stress will be a golden opportunity for these earth signs that they don't plan to miss. The key word for a Capricorn is "career." That's the one word that captures the goat, who's methodically moving up the mountain or the career ladder. And making it to the top or as near as possible is an achievable goal, so handling work-related stress is no big deal.

The downside to all this is that too much of anything is not good, including stress. Capricorns have a tendency to present a calm exterior while turbulence is raging internally. Their stomach and digestive system know for sure, though. Capricorns are accused of being workaholics, pushing themselves beyond the limits of what's physically and mentally feasible. In addition to exercise, which they're most assuredly involved in already, a hobby like gardening, needlepoint, painting or anything that's totally off the beaten path is what's needed to dilute some of the stresses in their life.

Capricorn rules the knees, joints and bones. Caps have aching joints, nagging knee problems, ailments related to the gall bladder, skin rashes and possible dental problems. Generous amounts of calcium are essential for their overall well-being. The Capricorn diet should be high in protein to fuel all their pent-up energy and running from pillar to post. The goats should eat plenty of dairy products and other foods rich in calcium, including milk, yogurt and low-fat cheeses, and greens. Eight glasses of water a day will keep the skin supple and rashes to a minimum.

Capricorn

One drawback for Capricorns is that often there's no one they can vent their problems to. That's when alcohol comes in as a substitute for honest conversation and shared feelings, an undertaking they have yet to master. They don't share their innermost feelings, and alcohol substitutes very nicely. The end results are nervous stomach or weight gain from alcohol and food used as a temporary solution. When they find themselves gaining a few pounds, most of the time they shed the unwanted poundage because they have the stick-to-itiveness and drive to achieve their weight loss goal. The problem is losing the weight may not be as simple because of the goat's inner struggle of not facing mounting problems that this earth sign needs to address, and eating may sometimes be a source of comfort. The solution is to stop trying to be there for everyone else, and not yourself, Cap. And if you take some time to get acquainted with yourself, and acknowledge that you need to open up more, the relationship won't be a bad one.

Famous African American Capricorns

Alvin Ailey
Muhammad Ali
Debbie Allen
John Amos
Tyra Banks
Julian Bond
Tom Bradley
Ruth Brown
Cab Calloway
Kim Coles
L.L. Cool J
Darryl "Chocolate
   Thunder" Dawkins
George Duke
George Foreman
Joe Frazier
Harvey Gantt

Zora Neale Hurston
John H. Johnson
James Earl Jones
Martin Luther King, Jr.
Butterfly McQueen
Walter Mosley
Odetta
Floyd Patterson
Sheryl Lee Ralph
Sade
John Singleton
Donna Summer
Mario Van Peebles
Madame C. J. Walker
Denzel Washington
Douglas Wilder
Dominique Wilkins

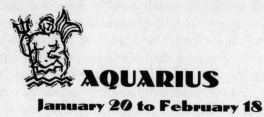

AQUARIUS
January 20 to February 18

Symbol: The Water Bearer

Positive traits: Charismatic, intelligent, independent, friendly, inventive, idealistic, intuitive, humane

Negative traits: Unpredictable, perverse, eccentric, tactless, disorganized, impulsive, rebellious

Ruling planet: Uranus is associated with independence and humane initiatives.

One of the first things you notice about Aquarians is their aloof demeanor—friendly but distant. But don't let that fool you. They seem distant because they are constantly thinking about the future, imagining the day when skin color will no longer matter because interracial marriage has made the world a wonderful shade of cocoa or, better yet, no one leaves the house because computers do everything. Aquarians are constantly thinking far off into the future—not next week or next year, but the next millennium.

In spite of this seeming aloofness, which we now know results from their contemplation of the world, the charismatic aura of the Aquarian will compel you to try to get to know this person. While you're conjuring up some kind of encounter, this air sign is not even aware that you exist—partly because they are one of the most modest signs of the zodiac and the last to notice that you are even interested in them.

It took one sister two years before she mustered the courage to speak to an Aquarian brother, since it became obvious he wasn't going to speak to her. They were both reporters and consequently covered the same stories. Once she said hello and asked him out to lunch, he looked at her as if he was seeing her for the first time. He was! Of course, he was intrigued and delighted by the invitation and wondered why he hadn't noticed this lovely creature before—and later refused to believe that she had tried everything but throwing herself in front of his moving car to get his attention. His head was probably in the stratosphere thinking, of course, how computer technology would eventually replace reporters.

Unlike the Leo, who thrives on attention, the Aquarian rarely seeks attention and tries to avoid it. Ironically, it seems that this humanitarian is in the limelight most of the time. For example, a financial administrator, new on the job, inherited a hornet's nest of responsibilities. The department had a long-standing negative reputation and all eyes were on the Aquarian to determine if he could do the job. Of course, he turned the department around, fired a few unproductive people and even kept the would-be lady wolves at bay. One of his first moves was to bring in the family photos, featuring the wife, children and dog, and prominently display them on his desk. This ended all the speculation as to whether he would "play." Maybe, but never in a volatile situation like this.

Aquarians are usually the ones with the latest haircut, clothing style, car or electronic gadget. They generally have slim builds because they are constantly on the go. They are usually walking briskly, head in the air with an "I know I'm tough" look of confidence, constantly looking at their watches or appointment books or talking on their cordless phones. But it's only a look. Aquarians are not the "I know I'm all that" type.

Part of their charm is that they don't understand how wonderful they really are. And this Uranus-ruled sign really is wonderful, as is evident in everything they do—whether it's picking up a hitchhiker, who falls asleep the minute he gets in the car only to be awakened later to a hot meal and a $20 bill, or staying up with you all night on a week night after you've called it quits with a companion, or having sex with you "for old times' sake" or just because you need it. I know the sex thing may sound crazy, but they are the true humanitarians in every sense of the word. They have a keen sense of what a person needs and wants (sex included), and they can and will rise to the occasion. They are the men and women of the twenty-first century.

What the Aquarian is thinking about now, the average person realizes or conceives ten years later. Once the Aquarians get their heads out of the clouds long enough to notice you and consider you a friend, your patience will be tested to the limit. The friendship that you're hoping will blossom into something more meaningful may take an eternity. This is not to say they have no interest in relationships. It's just going to be slow-going because of all of their many interests. New things pique their interest the most, and therefore after one goal is accomplished, they're usually off and running in another direction. (You will need new "running" shoes every six months to keep up, and most of the time you'll feel that you're losing ground.)

The Aquarius sister may initiate the recycling effort in her neighborhood only to discover that there's a need for a massive program for the entire city. Guess who's going to volunteer to head the city program? Or the Aquarian brother may start a Big Brother program after learning of the disproportionate number of black children in juvenile detention. He may even feel compelled to adopt several children, rearing them on a shoestring budget by growing his own food and at the same time teaching the children the elements of survival.

Their humanitarian outlook in general helps them to see beyond a rude comment like, "I thought all your people could dance." They divorce themselves from the comment and try to get to know the person who said it. They will take on the project of educating the person about racism and its degrading effects. Aquarians constantly take up the banner for good causes, whether it's welfare reform, the prolife-prochoice question or environmental issues. After all, they understand the far-reaching ramifications of these issues. Aquarians are also somewhat misunderstood at first. A lot of black people don't like them because of how this air sign is perceived. It's not that they aren't friendly and down-to-earth, because they are. Their uniqueness of spirit, dress and personality makes them an easy target for people who are less tolerant of this unusual air sign. But many blacks feel that if sisters or brothers don't use black slang and carry themselves in a certain acceptable way, those people are "acting white." They may even shun the Aquarian, who is not acting white, but just being himself.

The Aquarius Man

Girlfriend, you won't be able to help yourself. That's how tough this brother is. (There is something about them that attracts most people.) Usually when the brother walks in the room, presumably full of self-confidence and dressed to kill, all eyes are on him. He rarely notices, however.

This man keeps up with the latest trends, and he even sets a few. His dress is usually mild but definite. Although he has a tendency toward electric colors and wild styles, the understated elegance is usually there. Other times he is somewhat in disguise. He may wear Army fatigues, but may never have been in the service. Physically, Aquarians are quite appealing, with sensuous eyes that seem to sparkle, nice buns, big, juicy lips and no curls—I repeat, no Jheri curls.

You must be a friend first and he must respect your intellect before the wining and dining commence. For example, you may have lunch with him several times a month, hoping to push the relationship to the next level, but he won't make any overtures. Then just as soon as you've given up hope, he will call and ask you to lunch without being prompted. While you're deciding on the restaurant, you may ask casually, "What do you have a taste for? and he'll respond, "You."

Now in most exchanges that response may be the cue for the next level of the relationship. But you must be as spontaneous as the comment—laugh uproariously, but don't assume that this is an official beginning. You won't be able to predict when or if the relationship will start. He doesn't know the timetable any more than you do. There may not even be a timetable! You will need to ask the Aquarian directly. They love the direct approach, so don't beat around the bush with this impatient sign. He won't sit still for it.

Can you cook? This man would sometimes rather get down over a plate of greens, yams, ham and cornbread than pay attention to affairs of the heart. Also, talking at length to the neighborhood historian, an elderly brother who holds down the corner in front of the local barbershop (like the mayor in *Do the Right Thing*) delights him. "There may be potential for a book in those reminiscences, you know," your Aquarian explains.

The Aquarian man is complex, unpredictable and elusive. He understands all too well the ramifications of being a black male in America, but he doesn't allow himself to be stifled by such musings. There is, of course, the self-imposed pressure to live up to all of the expectations of trying to overcompensate for one's color, especially if he's the only black or the first black. But he will glide through most situations, be they racial, confrontational or otherwise, with a flair that will keep most wondering, "Who was that masked man?"

Intrigue and mystery get his attention quicker than answering your door in nothing but your garterbelt. This man is much more interested in what is not revealed. He wants the damsel-in-distress type, with her loose-fitting dress below her knees and legs clamped together like a steel trap and crossed at the ankles. Psyche! But you get the picture. The Aquarius brother will knowingly look for the woman who's trying to sneak by in her plain outfit and lackluster personality. Then he'll say to himself as she passes, "Wait a minute. . . . Not so fast." The more shy and self-effacing the potential companion, the more interested he is and the more time he'll want to invest.

The challenge for him is to behold the undiscovered treasures beneath the calm, reserved exterior of his potential mate. The prospect of seeing the controlled person become wild and wonderful fascinates him. He's very versatile: He can hang on the corner with brothers using street language one minute and address the importance of recycling in a speech to a group of hospital administrators the next.

In today's society, the emergence of equal rights for women and equal pay for equal work has many men looking for another form of equality—women picking up the tab during the date. Don't despair, ladies, the Aquarian has no problem spending money, be it yours or his. He's never let the mere lack of money stand in the way of what he wants. You won't be going to Wendy's for dinner. Most likely it will be an out-of-the-way place you never heard of, much like his out-of-the-way personality. He and the food will look good, the conversation will be engaging, and you'll think you've died and gone to heaven. If he doesn't have the money, he'll merely charge that expensive bottle of French wine on a credit card.

Trying to capture this sign is like trying to capture smoke or air. He is an air sign, you know—but he's a good catch too. Remember the saying, he's worth the wait, for you may wait, and wait and wait.

He constantly wants to fly by the seat of his pants and fears being bored. Aquarians believe boredom is a terminal condition, so they fight fiercely to maintain a certain level of excitement in their lives. They want to be busy or entertained every minute of the day with work or play. Once an Aquarian settles down, which is rare, he'll be an attentive friend. He reveres relationships that were developed early in life and those that have lasted through the years.

The flip side of all of the Aquarian's "wonderfulness" is that he can sometimes be very compulsive in those areas that are so minor that most would say, "Who cares?" A Libra sister paints this picture of her "anal-retentive" companion, a bank manager in Tennessee. He will plan weeks in advance for a weekend trip, calling every hotel in the preferred area to get just the right rate. And when he packs his clothes, they are folded and arranged in the suitcase for each day of the trip—Friday's clothes on top, then Saturday, Sunday and so on. She observes that he spends too much time planning and not enough time enjoying the weekend.

If these Aquarians get married, they usually marry very early to a high school or college sweetheart; otherwise they marry very late or not at all. Aquarian parents will handle their children in much the same way as the other elements in their life. They will promote independence in their children, but keep the lines of communication open. They will discuss just about anything. The emotional attachment between father and children will be a bit difficult, since the men deal primarily in logic rather than emotion. This sign is very comfortable being single. However, whether married or single, they maintain their independence.

Black Sun Signs

The Aquarius Woman

When you meet this woman, you will be thoroughly entertained, interested and intrigued, initally. She's exciting, she puts you on the edge of your seat, and you'll find yourself wanting to know more about her, her life and how you can fit into the complex scheme of things. In fact, during the encounter, you will immediately begin making plans for subsequent dates. If her smile, friendliness, intellect and all-around good looks don't reel you in, her outgoing personality and true interest in your well-being will. Stop! Hold it! Don't be misled. This air sign is like that with everyone. This woman is like no other sign of the zodiac.

The women embody both beauty and brains. The road to her heart is jammed with twists, turns and dips. An eventual courtship is going to be a tough one. Her expectations are high and she expects her companion to be responsible and forthright in the relationship. She guards her independence fiercely. Like the male of this sign, she takes love seriously. Just because you say you want a relationship, in her mind, that's not enough. She will know you intimately before the courtship begins.

I once knew an Aquarian who repeatedly told her date that she wasn't going to a hotel room with him. He rented the room anyway, and while he was standing at the registration desk, she quietly drove away. He made the fatal mistake of thinking simply because the evening was a huge success and she was her charming and alluring self, he'd score that night.

Just when you think you have her undivided attention, she will appear to be so removed from the relationship that you'll feel you're back at square one. You probably are. They are very intuitive and can almost read minds. If you're fantasizing in her presence about potential bedroom exploits, she'll sense it and be turned off. One suggestion: When you feel the fantasies coming on, think nursery rhymes instead. You know—"Mary had a little lamb," "Jack Sprat could eat no fat," or "Little Miss Muffett sat on a tuffet,". . .

Physically, the Aquarian woman is usually slim, with long, shapely legs, and her hair is either cut short or shoulder length for a variety of hairstyles. She's always stylish, even in her most casual dress or cutoff midriff T-shirt and jeans, and will expect you to be neatly dressed as well. If you want to get her attention, don't show up in light blue polyester bell bottoms with a matching Hawaiian shirt. It's not that she expects you to be sharply dressed all of the time, but she expects whatever you wear to be in fashion for the present decade. She collects antiques; however, she doesn't want a human one.

The Aquarian woman will always be full of surprises. You might meet her for dinner and she'll greet you in a navy business suit, scarf, pin, the works. But later, during a more intimate moment, you will discover that she has on thong underwear underneath. On the other hand, during a very impulsive moment, she may decide that this is the day she wants to lose her virginity. She may reason that since you're ten years her senior, you'd be a perfect teacher. To your way of thinking, the reasoning may be totally bizarre. One Aquarian woman, age eighteen, did just that but had to deal with a slight problem. After the encounter, she went back into the social setting with her shirt on backwards and inside out.

Aquarian women will not readily buy into black men blaming others for their problems or lack of success in life, for she believes that men, both black and white, should have a commitment to their philosophy and ideals of life and be able to deal with problems without a lot of bellyaching. A brother's good looks are not that important to her. And having plenty of money and a five-bedroom house won't get her either, but she will expect you to be a good conversationalist, warmhearted and considerate. Don't worry about the boudoir. If you're teachable, there will be very few problems.

Like the Aquarian man, the woman will want to know you as a friend first. She will also have to respect you as a human being before any romance or eventual marital bliss can take place. An evening at her place could include a delectable candlelight dinner, with all the fixings made from scratch.

Although the Aquarian sister can function pretty well as a parent, she may be an inconsistent disciplinary, especially if she's a single parent. Other factors such as a high-stress job and an unfulfilling love relationship can throw the sensitive nature of the Aquarian off. If a roommate pitches in, the Aquarian will be eternally grateful. However, the situation of sharing the responsibility of a child can get out of hand if guidelines aren't addressed. For example, the Virgo roommate of an Aquarian sister ended up rearing the Aquarian's three-year-old child. The Aquarian's schedule was irregular. The Virgo agreed to help with the child. But before long, the Virgo would get the child ready for school, take her to school, feed and monitor her homework. Over time some resentment began to build after there was some confusion on the part of others as to who the parent was. Finally, the Virgo roommate moved out of the apartment after the child became confused too.

Aquarians are very comfortable being single. One Aquarian counselor had difficulty convincing potential mates that all she wanted was a roll in the hay occasionally with no strings attached. The brothers simply couldn't understand that she didn't want a commitment, because "this sounds like what a dude would say." But what may be impossible for some, is very plausible for the Aquarian. Aquarian people have brilliant minds. With far-reaching projects like life on the planet, world hunger, and the cost of living in the year 2300, the likelihood of the Aquarian being sidetracked with a serious "Baby, please don't go!" relationship is very unlikely.

Love Connection

Now that you have some indication of what's ahead, if you're a brave soul with a lot of heart, read on. Even though initially finding the way to this air sign's heart will be an uphill climb, the journey is well worth it. If the Aquarian sister enters your life, you won't ever be the same. You'll go with her to the gourmet cooking classes, learn to play racquetball or help her spearhead her new project—getting the buildings in her neighborhood on the National Registry of Historic Places. She expects her mate to be close and connected; consequently, her companion will be expected to understand and know her needs before they can be verbalized. Sounds demanding? She is! But, she gives back 150 percent in any relationship. If or when she gets married, her mate will be in heaven. But she may not stay that way—married, that is.

Love matters with the Aquarian brother will move at a snail's pace. This Uranus-ruled independent person must weigh all of the pros and cons, the long-term effects on his well-being. You'd think he was about to take up smoking or mountain climbing. These brothers are so fiercely independent that they may choose celibacy until they decide what they want to do with their lives and with whom. It's not a big deal for them to be given the eye by members of the opposite sex because it happens all of the time. What they're looking to do, more times than not, is to learn how to hide or defend themselves from the onslaught of admiring women. Some Aquarian brothers pretend a lot. They pretend that they don't see the adoring looks. They can also pretend that they're only there in an official capacity with business cards in tow. But get this, folks, they're aware of everyone in the room, the innuendos, the gestures, and all of the above.

An Aquarian brother, who's involved in putting together investment portfolios for clients rarely if ever wants to discuss the details of a courtship with his companion. He feels for the most part that women are only attracted to him because of what he does for a living. He decided way back that he shouldn't be honest with his would-be companions because his honesty and openness about the relationship gave the sisters an extra edge. And in his mind, he didn't want the sisters peeping at his hole card. What he didn't realize was that regardless of what he tells his companions makes no difference to the sisters. The ladies of all walks of life will forever be attracted to this elusive, distant, but at the same time caring brother that everyone wants to know, even the dog.

Physically, there's always a unique sexiness about Aquarius people. This subtlety comes in the form of sparkling, penetrating light brown eyes against deep, dark ebony skin or the reverse: light papersack-tan skin and eyes that are so dark they look black. Eye contact is all-important to Aquarians. They must have eye contact to connect with the person and sharpen their intuitive powers when they delve deep into a person's cool, controlled exterior. When you start feeling a bit uncomfortable and hot under the collar, you'll know that you're probably talking to an Aquarian.

If you want to meet an Aquarian, jog on over to the high school running track about six in the morning—the earlier the better or attend a rally in support of a new health-care plan or a lecture on astronomy and its applications to everyday life. The Aquarian will be there, raising the controversial questions, leading the crowd in song or just soaking up every word for contemplation later.

Sexually, the Aquarian woman is a slow starter. If she was a teenage mother, many men may assume that this sister is an easy lay, but the assumption is wrong. Once she feels comfortable in the relationship, the sexual encounter will be the experience of a life-time. The experience might begin with an erotic short story that she's written, a fantasy of the two of you in an unusual setting like a hot air balloon or an airplane or in your office doing the "wild thang." And later the story will be acted out in real life. (I'm just trying to prepare you for what's to come.) So if you're working late, be mindful of Aquarians dressed as cleaning ladies, night watchmen or security guards.

When Aquarian sisters are aroused, they're extremely creative in bed. Some men are turned off by this need for variety and creativ-ity. If she determines that you're a prude, and she gets negative vibes from you, she'll be gone before you have time to catch your breath. On the other hand, if there's some underlying reason why your attitude toward sex bears looking into . . . well, that's another story. For example, an Aquarian sister, who worked as a manager in corpo-rate America, was totally speechless after she learned that her Leo date had been celibate for the last year. After enjoying the luscious dinner that her Leo prepared, and the intimate conversation during the preparation, the word celibate was the last word in the English language she expected to hear. She felt as if someone had just signed her up as a card-carrying member of a convent. Once she understood his explanation of the whys and wherefores, homegirl settled back and reluctantly supported his philosophy. It was definitely a nail-biting, traumatic experience, but she hung in.

To get things rolling with the Aquarian brother, verbal stimula-tion is always a good idea. Talk dirty—they love it. Massage the calves of their legs—they love that too. Aquarians don't even realize that their erogenous zone is the calves of the legs, in part because the zone is a part of their lower extremities and they're usually so impatient, they probably never explore down that far. But Aquarians love to place their legs in your lap. I suppose, there is a subliminal message there. Aquarius rules the ankles, calves and circulatory system. These are vulnerable areas for this sign.

But now that you've succeeded in getting these humanitarians hot and bothered, you need to settle in for the evening. Both the men and the women of this sign are highly experimental, which means that they will try just about anything once. That anything could be homosexuality and bisexuality. They detest being bored and the bedroom is no exception. So in the beginning if you feel you're going to need some tutoring, let the Aquarian know and he or she will be glad to accommodate. *Warning:* Don't get this air sign out in the middle of the stream and then announce that you can't swim. They won't appreciate the fact that you weren't up front, and you'll be left wishing that you had remembered to bring a life jacket.

When the Aquarian male or female finally falls in love, watch out!!! They are totally devoted. They will not, I repeat, not, play around, provided all their varied needs are being met. Remember, the sun came out to shine on their mate exclusively. But when the party's over, don't worry about feeling guilty about the relationship breaking up. They probably anticipated it long before you knew what was going on.

For the most part Aquarians are compatible with the two other air signs, Libra and Gemini. These people are independent, logical and impulsive. Aquarians are also attracted to Aries and Sagittarius because these fire signs are, like the element fire, hot-tempered, aggressive, uncontrollable and unpredictable. These personality traits work well with Aquarius.

But the Leo-Aquarius combination will be a one-day-at-a-time kind of relationship, because aside from wild, passionate bedroom antics, there's not much else to keep them interested in each other. Opposites attract, but that doesn't mean they can maintain a long-term relationship. Leo will require the Aquarian's undivided attention, and with constant stroking. But Aquarians are generally too preoccupied with world issues and far-reaching humanitarian challenges to even notice the lion. It's Doomsville for this pairing. The only advice I can give is, prayer changes things. Let us pray.

How to Get Next to an Aquarius

• Be spontaneous and flexible. The predictable and routine bores Aquarians to tears.
• Be fashionable, wear the latest in clothing and wear bright colors. Wild shades of blue are among his favorite colors.
• Don't nag. Remember they're constantly thinking in the future, so nagging about the same old thing makes them more elusive.
• Get involved in many of their humanitarian causes or projects.
• Maintain a good sense of humor. You will need one to deal with this unusual sign of the zodiac.
• Don't cling or be controlling. If you do, you will lose her completely.
• Don't try too hard to impress or be too eager to please. Be yourself and it will pay off.
• Aquarians don't like to be bossed around or given a long list of demands. They can't stand to be dominated.
• Aquarians cannot stand to be around dummies—those persons who are clueless about what's going on in the world. Good looks are secondary to intelligence.
• Material things, though attractive, won't hold Aquarians' attention either.
• They don't like snobbish people. They will get to know everyone from the janitor to the president of the company.

The Aquarius Child

Remember, don't try to change the Aquarian child according to how you were raised or in terms of how your firstborn was brought up. It won't work. The key here is to try to understand this unusual little person, who will grow up to be an unusual big person.

They are above-average students who can make B's without much effort. They will show their need for independence at an early age. Even as early as age six, control over clothing, toy or recreation selection will be a must. They will be the center of attention without even trying. They will display somewhat of a bossy nature, orchestrating playtime with friends, but when they're challenged, they will relent and occasionally allow their friends to run the show as well. Aquarian children will dominate if you let them, but their overriding characteristic is that they are ahead of their time and know what they want. It matters less to them whether a certain person runs the show to attain certain goals. Aquarians know that they set goals too, and they will go along for the ride as long as they can benefit from the end results.

When teenagers started some new fad, like wearing baseball caps backward, it was probably an Aquarian who initiated it. Basketball player Michael Jordan, an Aquarian, wanted baggy pants for his uniform to allow for room when he played—thus, the baggy look. And Jordan was wearing his head bald long before the fad began. Aquarians are trendsetters.

Mothers, tell your Aquarian daughters about the birds and bees early. Age nine is a good starting point. Remember, this child is definitely ahead of her time. She will thank you later because you will not be able to keep her from experimenting early. The Aquarian child should be encouraged to be creative, inventive and independent. Above all, don't stifle her creativity.

As he develops, he will readily understand what life is about and how he fits into the scheme of things. The teenagers will experiment with everything, including sex, at an early age. In an effort to understand the mysteries of sex, the boys will initiate the "show me yours and I'll show you mine" game. Sometimes, however, an Aquarian child is more interested in how to orchestrate taking his girlfriend to the movies—the negotiation and maneuvering. Once the girlfriend is in the car, the end result is sort of anticlimatic.

Parents, you must allow these children to be themselves. If he requests a chemistry or erector set when other children want Nintendo, get him what he wants. He is a unique person in every sense of the word. Try at an early time in the child's life to gain his confidence and trust. If the Aquarian child trusts you and takes you into his confidence, try not to be shocked by what you hear. Your mouth will drop open constantly in amazement.

And if by chance you're the Aquarian parent, think of your child and how some of your off-kilter behavior may affect her. Yes, you're ahead of your time, but your child is not. For example, an

Aquarian single parent turned to lesbianism and decided to relate to her only daughter as a father figure, in that the Aquarian rarely bathed, cuddled or combed the child's hair. And most interaction with the child was primarily when disciplinary actions were needed. She was also the breadwinner, so the hands-on rearing of the child was left to the Virgo companion. Of course, this was very confusing to the child, who turned to her maternal grandmother for understanding. But the child never fully understood until she became an adult.

And parents, in most interracial high school settings, curiosity about interracial dating is normal. Many black male teenagers will get flirtatious looks or suggestive inferences from girls of other races. Don't freak out, parents: the Aquarian teenager can handle it. He's mature beyond his years and has an uncanny ability to handle sticky situations without much fanfare.

Besides the general stereotypical notions about blacks—and yes, the children have heard these same myths, either from their parents or peers—the added pressure of the "Mandingo slave" theory of sexual prowess is everpresent in the teenager's life. There is pressure from peers to perform, to drink and to maintain somewhat of a macho image. Be aware of this possible pitfall by constantly communicating with your Aquarian teenager.

The Aquarius Employee

Although Aquarians can do most jobs effectively, routine jobs will bore them. Creative control is more important than money with the Aquarian employee. (Don't get me wrong! This sign loves money and will "buzzsaw" through an operating budget or a bank account in record time if given the go-ahead.)

Even though the money would be sufficient, working at the Ford plant anchoring the steering columns of cars is not his idea of a rewarding position. Allow him the chance to design the steering column to create more space in the car or as a money-saving feature for the company—this would be more to his liking and will bring out his creative inventiveness. He will design a model that will last far into the future but will be practical today. It was probably an

Aquarian who initiated the idea of day-care centers in the workplace fifty years ago. Of course, the idea fell on deaf ears. Today, with so many women being an integral part of the work force, day care in the workplace is not only essential, it's proving to be cost-effective, as well.

The Aquarian's eccentric nature and unconventional way of approaching any task makes an employer a little leery of allowing this free spirit to do things her way. Make no mistake, however, the Aquarian knows what she's doing on and off the job. A boss should never try to mold the Aquarian into his own image of the perfect employee. It will never work. And if you try to mold a black Aquarian you run the danger of misinterpretation. She's her own woman, preoccupied with the world in her head. The work will get done, and done well. Molding is counterproductive.

Aquarians are assets to your company. Yes, they are disorganized, preoccupied and not grounded in the way that the average person is—but they are brilliant and ingenious in their unique approach to life and work.

Don't nitpick about being five minutes late, why he wore that fuchsia shirt and matching socks or why her desk is messy. They don't know the answers any more than you do. And don't confuse those things with incompetence. Whatever the job, Aquarians do it a little bit better than anyone else could. You won't get them to write an outline or a blueprint or formulate a plan for how they execute their jobs. They just do it. It's all in their heads.

You won't have any trouble finding the Aquarian's office. It will be the one that looks like a museum, with oriental rugs, antiques, African masks, abstract paintings and exotic artifacts from all over the world.

Skittish bosses, especially those not used to a black employee, might misinterpret what they see in the black Aquarian. These air signs are often the only black, or one of two, in their office because they choose occupations such as doctor, writer, scientist or environmentalist—occupations that appeal to their humanitarian interests. Blacks are just beginning to join these ranks in significant numbers. This is not a problem because, as with most things, Aquarians pride themselves on looking beyond the surface of skin color to the person below and benefit from what a coworker or boss has to offer. Aquarians quickly grasp the big picture in the workplace and the positions of each player and how everything fits.

Aquarians can handle racism in the workplace without feeling intimidated and diminished self-worth. Of course, if the N word is used, they will set the coworker straight either by explaining in great detail about the origins of the word and why it's so inappropriate or by going off like the Incredible Hulk. With either approach, the coworker will get the message.

Although Aquarians are friendly, warm and loyal and have a nonaggressive nature, they must be treated with respect. If there is any sort of malicious intent lurking in the workplace, particularly from the boss, this intuitive sign will pick up on it immediately. The office museum you visited on your break will be closed permanently. They will vanish as mysteriously as they appeared.

Aquarius is an air sign. They will not be controlled or harnessed in any way. Give them leeway and leverage and watch the company benefit. Both men and women of the sign have a quiet power and charisma. The women will be swooning over the Aquarian men in the office, and the men will be in a quandary about how to approach this Aquarian woman powerhouse for a date.

Health Matters

Aquarians are generally slim and have very few weight problems, but that's because they're always on the run. Grabbing a bite in the car, at work or in a meeting is normal for the Aquarian, who's constantly on the move. Because this air sign is so busy with various projects, vitamin supplements are very important. Oftentimes, they're so busy they forget to eat. Most Aquarians pride themselves on being physically fit through regular exercise, sports of some sort, jogging, weight lifting or simply running around all of their lives. But being constantly on the run with a hectic schedule without taking the time to rest, relax and eat healthy foods can take its toll on Aquarians, who rarely stop until they drop.

The key to a healthy constitution with the Aquarius is to end all of the snacking and fast food in which they overindulge. The Aquarian sister who is late for the Saturday appointment will grab a hamburger at 10:30 in the morning instead of the traditional break-fast. It's whatever strikes her fancy at that moment. And the Aquarian brother may eat the leftover pizza from the set he had with his boys the night before because he simply doesn't have the patience to prepare a well-balanced breakfast most of the time.

For the Aquarian, alcohol consumption is very rarely a problem. Aquarius people simply won't stay still long enough to consume an overabundance of alcohol. But cigarette smoking may be another story. An early introduction to cigarettes by an older sibling may find the Aquarian still smoking later in life. Aquarians may experiment with drugs because of their willingness to try new things, but generally, drug addiction and alcoholism are rare.

Grocery shopping for this air sign seems to be a traumatic experience and something they try to avoid. Dashing into the store at a moment's notice without a grocery list is usually how they operate. In an effort to try new products, sometimes they will shop for hours picking five different brands of window cleaner or skin care products to determine which they like best.

Aquarius rules the calves, ankles and circulatory system; consequently, these areas are prone to health problems. Aquarians are prone to varicose veins, hardening of the arteries, swollen ankles, anemia and muscle spasms. To offset some of these health problems, avoid excessive amounts of fatty foods and sweets. Load up on fish, chicken, fruits high in vitamin C, leafy vegetables and lots and lots of water.

Aquarians tend to enjoy and function best in a warm climate. Sometimes because of poor circulation, Aquarians can get chilled very easily. They must pay attention to their body. There is so much in the world to contemplate, that in addition to not eating right, they often don't dress warmly for the cold weather. In this case, they find themselves with bronchitis, severe flu and even pneumonia. And they're usually the first to ask, "Why am I sick?" Of course, they simply don't remember the day they walked out of the house wearing only a sweater, because they were too preoccupied with the physics problem on the test they just flunked. That was the day the temperature dropped to almost the numerical score he received on the test, 35.

Black Sun Signs

Famous African American Aquarians

Hank Aaron
Marian Anderson
Ernie Banks
Eubie Blake
Barry Bonds
Bobby Brown
Jim Brown
Les Brown
LeVar Burton
Natalie Cole
Gary Coleman
Angela Davis
Sharon Pratt Dixon
Charles S. Dutton
Roberta Flack
Arsenio Hall
Sherman Hemsley

Gregory Hines
Benjamin Hooks
Langston Hughes
Michael Jordan
Eartha Kitt
Toni Morrison
Gloria Naylor
Huey P. Newton
Billy Ocean
Rosa Parks
Leontyne Price
Jackie Robinson
Bill Russell
Robert Townsend
Jersey Joe Walcott
Alice Walker
Oprah Winfrey

PISCES
February 19 to March 20

Symbol: Two fish swimming in opposite directions

Positive traits: Emotional, intuitive, romantic, imaginative, compassionate, sensitive, adaptable, receptive

Negative traits: Secretive, careless, impressionable, weak-willed, indecisive, vague, out of touch with reality, unworldly

Ruling planet: Neptune is associated with illusion, glamour, mystery and deception.

Pisces people are the great pretenders. You'll never realize whether the smile is "just a frown turned upside down," as the song says. This water sign knows how to put on the happy face to please the crowd, when all the while the internal seas are rough and choppy. Don't waste your time trying to figure out the psyche of Pisces people. They will only allow a select few into their private domain. Unfortunately, you'll never quite understand this complex person fully because they simply don't quite get it themselves. Their ruling planet is Neptune, which is associated with mystery, illusion and deception. Need I say more?

They're confined to quarters, you know. That is where all of the pretense, the guard, the "game" can be put aside. Their key word is "confinement." They don't have to leave the area because as long as they feel safe, and can put away the facade and have the necessities —like a good book, some soothing music and a bottle of wine—at their disposal, all is right with the world.

Pisces people are very creative and innovative, but although they may have aspirations to succeed in life, they rarely have a plan of action or follow through. Therefore, they are generally resigned to not being successful. And with this perception, it's almost like a self-fulfilling prophecy. Besides, they would rather be sailing, fishing or simply lounging in the bathtub enjoying the only solace and solitude they get. Money means very little to Pisces; they simply want what it can buy. You won't find the Pisces person trying to conquer the world or make a million dollars.

These creative water signs are the artsy-craftsy types, usually directing plays, teaching needlepoint, painting, playing in a band, cooking, writing or putting together a proposal for funding a work-shop to help underprivileged kids. Pisces people are more interested in the softer side of life, the side where they feel lies all life's true meaning. If you asked the Pisces person why she quit a lucrative job in corporate America to help the underprivileged, she may answer, "This is what the Lord told me to do." Or "I don't know why, but somebody has to do it." The point is, there won't be a clear-cut explanation for their actions.

Pisceans are the dreamers of the zodiac. They look at the world through rose-colored glasses, and of course, they see a world free of racial strife, sexism, violence and wars. I realize that this is a pretty tall order. They're constantly conceptualizing how they want the world to be and how they want all the key players—family, friends, companions and bosses—to fit. When you're with a Pisces, he will probably want you to sit with him and watch the Doberman romp and play on the grass. There won't be much hustle and bustle in their lives. The requests will be simple. And more than likely you will marvel at the simplicity of their lives. Generally, they want to be left alone to dream their dreams, and not entertain the realities of what the dreams represent. Those dreams may include becoming a poet, artist, musician or writer, but the realities of what is required to fill one of those revered positions sometimes won't be entertained by the Pisces. Their position is, just let them dream. And they won't be rushed. They are the consummate laid-back brother or sister.

Pisces is a water sign. These people are highly emotional, easy-going, sympathetic to the problems of others and generous to a fault.

Pisces people find themselves giving much more than they have to give and receiving little in return. A Pisces brother will lend a friend his last dollar, knowing full well he needs the money himself. The Piscean must learn to say no. It's called self-preservation.

The symbol for Pisces is two fish connected by a string and swimming in opposite directions. One Pisces is like the fish that swims upstream against the current, against all odds, eventually attaining his goals. Another is like the fish that swims downstream, takes the easy way, goes with the flow. This Pisces lacks ambition and direction and is even lazy, simply wanting to be left alone, writing a poem or song every now and then earning just enough to make ends meet. There's an ever-looming chance that the Pisces will become a victim of overindulgence in alcohol or drugs. If this happens, well, they may associate with street people, addicts and the downtrodden. Those who share a kinship of fate must lend support to each other. The Pisces could be the ringleader of that mix.

Pisceans are generally small in stature, and their faces are usually oval. Most Pisceans are attractive, but have unusually large eyes that project inquisitiveness and surprise. Their complexions are smooth and blemish-free. The sign of Pisces rules the feet, which, like the hands, are usually small in proportion to their physical size. The feet are usually beautiful, with either high arches or fallen arches. Later in their lives, Pisces people usually have weight problems because they enjoy being confined to home or other places where physical activity is at a minimum.

Pisces are highly intuitive and can predict the future. If a Pisces has a gut instinct about something, listen, because more than likely he's right. For example, a Piscean brother who had started a catering business predicted, even before he reached the park for the competition, that he would win the barbecuing contest in his hometown of Memphis for the second consecutive year. And he did! The trouble is, this water sign possesses the gift of prophecy about everything except believing that he indeed has the ability and wherewithall to succeed at whatever he puts his mind to. Before he won the first contest, he addressed it with the same uncertainty with which he dealt with most areas of his life.

Pisces people want to be impressive, well thought of and respected. And sometimes in an effort to be all of the above, they will overplay their hands. They will try their hardest to be impeccably dressed even if they have to borrow that impeccable dress or suit. Being dressed in the latest style with mild but definite elegance is a must for the Pisces. If the outfit is not phat, bumpin' or hittin', the Pisces won't be sportin' it. For example, a Pisces woman, who could ill afford to be sharply dressed all the time or compete with her friends who had more lucrative jobs, learned to sew and then later turned her sewing skills into a profitable side business. She could make whatever her friends wore in two days at one quarter the cost. Whenever this sister stepped into church on upscaled occasions, all heads turned because every stitch was coordinated, shoes, hat, gloves, jewelry and so on. But the Pisces look is all a part of the plan of turning heads, being ultrafeminine and being the woman of every man's dream. The Pisces woman ought to take this approach to the patent office because she's got it all down to a fine science—just ask the average male in Anytown, USA. In addition to being dressed and sporting the latest cologne, a Pisces brother may comment about how young he looks, adding that he's only echoing what his friends say. The comments may sound kinda tacky, but it's only his insecurities talking.

The Pisces Man

You'll be whipped in this relationship with the Pisces man. Most of the time, you'll be hopelessly in love, and so will he, but you won't ever be able to figure out completely what this complex, emotional, somewhat timid, caring, introspective brother is thinking, who he really is or what he wants out of life. Those are the $64,000 questions.

For starters, this brother wears several hats. He'll be the dear friend who will lend you half his paycheck to catch up your house notes. He'll be the one visiting the family of a loved one who's died. He'll also be the caring brother who takes a potential companion out for a night on the town, not expecting anything in return. (The last thing on his mind will be sex in this instance.) And by chance, if sex is an option after the date, more than likely the preoccupied Pisces won't take it.

Like the Pisces woman, the men of this sign are also curiously attractive to the opposite sex. The Pisces brother is what some may think of as the "nonthreatening" black man, in that he's in his own world and he doesn't pose a threat to society or himself.

But don't think he's timid and shy when it comes to bedroom matters. He definitely isn't. He feels, however, that sex should be at the right time and place—maybe two or three months into the courtship, but definitely not on the first or second date. I know you may be wringing your hands and biting your nails by then, but what can I say? If the sex thing is rushed, he'll only end up telling you not to go away mad, but to go away.

Every Saturday when this single Pisces brother, a former athlete and college graduate is working in his yard, the neighborhood women, sending out vibes galore, come out and sit on their porches to watch this hunk at work. Of course, he enjoys the audience, but has a real problem responding to overly aggressive women. He's not taking the bait because he feels he must be in control of the situation. Oh, well.

On the other hand there's that other fish swimming downstream. If given an opportunity, he'll have sex on the first date, and any other date, too. Most Pisces brothers, once they are assured that they won't be found out, will do just about anything in the way of sexually related manuevers. For example, a long-distance truck driver, announced to his potential mate that, physically, he was at her disposal. What she liked sexually or otherwise, he'd do without any qualms. Of course, he didn't live in her city, and no one knew him. Therefore, his declaration could be made with very few misgivings. So, girlfriend, find you an out-of-town Pisces and you're set!

Pisceans are extremely private people and keep secrets. When a Pisces man overheard his Virgo wife being interviewed on the telephone for this book, he insisted on knowing who she was telling "our life story and all of our business" to.

A courtship with a Pisces brother (I didn't say marriage), will expose you to a world of fantasy and romance like you've never had before. That's the whole purpose—like you've never had it before. Also if you've just met this man and he's doing the wining-and-dining routine, sending flowers and doing all of the right things you've seen at the movies, he's watched those movies, too. And ideally, your Pisces is a hopeless romantic. He secretly wants his life to be like the guy in the movie who gets the girl and then rides off into the sunset with her. The predictable ending here is driving off into the horizon, with her cute little terrier bobbing along friskily in the backseat of the car. Or how about the scene when the Pisces plays a song he wrote "just for you" on the piano as you sit atop the baby grand, legs crossed, kneecaps showing and hair softly framing your face. Excuse me, nice try, but this won't take you over the long haul. What happens after the movie ends is that the audience leaves and returns home to reality: the dirty dishes, crying babies, burping live-in companions and barking dogs. And if there's a piano involved, it needs tuning and the kids are usually playing chopsticks nonstop.

The Piscean approach to marriage or courtship is romance, moonlight and music. This man has an idealized view of companionship or marriage. But the problem surfaces when your Piscean mate begins to believe that the relationship can actually be like the last movie he enjoyed. After a while, both of you become frustrated.

The scene plays itself out similarly during marriage. Piscean husbands have a 50–50 chance of succeeding in marriage. Again, he is the dreamer—the little house with the white picket fence, the lovely wife and 2.0 children. But usually when reality sets in—the dental bills, the mortgage and money for the children's education— it hits him squarely between the eyes. This can be too traumatic for the Piscean to deal with.

A Piscean truck driver and former high school football great married his high school sweetheart, a cheerleader. The marriage ended after two years because the Piscean couldn't settle down to being the doting husband. Long after his wife would fall asleep, this brother would sneak out the window and hang out with the "posse." He even started dating an older woman. After his wife filed for divorce, guess who had regrets and wanted to renew the commitment?

In addition to the inability to face reality, Pisceans try at all costs to avoid confrontation and chaos. When the son of one Pisces brother broke a boy's nose during a confrontation, the Pisces parent didn't go to the school to get to the bottom of what happened, but simply allowed his child to accept the home suspension. In fact, the other child had called him a nigger.

The Pisces Woman

This sister knows how to be captivating to a man. When you meet this woman you won't be able to forget her. And you'll definitely try to follow up for a second date or second anything. She knows at a very early age what her strengths are in terms of attracting the opposite sex, and she uses these assets to the fullest extent of the law. The Pisces knows the effect she's having on her prey—excuse me, "potential companion." Since early childhood, her charisma and charm have been a part of her makeup. She knew how to wrap daddy around her tiny finger to get anything she wanted. These women will affect you subtly. It'll feel like you're being run over by a truck, only in slow motion—a little at a time.

The Pisces sister's needs are simple. All she wants is a strong, supportive and confident man whom she can spoil and surrender to fully. And with that philosophy, the line forms at the left. On the other hand, the Pisces career woman knows exactly what she wants out of life, but she needs companionship to make her feel complete. For example, a Piscean sister with a successful teaching career got a divorce after her husband treated her like a prisoner and watched her every move. This sister wanted companionship, but she didn't want the relationship to dominate her entire life. Her husband had other plans. He left the Catholic Church and wanted her to follow, but she did not. He wanted some say-so over her use of birth control, and she wouldn't have any of it. Although the Pisces woman may project the helpless, innocent, vulnerable image, it ain't necessarily so. A Pisces college professor at a small college in the East was hired by the college president, a friend, to be his right hand in orchestrating the accreditation process. But when foul politics became a part of the equation, the Pisces, undaunted, moved to Boston with her child and stayed with a friend until she found another job two months later.

If you're thinking about dating a Pisces, this perceptive woman will strip you naked with her powers of intuition. You'll have to come clean. Leave all of those perverted musings at home, because all that you leave out will be filled in by her innate ability to read you before you even realize what you're going to say or do. But the encounter with a Pisces woman is mutually satisfying, for she is genuinely interested in your welfare. And she'll listen attentively to your every word (even if she's bored to tears).

You can tell the Pisces woman your deepest, darkest secrets and no word about it will ever be uttered. They're secretive, too. The female fish will be a devoted and supportive friend. As parents, Pisceans can be very doting, overindulging their offspring in most every aspect of life. Piscean parents are so easygoing that they lack the ability to administer discipline in a consistent manner. Although the children of Pisces will be exposed to the arts and other social areas of their parent's life, the children will also be taught responsibility for household chores, homework and self-organization.

Piscean women have an inner strength that may not be evident to those on the outside looking in. These women will be supportive, attentive and excellent homemakers and create a haven you will not want to leave. For example, an elderly Piscean woman, the classy matriarch of her family and, seemingly, the neighborhood, made all the prom dresses for the neighborhood children in addition to sewing for her own six children. This woman was an only child whose father was a teacher at one of the local colleges in Alabama. As a young adult, she was even sent away to New York in an effort to separate her from the man who eventually became her lifelong husband. Unbeknown to the Piscean woman, all the teenagers in the neighborhood adored her and looked at her as a role model. Years after her death, these same teenagers, now in their forties and fifties, reflect back on how this African American Pisces woman affected their lives and made them feel special.

Yes, the Pisces woman does thrive on romance, but romance alone is not enough. Pisceans are not too hung up on your occupation as such, but you do need to have a job. Don't tell her, "I haven't worked in two years because I hurt my back on the job. I've applied for disability." The Pisces woman functions best in a solid relationship. But invariably, this water sign has an uncanny way of choosing mates who are either too domineering or who just don't get it or just won't get it—a job that is.

In a workplace where there are only a few African Americans, the Pisces's self-imposed pressure will be an additional burden. The ol' "I've got to be the best" and then some, will be quite evident. She'll work the extra hours, volunteering for overtime and work on weekends. What the Piscean doesn't understand is that she is the best, or certainly one of the best employees. The ability of a Piscean is evident to everyone but her.

Love Connection

One of the most important things to a Pisces is the emotional, spiritual and romantic character of a relationship. The Pisces brother will read you his favorite poem or even write a poem for you just because. If that's not romantic enough, he'll invite you to Milan or Paris for a week with only seven days' notice. He may blow a month's salary, but it'll get your attention. For the woman of the sign, romance is all-important. For example, one Piscean loves to prepare dinner, then play, and a long walk piques her interest. And if you're invited to dinner at her house, bring a nice bottle of champagne. No-name brands are a turnoff—you must give the impression that you know what you're doing even if you haven't a clue about good wines or champagnes. Ask the clerk at the liquor store.

It may take you a while to make the trek to the Pisces' bedroom because Pisces guard their privacy fiercely. One Piscean who had known her suitor for years was more than disappointed with their first sexual encounter after both were stuck at his hotel in a snowstorm. When it came to bedroom matters, homegirl thought that she would be in for the experience of her life. Wrong! According to Pisces, "He didn't know what to do with that thang."

These water signs will do whatever it takes, short of hiring a private detective, to ensure that you're worthy of their trust, but if you pass the security check with very few blemishes, well, then let the fun and games commence! This quiet demure epitome of womanhood can become a tiger in bed. And it will seem like you literally have a tiger by the tail. Looks are definitely deceiving in the case of the Pisces woman. She's in the exclusive no-holds-barred club. Piscean women enjoy sex to the fullest. Both the male and female will do just about anything short of death to please their partners.

The Piscean man is slow-moving as well, but after all of the amenities are over and he feels comfortable enough, his aim is to please. His goal to please his partner will be either in the spirit of cooperation or because he's in the mood to do whatever it takes.

Okay, let's cut to the chase—he's a freak! You'll be at peace with the world.

The women want intrigue and creativity in the bedroom. You'll be pretty astounded at the ease and creativity of any sexual encounter with a Pisces.

If you mess around and fall in love with a Pisces, you'll be "whipped." If you're looking for the whys and wherefores from me, I can't help you. They're water signs and there's something about being near water. It's soothing, it's comforting, it's calming and it's relaxing. The engaging sensitive people are easy to talk to. Women who are interested in a Pisces brother will more than likely pour their hearts out, explaining how some dude jilted them—and all the while the Piscean offers atmosphere, tissues and music. That first date will find the two of you staying up all night lamenting over past and present mistakes, loves or life's twists and turns.

Everyone who meets a Pisces person believes at first that they must be compatible because of their easygoing nature, nonthreatening appearance and lighthearted attitude. But on the flip side, the Pisces persona is a moody and pessimistic person who can pour water on the best-laid plans of the heart. Therefore some discussions of the compatible mate should be addressed.

Pisces is most compatible with the other two water signs, Cancer and Scorpio; these signs provide each other with the emotional support, romance and sense of protection they need. The two earth signs, Taurus and Capricorn, provide a nice balance for insecure, introspective Pisces, who would sometimes prefer to gaze out the window and write poetry than tackle more responsibly demanding endeavors. Earth signs, in contrast to water signs, are stable and steadfast; they promote harmony in Pisces.

The opposite sign for Pisces is Virgo. Of all of the opposites in the horoscope, the Pisces-Virgo combination is probably the only coupling that could work. Both are easygoing types that complement each other nicely. But bear in mind the concept of opposites: There could be trouble ahead.

Peace and harmony are key to a relationship with a Pisces. Consideration of others' feelings also helps. This relationship won't be a dictatorship. The Pisces woman might date three men simultaneously and then, after she's caught, will end the relationship with all of them. She simply can't stand to be found out.

How to Get Next to a Pisces

• Pisces women are drawn to the strong, silent type. They love to be able to feel totally secure around a potential companion.

• Pisces people are very creative and love the arts. Take them to a play, an exhibit or a poetry reading on the first few dates. You'll be glad you did.

• As for the weaves, braids and toupees or the men with permed hairdos, that won't be a problem. Sometimes Pisces people wear these enhancements too.

• Being well-groomed and dressed appropriately are musts for this water sign. If you plan to accompany them, you must look neat.

• Pisces love to eat out in fancy restaurants. This sign is interested in the ambiance first, and then their attention will be turned to you.

• They are great conversationalists and will chatter idly about a variety of subjects. Pisces will shy away from argumentative or chauvinist companions at a moment's notice.

• Pisces people love moonlight and music and any activity near water. Take your date on a midnight stroll along the beach, the lake or the river and watch the sparks fly.

• Loud, boisterous behavior will get you nowhere but a quick trip out of the Pisces life. Image is everything to this water sign, so there won't be anyone in their lives to reflect negatively on the Pisces persona.

• By all means, get rid of the Jheri curls and the polyester. If you don't, you won't have access to the porch, let alone the person.

• Pisces people oftentimes find themselves being socialites. Whether it's a black-tie or white-tie function, the Pisces will expect you to be dressed for the part and provide them with an impressive armpiece and other amenities to complete the look.

The Pisces Child

The Pisces child will definitely be hard to figure out. They will be little dreamers, who, like Peter Pan, will not want to grow up. They won't ever be in a hurry about anything, except maybe a first date or the prom. A regimented, taskmaster approach with the little fish is a waste of time. These children are easygoing, nonaggressive and cooperative. They will do what they're told and when they're told, rarely offering any resistance. There will be no need to browbeat them into submission because this approach may cause emotional problems later.

With the Pisces toddler potty training, walking and talking will be accomplished with ease and little or no fanfare. These little ones are intuitive rascals. A nudge, a warning or the mere threat of a scolding is all that's needed. However, if you spoil these youngsters by allowing them free rein, including using the hallway as the Daytona speedway or allowing them to use your clothes dryer as a playpen, you won't have anyone to blame but yourself.

Pisces youngsters function best when the environment is pleasant and serene, with very little arguing and bickering on the part of the parents or other siblings. These children need constant encouragement and support for their vulnerable, insecure natures. If a Pisces has a traumatic and unhappy childhood, it will follow him through adulthood. If the early years are less than supportive for this fragile youngster, he or she may need counseling to recover and become a productive adult.

A Pisces comedian remembers most of the intimate details of his grandfather's life, who was blinded at age thirty while working in a factory bleaching cloth. He remembers leading his grandfather around in rural Tennessee and, though his grandfather was blind, the people of the community respected him. The positive feedback and encouragement he received from his grandfather propelled him to teach and encourage others with comedy.

During the early years, an introduction to piano lessons or playing an instrument will promote the Pisces' interest in music. For example, a thirteen-year-old Pisces who taught himself how to play drums was able to get his first paying job as a drummer in a band of older teenagers, playing gigs at fraternity parties. The experience, though somewhat threatening because of the venue, enabled the Pisces to become more adventurous and not too cautious with new challenges.

Like the adults, Pisces children spend a lot of time looking into the future and thinking about the past. For example, a Pisces brother, the oldest of five children, remembers with deep regret that he had no relationship with his father until adulthood. The Pisces constantly talks about how he wishes his father had talked to him, even if it was only about sports.

As youngsters, these children will be cooperative in every way. The boys will take an interest in helping mama, learning to cook or accompanying mama shopping. If the Pisces is a boy child, he'll usually be mom's favorite. The Pisces girl is everyone's favorite, including the boys of the neighborhood. She won't get dirty wrestling with the kids or trying to learn basketball. None of that! She's the dainty child, the ultrafeminine sibling of the family. Her role early on, and in subsequent years, will be to look and act like a little lady. She'll have no burning desire to compete with the guys.

However, as a parent, you'll need to monitor a Pisces child closely because you want to be able to determine their whereabouts sometimes. Even when they are sitting at the dinner table with the rest of the family, their little minds will be light years away, maybe somewhere over the rainbow. You won't understand why she wants to go to her room and skip dinner. She simply wants to be alone without the influences of the outside world, parents, rules and regulations and all of the other systems she simply doesn't want to deal with. Like the adults, the Pisces child has her own ideas and views about the world and how this fish fits into it. These children won't have any trouble playing alone. They have vivid imaginations. They can sit for hours in their bedroom reading, writing, playing with toys and simply gazing out of the window. As a parent you'll probably wonder why your child won't play outside with the other neighborhood children. When she is in the mood to play with others, including her siblings, she will, but not before.

In later years, keeping secrets may become a real problem with the little fish. The effort won't be in a calculating, malicious way, but just as soon as this Pisces youngster can think for himself on any level, there will be some parts of his life that neither mama or daddy will know about. And no one else will either, for that matter. These children simply must keep a part of themselves closed and hidden from the rest of the world. This measure, on a minute level, provides them with a sense of security.

Pisces children are extremely agile mentally, although during adolescence insecurities like acne, being awkward, goofy, geeky or whatever the Piscean's self-perception is, usually overshadow all the many accolades he or she receives during the high school years.

You'll find these water signs encouraging others, directing plays, hanging out in the band and choir rooms, in the art department or the president of the speech and drama clubs. It's much easier for Pisces youngsters to express their feelings by acting them out on stage than in the straightforward, honest manner parents expect.

If you're a parent of a Pisces child, I wouldn't worry too much about the mad dash to discuss the facts of life before age nine. These children are late bloomers. Growing up too soon is not something they readily aspire to. The way the Pisces teenager sees it, having a baby is way too much responsibility.

The Pisces Employee

There are plenty of variables with the Pisces employee that must be considered before you as the boss will benefit. First and foremost, the surroundings for this sensitive water sign must be conducive and pleasant. Chaos, confusion, and disorganization will have the Pisces employee feeling the same. They simply must have order and a system in place to function effectively on any job. For example, if this sister is a social worker for the welfare department determining people's eligibility for assistance, that's okay. However, if this Pisces employee is working in the child abuse department, she will be miserable and unable to function. The Pisces employee will internalize the suffering of the children and won't be able to perform the job effectively.

The Pisces employee must also feel that his labor will benefit humanity over the long haul in some way and has a purpose. Pisces people are the dreamers of the zodiac. If the Pisces' dreams of having a perfect world can be actualized, in some measure by the job they perform, then they're happy campers. Remember, these water signs are driven by their emotions. Consequently, they are extremely sympathetic to any pain and suffering of others.

If the Pisces is a machinist, a doorman, a computer analyst or any other job that he feels has no meaning, he'll be gone before you can figure out what happened. Money is not a real issue and wouldn't be an inducement to remain on. It's merely a means to an end. Pisces people don't really expect to have much of it anyway. And as the saying goes, you don't really miss something you've never had.

Pisces employees also take on jobs as nurses, teachers, college professors—jobs that give them a sense of promoting the big picture, being an integral part of the whole, and a real team player. The fish may also lean toward a religious vocation. Pisces people are willing to make great sacrifices on such jobs. Pisces people are also at the top of their game, for the most part, in jobs that are artistic in nature: writers, painters, poets, dancers, actors or chefs.

The Piscean has no use for those who allow their positions to go to their heads, thinking they are the job instead of being a person on the job. The Piscean is a team player. He could very easily be the manager or the coach of the team, but he has little interest in becoming a supervisor. He knows that the team, a network of players, wins the game, not an individual. And he is willing to carry his weight on the job.

The Pisces employee must feel that she's got some sense of purpose on the job. She will invariably need a source of inspiration, a mentor, best friend or someone who's at the top of the game to encourage this unsure, insecure water sign. It's not that she doesn't have the ability, talent and intelligence, but the Pisces simply won't accept her abilities, not readily, anyway. She may never do so, and this could translate into unrealized and unfulfilled dreams.

If you're considering a partnership with a Pisces, he or she will be able to come up with all the wonderfully creative ideas. But a nuts-and-bolts person needs to be a part of the equation. If not, the project may turn out to be another Piscean dream that never sees the light of day. For example, if you and the Pisces decide to open a state-of-the-art spa, leave the decorating and hiring to the Pisces. With his sixth sense, he's a good judge of character and can strategically map out where the players fit. And he'll definitely be able to choose all of the right shades of sea green, ocean blue and mauve. But you or someone else must take care of the business plan and financing right down to the rolls of toilet paper. The Pisces employee is usually well-organized, but a system absolutely must be in place already. Meticulous, detailed work is no problem for Pisces. If she works for a television cable company, she will sit there all day figuring out why the customer's videocassette recorder won't work when the cable line is connected. Or as the obituary writer for a newspaper, she'll patiently listen to the widow of a police officer killed in a shootout even though her deadline is minutes away.

In the workplace, the Pisces employee will be the odd person out. The moods of Pisces people come in many colors, and when they get in one of those moods for no apparent reason, leave them alone. Otherwise, you might get your head bitten off. But these water signs are supersensitive to the moods of the boss and fellow workers. If there's a rat anywhere, the Pisces employee will smell it. Pisceans with their sensitive natures are keenly aware of unfair behavior and favoritism on the job. They're loyal employees so long as you're fair. But don't patronize or engage in deviant behavior, because they won't stay around for the explanation.

Health Matters

Many of the health problems the Piscean suffers from are emotional in origin. Like Cancer and Scorpio, Pisces is prone to internalize emotional stress and strain to the point of becoming physically ill. The health of the Piscean ranges from fragile to sturdy. Problems occur for the Piscean man or woman because they take on the burdens of friends and relatives, along with their own problems. Their constitutions are not strong enough to withstand the rigors and emotional stress dealt by life.

Pisces people love to snack. Like the Scorpio and the Cancer, Pisces people are highly emotional and intuitive. But they are dreamers. They enjoy daydreaming about what they want their ideal weight to be and what steps they plan to take to accomplish this goal. In reality, those measures don't ever quite get off the ground. When the

Pisces man or woman enters the grocery store, they know to purchase healthy foods, including fresh fruits and vegetables and lean meats, but for some reason they will invariably find themselves in the aisle with all of the cookies, pastries and candy. After this water sign puts at least two kinds of sweets in the basket, he'll try to justify it by telling himself the sweets are for the neighbor's children or other company. Yeah, right!

One major hurdle for Pisces people is not to overindulge in alcohol. Tranquilizers, even those legally prescribed by a physician, can take their toll on the overall health of Pisces people. They will sometimes tell themselves they need the tranquilizer because they have had such a rough day, but there are always going to be rough days. And Pisces must realize they must face the music without becoming dependent on prescription drugs or other aids.

This water sign should get plenty of rest because their energy levels can plummet very easily, especially when their emotions are involved. They simply don't have the drive to keep going without proper nutrition and plenty of rest. Leave them alone in the morning. They aren't morning people who spring out of bed, and jog while they're in the shower. It'll never happen.

Pisces people must stay away from alcohol because it serves as a source of comfort for them. And, as problems arise, the ol' bottle of vodka that's hidden in the back of the cabinet in the kitchen will find its way to the Pisceans, who drink to assuage hurt feelings and for the added confidence that they perceive alcohol gives them.

The sign of Pisces rules the feet, including the ankles. These areas are susceptible to problems: bunions, falling arches, weak ankles. Other physical ailments to which Pisces are prone are alcoholism, gout and allergies. Comfortable shoes are a must for Pisces because of potential problems with the feet. A good foot massage is always a good way for Pisces people to relax. Exercise is another way for a Pisces to release some of life's tensions. Swimming or relaxing in a whirlpool or hot tub is fun for this water sign and a good way to unwind.

Pisces people love fish, so any sort, if it's not fried, is good healthy eating. A high-protein, low-fat diet is a necessity if this water sign doesn't want the excess pounds. Also drink at least eight glasses of water a day. Foods with lots of iron will help Pisces people get rid of fatigue.

Generally, Pisces people aren't too gung ho about any form of exercise, but they know they must make up for all that late-night snacking. If Pisces does exercise, the commitment tends to be sporadic. Pisces will sign up for the three-year membership at the health club, then attend religiously for three months and disappear for the remainder of the year. Consistency is the key here.

Famous African American Pisceans

Ralph Abernathy

Charles Barkley

Marion Barry

Louise Beavers

Harry Belafonte

Godfrey Cambridge

Nat King Cole

Fats Domino

W. E. B. Du Bois

Bill Duke

Ralph Ellison

Charlayne Hunter-Gault

Michael Irvin

Monte Irvin

Al Jarreau

Quincy Jones

Barbara Jordan

Jackie Joyner-Kersee

Spike Lee

John Lewis

Bobby McFerrin

Garrett Morgan

Shaquille O'Neal

Sidney Poitier

Charley Pride

Ishmael Reed

Smokey Robinson

Raymond St. Jacques

Willi Smith

Herschel Walker

Marsha Warfield

Vanessa Williams

Nancy Wilson

James Worthy

Andrew Young